Con

From the Road

Notes from a Wayfaring Stranger's Journal

Caleb Pirtle III

An Imprint

Of Venture Galleries, LLC.

Produced by Venture Galleries LLC
1220 Chateau lane
Hideaway, Texas 75771
214-564-1493

ISBN: 978-1-937569-91-4

Manufactured in the United States of America.

Confessions from the Road/Caleb Pirtle III
Notes from a Wayfaring Stranger's Journal
Partly Fact and Partly Fiction
First Printing
Formatted by Enterprise Book Services, LLC

Venture Galleries.com
calebandlindapirtle.com

Dedication

To Josh and Taylor Pirtle:
The journey
would not have been worth taking
without you.

Contents

Confessions From the Road

Acknowledgements

To those writers and critique partners who have put up with my eccentricities and made a difference in the way I look at words, stories, and the world around me: Linda Pirtle, Stephen Woodfin, Richard Hollingsworth, William Burgdorf, Beverly Sable, Ryan Martin, Nancy Larson, Brinda Carey, James R. Callan, Jim Ainsworth, Gene Shelton, Patty Wiseman, Nancy Hudgins, Gay Ingram, Galand Nuchols, Sue Coletta, and Scott Bury.

Prologue

I GREW UP in a world occupied by storytellers. Their stories were better than books. Their stories became books. After all, life is just one story piled on top of another with page numbers.

I would sit in the back of Mr. Wyche's Country Store while men played dominoes, or at least talked about playing dominoes, and traveled the forgotten roads of their memories.

"Homer left yet?"

"Didn't know he was going anywhere."

"Neither did he."

"Why do you think he's leaving?"

"Agnes bought a shotgun."

"Agnes never shot a shotgun."

A smile.

"She has now."

What's truth?

What's fiction?

Who cares?

I stood on the front steps of an underpass in Leverett's Chapel where we all had gathered when the big storms came rampaging through East Texas. It was a time of tornadoes.

Our world was thick with oil derricks. The winds weren't always kind to them.

So we went underground to watch the lightning flash with rattlesnake tongues to strike the oil fields and hear thunder growl in a distance sky while the men told stories.

Past storms.

Past lives.

Past loves.

Pass the bottle.

In those days, storytellers did not know they were telling stories. They were simply carrying on a conversation. I never outgrew their stories. Nor did I ever stop listening to conversations that hopscotched their way along the side of a wayward road.

The voices stay with me. So do the stories they told me.

The voices may come from down the road apiece, at the counter of a diner, on the bar stool in a beer joint, sitting in the front yard of a mountain cabin, along a stretch of spun-sugar sand, back in the darkness of a pine thicket, amidst the downtown traffic jam of a city at sundown, or from the faint memories of a distant past.

Everyone who crosses my path has a story to tell. It may be personal. It may be something that happened last week or the year before. It may have been handed down for more than a single generation. It may even be true, but who knows anymore?

Mountains fade into the distance. Beaches are timeless. The tides come and they go, but once they have gone, they are gone forever. New tides arrive at their appointed hour, but the old ones have washed back into the mysteries of a timeless sea.

The city is an abstract sculpture of steel and glass, but so is the next one, and the next one. The cities, in reality, are only small towns separated by sidewalks instead of city limit signs.

Voices remain eternal.

Some people collect coins and stamps, model ships and lighthouses, driftwood and seashells, cars and boats, paintings and homemade crafts.

I collect stories.

The winner of a beauty pageant whose talent was standing on her head with a mouthful of pennies, humming John Philip Sousa's Stars and Stripes Forever.

The old rancher who bought the entire town of Luckenbach so he could keep the beer joint open and have a cold beer anytime he wanted one, day or night.

The old man who camps beside the cemetery so he won't have to leave his wife.

The beachcomber who came to Padre Island to die after World War I. His lungs had been ruined in a mustard gas attack. Sixty years had passed. He was still combing the beaches.

The cowboy artists who said he didn't want some critic criticizing his art until he had worked the hind end of a cow at branding time.

The drunk who crawled out of a wrecked car in the middle of the night. He staggered to the edge of the freeway, looked at the blue and red lights on the police car casting strange beads of neon down the concrete, turned to the officer, and said, "Hell, you're creating a bigger disturbance than I am."

The miles are endless. So are the stories. I find them most when I listen to other voices while traveling to other towns. I began in Texas, writing feature stories for the Fort Worth Star-Telegram, spent a few years promoting Texas with Governor John Connally's Texas Tourist Development Agency, and finally moved on through the South as Southern Living Magazine's first travel editor.

I couldn't read a road map.

So I took back roads.

Crossroads.

Paved road.

Dirt roads.

Wrong roads.

Ruts where only the wheels of wagons had gone before.

I was little more than a lost ball in the tall weeds.

But I found towns I wasn't supposed to find and was always a stranger among strangers where the next story was just down the street, around the corner, across the river, past the cotton gin, and if you go too far you'll miss it, and if you go even farther, the road runs out.

Not all of the places are on the map.

Not all of them want to be.

Let the journey began, as I began, in Texas.

Every Road Has a Different Story

"WHAT'S IT ALL ABOUT?" I asked the old man sitting in the back chair at the back table of a NETWO writer's conference in Mt. Pleasant.

His hair was white. His face had been carved from a poor grade of granite. He looked at me strangely, a puzzled expression on his face.

"You a writer?" he asked.

"Writing a novel," I said.

"Do you know anything about life?" he asked.

"Not a lot."

He shrugged as though I was helpless, and he was probably right.

"Learn about life," he said, sipping on a free cup of cold coffee. "Then you'll know how to write a novel."

He paused and watched a spider wander aimlessly across the ceiling.

The speaker droned on.

Hadn't said anything yet.

Doubted if he would.

"It's all about choices," the old man said.

"Life?" I asked.

"Novels, too," he said. "Stories are about the choices we make. Nothing more. Nothing less."

"What kind of choices?" I wanted to know.

"When I was a young man," he said, "I could go to work, or I could go to college. I had a choice to make."

"What'd you do?"

"Went to work." He shrugged again. "Couldn't afford college."

I forgot the speaker.

I gave the old man my full attention.

"If I hadn't gone to work," he said, "I would have never gone to Oklahoma City."

He grinned.

"If I hadn't gone to Oklahoma City," he said, "I would have never gone into the Boots and Saddles bar."

The old man leaned forward, his elbows on the table.

"If I hadn't gone in the bar," he said, "I would have never met Debra Ann McKinney."

He was cleaning out the cellar of his memory now.

"If I had never met Debra Ann McKinney," he said, "I would have never quit my job and took the train to Omaha."

"Why the train?" I asked.

"Didn't have a car."

"Why did you leave Oklahoma City?"

"Debra Ann McKinney was a married woman." He took another sip of his coffee. "I had a choice to make. I could stay, or I could run."

"Was she worth fighting for?" I asked.

"She wasn't worth dying for."

"You think her husband would have killed you?" I wanted to know.

"He had a choice to make," the old man said. "He could shoot me, or he could forget it, forgive Debra Ann, and let the whole sordid affair go."

"He didn't let it go, I guess."

"Shot at me twice."

"Hit you?"

"He wasn't much of a lover, Debra Ann told me. He was an even worse shot."

"What happened to Debra Ann?" I asked.

"She had a choice to make," the old man said. "She could stay with him or leave."

"Where would she go?"

"Certainly not with me."

"How about divorce?"

"That was his choice."

"What did he decide?"

"He and Debra Ann took a second honeymoon to Estes Park in the Rockies," he said. "Love is a wonderful thing. So is forgiveness. They went hiking early one morning. She came back. He didn't."

"She kill him?"

"She said he fell."

"Did they ever find the body?"

"The Park Ranger had a choice to make," the old man said. "He could investigate a crime or spend the night with his primary suspect."

"What'd he do?"

"Never found the body."

"Anybody ever look for it?" I asked.

"No reason to."

"Why not?"

"The missing man was never reported missing."

The old man grinned.

The speaker was through.

And so was he.

I looked at him strangely, a puzzled expression on my face.

"Do you expect me to believe all of that?" I asked.

"Don't care if you do," he said. "Don't care if you don't."

His grin grew wider.

He stood up and ambled toward the back of the room for another cup of coffee, as bitter as his life had been.

"That's the choice you'll have to make," he said. "When you come to a crossroad, it's all about choices."

"How will I know which road to take?"

"Doesn't matter," he said. "There is no wrong choice, but each choice has a consequence you have to live with for the rest of your life."

Those were the last words I heard him say.

I waited for him.

There were other questions I wanted to ask.

But he was like the man on the mountain.

He didn't come back.

I climbed into the car and headed toward sunset.

Didn't know where I was going.

Didn't care.

I knew, as always, a story was waiting somewhere ahead by the side of the road.

People tell me their secrets.

I hear their confessions.

Their stories aren't always pretty.

But they are always intriguing, maybe even enticing.

And sometimes they are true.

Nobody ever remembers a lie.

But then, that's their choice.

Life is not unlike the confessions I hear on the road. Stories are remembered as they are lodged in a single memory?

In the words of the great Kris Kristofferson, stories handed down from one telling to the next are partly fact, partly fiction, partly truth and contradiction.

Is that really the way it happened?

Maybe.

Maybe not.

I don't know.

I'll never know.
But it's close enough

Saga of the Stripper and the Preacher

The men who hung around Fort Worth with money in their pockets and watch chains on their vests were worried. They wanted to bring dancing girls into the city, and some of those long-legged ladies might be naked, or at least give the faint appearance of being naked if the shadows from the footlights failed to properly hide them, and men with money and watch chains were betting on a flash of flesh even during the darkest of nights.

There was, however, a hellfire and brimstone preacher man across town who, they feared, just wouldn't stand for any hint of sin, much less the sight of a lovely line of dancers who had misplaced their skirts and stockings.

J. Frank Norris did not like sin, and he was, he said, the chosen one to kick sin and all of its illegitimate offspring out of Fort Worth, or at least leave the remnants of iniquity smoldering beneath the brimstone he personally called down from of heaven.

J. Frank Norris knew how to preach hell so hot that his congregation down at the First Baptist Church could feel the heat blistering the napes of their necks even during the chill of winter. Some swore, as much as a Baptist dared in 1936, that they could smell the smoke and Sulphur when the right Reverend Norris warmed up and began sermonizing about damnation in that pit of everlasting fire. He would never understand that those naked dancing girls just might chase away the Great Depression, or at least the hard-scrabble blues it had left scattered and blowing in the streets and .

The men with money in their pockets and watch chains on their vests only sighed and prayed that the good Brother Norris would turn his head and look the other way when Sally Ann Rand undressed behind those now-you-see-it, now-you-don't flimsy curtain of fans, and they knew he never would. Their prayers fell on deaf ears.

Fort Worth ached in the grip of hard times. Jobs were scarce, and money always belonged to somebody else.

Bellies growled, and children slept in wagon beds. A bite of day-old bread was the taste of luxury.

But in1936, Texas decided, in spite of the depression, to honor its hundredth birthday, and the Centennial Commission – a band of holier-than-thou historians and politicians – handed Dallas three million seed dollars to produce the celebration.

No funds were given West Texas, the commission explained, because West Texas had nothing to commemorate.

Fort Worth exploded.

By Gawd, said the men with money in their pockets and watch chains on their vests, they would just have a little shindig of their own.

Into town rode Billy Rose, the producer of Broadway's sensation "Jumbo." He would create an extravaganza if anyone could, and besides, the men with money in their pockets and watch chains on their vests, had agreed to pay him a thousand dollars a day for a hundred days. Rose merely grinned and said, "You people stick with me, and I'll make a big state out of Texas."

Across town, the Rev. J. Frank Norris knelt on bended and troubled knees. He had faced controversy eyeball-to-eyeball before. Brother Norris had once talked the minister's association into hiring a detective to investigate the filthy innards of Fort Worth's Hell's Half Acre, and he discovered that eight owners of the area's eighty houses of prostitution were influential and socially prominent leaders of the community.

They were the ones who gave large donations to the churches. One was even a deacon.

All the ministers had agreed to stand up in their pulpits and publicly read the names of the men who ran the bawdy houses of ill repute.

All backed down, save one.

J. Frank Norris preached that Sunday on "The Ten Biggest Devils in Town and Their Records Given."

Back in 1911, he had fought for state-wide prohibition, and gunmen were hired to assassinate him.

They fired their best shots.

They missed.

Beneath an old circus tent, Brother Norris began a ninety-day revival against the transgressions of alcohol. But six days before the liquor election, firemen chopped the tent down, saying it was a fire hazard.

The wets won by six thousand votes.

J. Frank Norris was no stranger to the battles against sin.

Billy Rose, perhaps, had met his match. Rose didn't think so. He was not at all worried or concerned about a preacher. He was only looking for new ways to beat the pomp and circumstance, culture, and refinement of the almighty Dallas Centennial show.

"How will you compete?" he was asked.

"We'll give them a ball of fire," Rose answered. "We'll have a 'Lonely Hearts Ball' weekly where all the lonesome women can come and find a partner in a drawing. I'll get Shirley Temple, Mae West, Guy Lombardo, Jack Benny. I'll get one thousand beautiful girls for the Frontier Follies. I'll have two thousand Indians and a thousand cowboys, and guess who wins? I'll have a chorus line of five hundred pretty girls."

And most of them would be naked, more or less.

Rose continued, "Dallas has all that historical stuff, so we don't have to worry about that. We can just show the people a good time. I plan to drive Dallas nuts. Every time Dallas says something about its exposition, I'll give them Shirley Temple. This'll make 'Jumbo' look like a peep show."

At his first press conference, Billy Rose told the newspaper reporters that his production would have neither nudity nor smut. Only once, he said, had the public ever responded to smut.

Fort Worth Star-Telegram Publisher Amon Carter, who had money in his pocket and a watch chain on his vest, quietly told Rose, "I heard you mention smut."

"I did."

"You said the public responded to it once."

"The public did."

"Where?"

"At the Century of Progress in Chicago," Rose answered. "Sally Ann Rand had a nude act."

"Pulled them in, did she?"

"By the thousands."

Amon Carter smiled. "Let's get her," he said.

He did, and what good was smut without a little nudity? He figured the reporters would give him the publicity he needed, and they did.

Sally Ann Rand may have been one of the most successful strippers in history, but she never removed her clothes on stage. She simply said, "I am an exponent of truth in advertising, and consequently I stick to the bare facts when selling my merchandise."

What she did was dance naked behind fans or balloons while bathed in a baby blue light. Most thought they had seen a lot more than they really did, and they would pay again and again for the privilege of finding out if they had missed anything, and they always had.

Sally Ann Rand was the belle of Billy Rose's ball.

He was a showman all right. But then, so was J. Frank Norris. The good Brother Norris, long ago, had learned – then polished to perfection – the power of sensationalism.

He condemned bootleggers, standing before his congregation, his face glistening with sweat, speaking with a voice that sounded a lot like God, and bursting fruit jars of moonshine against the side of galvanized tubs. It was said that he kept two bootleggers in business just bringing him enough illegal whiskey for his sermons.

Norris rolled up his sleeves and openly paraded monkeys around as part of his fundamentalist wrath against the falsehoods of Darwin's ideas about evolution.

He even filled a number-two wash tub with writhing rattlesnakes just so the crowds would come to see what he might do next. He was a magician in the center ring of his own religious three-ring circus. No one knew for sure what kind of serpent tempted Eve in the Garden of Eden. But inn Fort Worth, in the trembling hands of J. Frank Norris, it was a rattlesnake, and a damn big one.

The crowds came.

Norris condemned them.

He saved them.

He baptized them.

He knew, however, they would all, sooner or later, be heading down to Casa Manana to take a look at Billy Rose's naked girls before the baptismal water dried on their faces.

One preacher said, "If I had the money, I would rent a concession stand out there and preach morning, noon, and night."

That's where the crowds were. That's where the sin was piled deep. That's where he belonged. The Fort Worth Minister's Association adopted a resolution that condemned Billy Rose's advertising of bare-breasted ladies.

But the men with money in their pockets and watch chains on their vests were only worried about J. Frank Norris.

They shouldn't have been.

Amon Carter, in the dead of night, in a private meeting, far from prying eyes and the thumping of worn Bibles, had made a deal with the firebrand preacher.

"You might want to take a little trip out of town," he said.

"Why should I?"

"Well, we've got this centennial show with some nude girls, and we're going to sell whiskey."

"I'm against it."

"You've been preaching against it for years."

"So I have."

"I believe Fort Worth's gonna need a lot more salvation after the centennial than it does now."

J. Frank Norris nodded. Carter's reasoning made sense to him. "Well," he said, I have been intending to hold some out of town revivals. I guess I could start a little earlier than I had planned."

"This might indeed be a good time for you quit worrying about Fort Worth and save the rest of the country," Carter said.

"It takes money."

"I might be able to find a little." Amon Carter smiled.

J. Frank Norris packed his luggage. After all, if Fort Worth was dead set on losing its soul, and surely it would, he might as well go out and try to bring salvation to some other lost and wayward sinners.

Just how many, of course, depended on the size of Amon Carter's bag of money.

Sally Ann Rand rode into Fort Worth in a chocolate-colored Lincoln touring sedan, attired in a sunbonnet and calico granny dress.

J. Frank Norris was already on the road.

Sally Ann Rand spoke to PTA groups, bought fifty memberships for the civic music season, and donated time and money to underprivileged children.

The trail of J. Frank Norris left a wide swath of brimstone from one end of the country to the other. He had never preached hell so hot.

Sally Ann Rand, in tight shorts, gave a pep talk to TCU's football team, discussed crochet patterns and lemon chiffon pie recipes with reporters, and her winsome pictures appeared more than nine hundred times in Texas newspapers.

For J. Frank Norris, hell was getting hotter all the time.

One reporter walked into Sally Ann Rand's dressing room and found her lying on her stomach, reading the Bible and totally devoid of any clothes. She rolled over, smiled her sweetest smile, and covered her most private of parts with Psalms 35:17.

J. Frank Norris would have blanched.

During the summer of 1936, however, the fire and brimstone preacher traveled twenty-seven hundred miles, delivering the word of God, saving souls that didn't even know they were lost, while back home in Fort Worth, a naked Sally Ann Rand was given her own special day, was acclaimed and applauded for her consummate artistry, and thanked by the men with money in their pockets and watch chains on their vests for using her feathered fans and well-balanced balloons to bring "culture and progress to Tarrant County."

J. Frank Norris trusted God.

Fort Worth trusted Sally Ann.

Sally Ann trusted her fans.

The only difference between Heaven and Hell was a matter of trust.

Bury My Heart Beneath the Tears

FOR WEEKS, JOHN DAVIS had worked alone, nailing together a little log cabin where the scrub and cedar stubbornly held on to dirt that was as poor as he was. It wasn't much. But it was more than he had ever had before. And besides, John Davis wouldn't be alone for long. His bride was on her way, and she would forever walk with him there upon the land that belonged to anyone who was strong enough to take it, and he was.

At least he was as long as she was close enough to share his love, his hopes, his cornbread, and the blisters on his hands. They would raise their crops and their children down on the flatlands where the Brazos River kept the hills apart, and the yellow shade of the cottonwoods tried to turn back the heat of summer but failed.

John Davis soaked the sweat from his face in a faded red bandana and stepped back from the cabin. He wondered if the roof leaked and figured that it probably did. But the holes would cause him no grief until the skies rained, and there was no distant rumble of thunder nor hint of a cloud that seldom came his way.

The wind burned his face and left it tough as leather, wrinkled before its time, and he was grateful for the wind and the cabin and the good woman whose touch made him forget that times were hard and sometimes worse.

He walked through the front door and across the dirt floor, and John Davis was a troubled man.

Something wasn't quite right.

He had made a terrible mistake.

Davis immediately ran outside, hitched up his team of mules to an old wagon and headed south across the Brazos to Waco. He could find split lumber there, and John Davis wasn't worried about the cost, whatever it might be. He didn't have the money, but he could sure earn it.

He couldn't give his bride a lot, not nearly as much as she deserved. About all he could really give her was his name. But he could damn sure keep her from having to live the way her mama had lived and the way all of her neighbors had lived. He could flat keep her bare feet off the dirt while she cooked and swept and cleaned the cabin.

When she stepped across his threshold, the new Mrs. John Davis would be walking on wooden floors.

The ceremony was a simple one, but strong enough to keep the couple together, for better or worse, for richer or poorer, in sickness and in health, until death did part them. They rode the wagon down past the scrub and cedar that led to the little cabin, and the young girl with auburn hair truly believed that she must be the richest - or at least the most fortunate - wife in all of Texas.

She owned the only wood floor in the breaks and bramble bush of Palo Pinto.

Life was not an easy one, but no one had expected it to be. There were blisters and tears and a crop that wanted to die. But John Davis refused to let it. He kept the garden sprinkled with his own sweat and buckets of that muddy Brazos water, and he kept his family fed, provided they didn't want much, and they didn't.

He had to. He had no choice. By next summer, he would have another little mouth that would cry for food. The thought of having a baby crawling around that wooden floor kept John Davis smiling even when his muscles ached, and they almost always did.

The land and the heat began to take their toll. One neighbor nailed his door shut, packed up, and rode away. "I thought I had it all," he told Davis. "I owned a farm, and I owned cattle. But the dry weather made a hired hand out of me."

"It'll get better."

"I got to keep selling off land to make a little money," the neighbor said. "If I keep selling it off, I won't have enough dirt left to pull over my grave."

John Davis watched him go, but John Davis didn't run. He had staked his claim, and he intended to keep it. Besides, nobody in his right mind would ever ride away and desert the only wooden floors in all of Palo Pinto.

He and his wife settled down, wrapped themselves against the winds of winter, and waited for spring. There had been clouds on the frost, so John Davis knew the weather was bound to be bad. The ground froze, but he thanked God for the wooden floors beneath his wife's tiny feet, and she thanked John, and together they dreamed of warm weather when that other small voice would be added to their own.

The land thawed. But the bride beside John Davis remained cold and sickly. The chill had soaked down into her fragile bones, and even the early spring sunshine couldn't chase it away or warm them.

Don't worry, she would tell her husband, it's only my condition.

But she coughed a lot, and Davis mixed up a hot poultice of lard and fried onions to lay on her chest. She drank syrup of horehound tea and wild honey and said she felt better even when she didn't.

John Davis planted his seeds by day and held his wife's hand at night, and she would smile and remember the old tales her mother told her about babies. If you take the first louse you find on your child's head and crack it on a bell, she had said, the young 'un will be a good singer. A blister on a boy's tongue is a sure sign that he will be a liar. And she made Davis promise that he would never call the baby "angel." Babies called by that name never live long, she whispered. You can see them smiling in their sleep, and it's because they're already talking to the angels.

The spring was good to John Davis. The sky rained when it was supposed to, and the crops grew quickly in the wet ground, but his wife always made him pull his boots off outside to keep him from tracking mud across the only wooden floors in Palo Pinto.

He complained, and she laughed, always quoting the old superstition about the influence of a particular day on a child's birth: Sunday - never to want; Monday - fair in face; Tuesday - full of grace; Wednesday - woeful and sad; Thursday - a long ways to go; Friday - loving and giving; Saturday - work hard for a living.

John Davis hoped that his baby would be born on a Sunday, but he knew in his heart that the child would, more than likely, come kicking and screaming into the world on a Saturday just as his daddy had.

Early one afternoon, John returned home and found his wife crying. "It's because I'm happy," she said.

"Why?"

"Because I know you love me."

He grinned. "How do you figure that?" Davis asked.

"Because I'm the only woman with a wooden floor in the whole county."

The baby was born just about the time the first tomatoes ripened on the vine. John Davis came running from the fields, his heart pounding, when he saw the midwife step from the door.

From the look on her face, he knew he would have no reason to ever smile again.

That night, John Davis ripped up the only wooden floor in Palo Pinto. From the boards he made an oblong coffin, and he buried all his hopes there beneath the scrub and cedar that held stubbornly onto dirt as poor as he would always be.

Whatever It Was or Wasn't

THE LITTLE CARAVAN rolled through the gray rain of an East Texas night, four trucks that groaned, grumbled, and groveled their way past sleeping hamlets in the pines, and no one paid any attention at all to their passing. The big man with the worried eyes stared into a darkness as empty as his wallet. His razor-thin face sagged, and so did his shoulders. His circus was dying, and all that could save it was dry weather, and the rains kept stalking him through the Big Thicket country.

He glanced over at the bearded Hungarian who drove the lead truck down a narrow, winding roadway through a tunnel of pines. His hair was gray turning white, and he had more wrinkles than potholes on a bad road. "Maybe we ought to try and book some performing chickens," he said at last.

"Why chickens?"

"If nobody comes to see 'em, we can eat 'em."

The old Hungarian would have laughed if he hadn't been so hungry. There was an old superstition with the circus. If it rained thirty days during a season, you were out of business. Hell, thought the big man with worried eyes, that ain't merely a superstition. That's gospel, book one, verse one.

Nobody stood in the rain to see a goat ride a horse, even if it was a pretty goat, and his wasn't. The dwarf was a disgrace. He had eaten too many fried potatoes, too much fried okra and cornbread – dripping with red-eye gravy – and had grown to five feet tall. He would not fool anybody after a good meal. The big man with the worried eyes even tried to bill him as "The World's Tallest Dwarf," but that hadn't worked out either. Another month, and he would be the world's skinniest dwarf. No potatoes and okra to fry, and no cornbread to sop in the gravy.

His circus needed an elephant. Everybody wants to see the elephant. He could have gotten one, too. Cheap, the way he liked his elephants. But he could not afford to buy, rent, or steal a truck large enough to haul him around. The big man tucked his red checked coat tighter around his shoulders and closed his worried eyes.

He already had one star. He had Herman. But Herman was sick. The big man cursed silently to himself. He had always depended on Herman to draw crowds, even in towns too small to have a crowd, and Herman had never let him down before. But then, you just can't go on trusting a gorilla forever.

Herman wasn't particularly friendly, but nobody wanted to see a friendly gorilla. They wanted to stare with wide, fearful eyes into the saggy face of a creature straight from the backside of darkest Africa, and Herman looked as though he still had African mud stuck between his toes, even if he had never been closer to the dark continent than Plum Nelly, Georgia, where, the big man figured, the menacing freak show was on both sides of the cage.

The truck behind him began desperately flashing its lights, honking its horn, and the Hungarian eased to a stop by the side of the narrow country road that led to nowhere and never got there before dawn. The big man opened his worried eyes and watched as his cranky, white-haired assistant ran through the rain toward him.

"It's Herman," the man yelled.

"What about him?"

"We ain't got a show no more."

"Why not?"

"Herman's dead."

There was no use to mourn the gorilla or his streak of bad luck. The big man and the Hungarian slowly dragged the limp gorilla out of his personalized truck and dumped him gently into a red-clay ditch where the bluebonnets and red clover grew.

"You're not gonna just leave him there?" asked the assistant, his wide eyes as white as his hair.

"There's too much red tape if we haul a dead gorilla into town," the big man said softly. "Red tape costs money. We ain't got no money."

"It don't seem right to just leave him out here in the rain."

"It isn't. But Herman doesn't feel the rain anymore."

The little caravan was mired in the clutches of the Great Depression. Only the clown could have cheered the big man, but the clown with the painted smile had been fired five days ago, and he promptly ran away with the only daughter of the richest man in Rosetta, Mississippi.

For a moment, the big man thought seriously about just burning the circus down, taking his losses and the few insurance dollars he could earn, then walking away while he was still on his feet. But, alas, the matches were wet, and there wasn't enough gas left in the trucks to soak down the tents.

So he crawled into the cab of his truck, and the little caravan rolled on toward Saratoga. The warm April rains beat down around Herman, who, at last, didn't mind anymore.

It was late the next afternoon when a young boy, mudding home from school, stumbled across the body in the ditch. The sight of it took his breath away.

The thing – whatever it was or wasn't – was hunkered down as though it had grown rigid from too many hours in a straight-backed chair. It had long black hair and a beard. Its shoulders were stooped. And it was hard to tell whether the thing – whatever it was or wasn't – was grinning or grimacing, and its sagging chin was propped up against the knuckles of long, bony fingers.

The boy did what any self-respecting boy would do in 1931.

He ran.

He didn't scream until he caught his breath. His father didn't believe him, not at first anyway. But at last he ambled out of the barn and followed his son down to the red-clay ditch where the red clover and bluebonnets grew. Seeing the thing – whatever it was or wasn't – made a believer out of him.

"It's naked," the man told the farmer down the road. "It's just lying there without any clothes on. And it's barefooted."

"It say anything?"

"Not a word?"

"Is it dead?"

"If it ain't, it ought to be."

The East Texas farmers – most of whom had never even been outside the Big Thicket – came by the truckloads on that spring day to view the thing – whatever it was or wasn't – that had, without warning or invitation, intruded upon their land.

It's a prehistoric monster, some whispered.

It's from some world that ain't ours, believed another.

"It's the Anti-Christ," a preacher warned. "Read about the mark of the beast in Revelation, and I'm convinced this is the beast. The end is upon us, and I fear that it's too late to pray."

Finally, one suggested that Lance Rossier come down and look the thing over. He was a small man with wise eyes and a shock of white hair. His clothes hung loose on his bony frame, and he looked like he might have been either a professor or bootlegger.

Rossier had long been the sage of the Big Thicket. He had read a lot of fancy books, even when there weren't any pictures in them, and was a well-known traveler. It was rumored, in fact, that he, at one time or another, had even gone as far away as New Orleans although he did not brag about it nor confess any sins he might have committed in the Big Easy.

For almost an hour, Rossier studied the beast before him. He knelt beside it. He even dared to touch it. He noticed how rigid the thing was, as though it had spent too many hours in a straight-backed chair. He checked the stooped shoulders, the whiskered and sagging chin propped up on long, bony fingers. He stared at the mouth, trying to decide if the thing was grinning at him, or just grimacing like it had a belly ache. Rossier stood and stepped back, thrusting his hands back in his pockets.

"You know what it is?" he was asked.

Lance Rossier nodded that he did.

"Then don't keep us in the dark."

"Well," Rossier said softly as he headed on back down the narrow road toward Saratoga, "it ain't no mystery."

"It's a mighty fearful thing."

"I've seen plenty of them before," Rossier said.

"You think our women and children are safe?"

"Could be." Rossier shrugged, turned around, and glanced at the rigid creature with long, bony fingers and a whiskered, sagging chin one last time and said, "Boy, I believe what we have here is a deep East Texas domino player."

The farmers argued for a while, then finally passed around a bottle and a shovel, and they buried the thing – whatever it was or wasn't. In deep East Texas, that seemed like the proper and Godly thing to do, even for a domino player.

For the Best Little Girl in the World

ALVIN PARSONS PULLED the collar of his tweed coat tighter around his neck and squinted down the narrow roadway as snow and sand danced in the yellow beam of his headlights, puppets in the wind that howled at him and tried to squeeze its way past the rattling windows on his old Ford car.

He rubbed his tired eyes and shifted slightly in the seat to ease the dull ache that jabbed like a hot poker between his shoulder blades, trying hard to forget the sagging mound of dirt he had left behind on the high Texas plains of Dalhart. He would have planted flowers, but the wind would not have honored them, and flowers don't grow on the high plains of Dalhart when winter comes to numb the ground and kill the seeds and bury all hopes.

Alvin Parsons took the small gold locket from his coat pocket and clasped it tightly in a hand that bore the scars and calluses of too many days in too many West Texas oil fields. It had belonged to her, to the best little girl in the world, and he held it because he could never hold her again, and the locket was all he had left.

Parsons scratched a white beard that had grown much too long and ragged. He looked as old as he felt, and he began aging five years ago when the doctor looked down into the dark, sunken eyes of the little blonde girl and said one word: "Pneumonia." Four days later he had removed the gold locket for the last time.

A lone tear blemished her cheeks.

His tear.

Alvin Parsons shivered as he watched the dancing snow outside reach down and wipe away the dirt road from beneath his headlights. It was much like Parsons himself, always drifting and being blown from place to place, unsure of where it was going and not interested in staying anywhere for very long.

The man behind the steering wheel gently braked the car to a halt as the roadway swung sharply to the right, or maybe it went on straight. Alvin Parsons wasn't quite sure anymore. He rubbed his eyes again. The cracked windshield was fogged, and the road was gone. His headlights lost it, and the weather wiped it from the plains.

Leaving the old Ford behind him, Parsons trekked out across the new-fallen snow, knee-deep in some places, and followed the strands of a barbed wire fence that stretched on into the darkness, trudging uneasily toward a dim flicker of light that beckoned from just beyond a thicket of mesquite trees. The night was silent but not still, and the tiny flakes of ice and sand stung as they bounced against the chilled face of Alvin Parsons.

The light grew larger, then brighter, a lamp in the window of an old nester's farm house that nestled beneath the whine of a windmill that kept complaining in a rusty voice about the wind. It was as though someone was waiting for him, and Alvin Parsons laughed bitterly at the thought. No one cared about him anymore, not really, not since the best little girl in the world had been taken from him. A frown shadowed his face as he again touched the gold locket. It seemed so thin, so fragile.

Parsons knocked. The door eased open. And he stumbled like an unwanted gust of winter wind into a room where a blazing log fire chewed at the gnarled mesquite logs and fought back the December chill.

A farmer in faded overalls stared at him without a word. His wife looked up from the stove where she slowly stirred a bowl of weak soup, adding water because she had run out of potatoes. Near her, a little girl, maybe six, maybe just small for her age, was carefully winding a strand of popcorn around a scrub cedar tree that sat in the corner.

Her eyes were wide with fear - or was it excitement? - as she watched the snow glisten and melt on Alvin Parsons' white beard. His face was ruddy, and she thought, for a long moment, that she had seen a twinkle in the old man's eyes. Her last breath was left hanging in her throat.

"I lost the road in the snow," Parsons said to the farmer. "I need someplace to stay till morning if it's not a bother."

The farmer nodded. "I got a barn," he replied. "It ain't much, but it'll keep the wind and some of the snow off you."

"The barn will do fine."

"Are you hungry?" the wife asked.

Parsons glanced at the three empty bowls on the table and the pot of weak soup that bubbled on the stove. "No," he answered, "but thank you." He hoped that no one heard the low growl in his stomach.

The farmer had been right. The barn wasn't much but more than he expected or probably deserved. Parsons snuggled down in the hay, cold but dry, and tried to sleep, listening to the wind as it roared angrily outside, unable to reach him and quite upset about it.

Sometime around midnight, he heard a noise echo in the night and opened his eyes as the small girl tiptoed into the barn, carrying her scrub cedar tree with her. It had been wrapped heavily with strands of popcorn. Wooden spoons - painted red and blue - hung from the slender branches, and a paper star was tied on top. The small girl knelt beside Parsons and stared for a moment in silence. Then a smile broke through the seriousness of her eyes as she gently touched his beard with trembling fingertips.

"Are you Santa Claus?" she asked softly.

Alvin Parsons' frown turned as dark as the inside of the barn as he suddenly sat up in the hay.

Christmas.

He shook his head.

He had somehow forgotten about Christmas.

Somehow, he always did.

"You didn't come last year," the girl whispered. "Mama said you got lost."

Parsons looked down into the childish innocence of her eyes. Wide. Believing. It was as though he had seen them before.

"I didn't have a tree then," the small girl confided. "Mama said you couldn't find me without a tree."

"It's a beautiful tree you have now," Parsons said, his voice as raspy as sandpaper rubbing against barbed wire.

"Daddy cut it."

Parsons nodded.

"Mama made the star."

Parsons pulled the collar of his coat tighter around his throat, although he didn't feel quite so cold anymore.

"Daddy said you wouldn't come this year either," the little girl said.

The old man sighed. He was cold and tired, and his back ached. "Maybe I'm not Santa Claus," he said.

"It's Christmas eve," the little girl replied, her words coming in short breaths. She was staring hard at his white beard, searching for another twinkle in his eyes. "Who else would you be?"

At the moment, Alvin Parsons didn't know.

"Santa Claus doesn't bring gifts," he said softly. "God does."

"What does God bring?"

"Little girls."

The smile on Alvin Parsons' face eased the hurt in his chest. He tucked her scrub cedar tree under his arm and carried the little girl back through the snow to the warmth of her home.

When she awoke on Christmas morning, he was gone, but on the lower branch of her scrub oak tree there hung a thin, fragile gold locket with a hand-scribbled note that said, "To the best little girl in the world."

She ran down the road, but the car had left, and the snow had blotted out the tracks, and maybe it had not been there at all.

Every year she would wait in the barn, but she never saw Santa Claus again. And when she became a young wife, she looked one December morning into the tiny eyes of a baby girl and finally realized what Christmas was all about.

The old man had been right.

About God.

About gifts.

But mostly about little girls.

She at last removed the gold locket from her neck. The time had come to pass it on to another.

The Stage That Refused to Stay Dark

THE STAGE WAS as dark as a harlot's past. But then, that's the way it had been for almost six decades, and rats ran hungrily amidst the rubble, and cobwebs reached out to torment the footsteps of JoAnn Miller. She paused for a moment to gaze upon the ruptured grandeur of the old Granbury Opera House, crippled by age, an outcast that had lost its glamour and its inheritance.

A woman had killed it.

Maybe a woman could bring it back to life again.

Back during those reckless days, the rough and rowdy days that drank themselves past the turn of the twentieth century, Granbury had boasted wine, women, and song, but it did not spend a whole lot of time with a songbook. There were seven saloons around the Hood County Courthouse, and sin could be found panhandling on the street corners most every night. It wasn't big business. It was just simply the best business in town and probably the most honest.

Then came the day when Carrie Nation - in her pious tirade against the evils of demon rum - marched down to the square, pulled out her trusty little hatchet, and cut the drunken laughter short. She closed the saloons, and whether Carrie intended to or not, she brought the curtain down on the opera house as well. Actors, it seems, had a bad habit of refusing to perform when there were no potential ticket buyers headed to town. Only a few rode to Granbury, Texas, after Carrie Nation rode away. They were the cowboys.

Cowboys didn't count.

To them, culture was about as useless as a windmill without water and not nearly as common. They weren't upset because those God-fearing, Good-hearted little temperance ladies had nailed the door shut on the saloons. They simply ordered their liquor by mail, then picked it up down at the freight depot, sneaking into the dark, dank innards of the old opera house to empty their bottles and fill their bellies and hiccup their way through what was left of the good old days.

The opera house became as tainted as the sour whiskey stains splattered on its walls. For a time, it suffered the indignities of being a warehouse, and someone else stored peanuts in the corner.

That was the legacy that JoAnn Miller found crumbling on the square of Granbury, a derelict whose soul was lost and probably not worth praying for, much less saving.

She had come to town to play golf with Lu and Joe Nutt, whose long-ago ancestors had molded Granbury into shape in the first place. JoAnn Miller was a celebrity, an actress who had starred on Broadway, a singer who had toured the country with Tommy Dorsey, a band leader and director who had once owned the famed Cooperstown Playhouse in New York.

JoAnn Miller had never been to Granbury before. She had no business being there. She wondered why it felt so much like coming home. Lu and Joe Nutt proudly showed her the decaying shell of the old opera house. They had bought it, had even formed an opera association to revitalize it again. "But we need help," they confessed.

"You need money," JoAnn Miller told them.

She shuddered. The roof had collapsed. The wooden floors were rotting away. the lights and plumbing were gone. Rats were nibbling at her shoes.

For some, the opera house might be a dream.

In reality, it was a nightmare.

JoAnn Miller, in the year of 1974, was ready to leave. She never did. After all, the opera house needed a managing director as much as it did a new coat of paint, so she resigned her job with a summer stock theater company to become one.

She must be insane, JoAnn Miller thought. It would take thousands of dollars to restore the opera house and produce good theater, and where was Granbury going to get that kind of money? Those who lived there couldn't pass the hat. It had a hole in it. So did their pockets and most of their shoes.

JoAnn Miller had one hope.

It might be her only hope.

The Texas Historical Survey Committee had funds for worthwhile projects. Perhaps, she might be able to tap the good folks down in Austin for a grant or two. The committee members listened to her plans and her tales of woe, smiled their best political smile, leaned back, propped their patent leather shoes on that rich mahogany desk, and said, "If you all can raise a hundred and ten thousand dollars, we'll match it."

In Granbury, that seemed like all the money in the world.

But the opera house must be preserved, JoAnn Miller decided, so she toured the countryside, preaching and singing the plight of the grand old structure, passing the hat with a patch on it.

Local plumbers went to work on the opera house's water system. Volunteers poured concrete. The Granbury Jaycees framed the stage. Girl Scouts held bake sales. Dallas architect Ed Beran offered his services, and they came without a price tag. The ladies had another bake sale.

JoAnn Miller kept singing, and the old hat was becoming threadbare. Don Byrd, an expert mason, would ride bulls in a rodeo, then hurry home to work on the crumbling stone walls.

The first bid to remove the dangerous, decrepit roof came in at seven thousand dollars. JoAnn Miller broke out in a cold sweat. But a businessman stepped forward and agreed to tear it down for four hundred bucks, and he apologized for charging that much. A retired cabinet maker matched the original design on the doors and windows, which had suffered as the ignominious victims of worms, mold, and rain.

A woman hurried up to JoAnn Miller on the street and confessed, "My husband has a plastering firm. I'm volunteering him if you want him."

If he were a working man, JoAnn Miller wanted him.

She was running out of songs and towns, and she needed a new hat. Granbury had grown fat from bake sales. The days weren't long enough, and sleep was as rare as rain in West Texas. But JoAnn Miller was desperate, and desperate women were capable of just about anything.

The days were drained of energy early, but she wasn't. Within six months, Granbury had earned its hundred and ten thousand dollars, and JoAnn Miller, quite pleased with her efforts, drove off to secure the matching funds with a new song in her heart.

The notes quickly soured in a hurry.

The Texas Historical Survey Committee members listened intently to her plans and tales of success, smiled their best political smile, leaned back, propped their patent leather shoes on that rich mahogany desk, and said, "It'll be a year before we can give you the money."

JoAnn Miller felt a little like dying, but she was too angry for her heart to stop.

"What'll we do?" the opera association asked her.

"We open anyway," JoAnn Miller snapped.

Over in Stephenville, she talked Tarleton University - a member of the Texas A&M System - into giving credit for any student in drama who took her summer workshop, and it did not hurt a bit that the president of JoAnn Miller's board also happened to be the president of the Texas A&M board of regents.

Thus she had a resident company, one whose song-and-dance productions would earn the Granbury Opera Association eighty thousand dollars that summer. It wasn't all the money in the world. But, to JoAnn Miller, it seemed like it was.

One night the phone rang behind the stage where rats had nested and cowboys had once spilled their whiskey. It was the historical survey committee saying, "We have your money now." The committee, a band of historical bureaucrats, had been watching from afar, and now, it, too, wanted to glory in Granbury's artistic success.

JoAnn Miller listened intently, smiled her best political smile, leaned back, propped her scarred leather dancing shoes on a rain-warped desk, and said softly, "We don't need your money anymore."

It was, she believed, her finest performance.

Curse of the Sanctified Sisters

GEORGE MCWHIRTER LOOKED with dim eyes around the small room atop his downtown mercantile store and guessed that he would be dead by the time he left it. He had only one regret. He hated to die alone, but that's the way it is when no one comes to sit at your feet except the angel of death, and God's final messenger was already shuffling up the stairway on the far side of the door that George had never seen any reason to lock.

He lay in the wooden bed his wife had deserted the day she traded him in for Jesus, and George McWhirter tried to unravel the thoughts that troubled him about Martha.

She was sanctified. He wasn't. At least she said he wasn't.

His wife dreamed dreams. He didn't. At least his dreams came and went as quickly as the night, and they were just about as dark.

Martha heard the voice of God. George heard the town laughing, not a chuckle nor a snicker, but a genuine down-in-the gut belly laugh, and it hurt him, even though the town wasn't laughing at him.

Martha was being ridiculed. He was merely pitied. George McWhirter sometimes decided that it was difficult to tell the difference. He never could. He never really tried.

He and his wife had come rolling out of Tennessee back in 1855, finally settling down on the banks of Salado Creek in Belton, Texas. McWhirter built a business, and good old Martha did what any self-respecting woman should have done. She had babies.

George became prosperous. His wife became sick, mostly in the mornings. George gave Martha a fine two-story home. Martha gave George twelve children.

George was king.

He lost the queen.

For weeks, a revival meeting had kindled the fire and brimstone in the back streets of Belton. Martha prayed and she wept and she prayed some more, but mostly she begged for the Good Lord to reach down and save her passel of unsaved children. If He tried, they ducked. The preacher ranted, and he raved. The children closed their collective ears.

One night, as Martha McWhirter walked home in the darkness, a voice whispered softly to her. The revival is all wrong, it said, not even a ripple in the silence. The revival is the work of the devil, the preacher his messenger, and the scriptures his lies.

She never saw who spoke to her, there in the darkness, there in the solitude beside Salado Creek, but the voice's words seared her soul, and Martha McWhirter didn't sleep at all that night. She prayed. Lord, how she prayed. And she wept until her pillow was damp beneath her face. By now, she was used to it, the lost nights, the weeping, her being the mother of so many unsaved and sometimes unsavory children.

The next morning, as she rattled her pots and pans in the dishwater, comfort came at last to Martha McWhirter.

"I've had it," she told her husband.

"What?"

"A divine revelation," she said.

He shrugged, not having had any revelations himself, especially not any divine ones.

"I've got it," Martha told her husband.

"A revelation?"

"Sanctification," Martha McWhirter said.

She had simply arisen that morning, crawled out of her husband's bed, and never bothered to crawl back in. The voice of God – it must have been God since there was no one else around in the still of the night – had gotten her attention, and she vowed to live a life completely free from any sin, shame, or degradation. And that, of course, meant no sex. She was sanctified. Her body was pure again, maybe even virginal, and the righteous Martha McWhirter intended to keep it that way.

"Keep your hands off me," she told George.

"That's ridiculous," he exclaimed.

"That's old-time religion," she said.

George McWhirter was flabbergasted. He didn't mind feuding with his wife. He had done that before. But George wasn't too sure about quarreling with God, and Martha said He was on her side, and George did not doubt it for a moment.

The year of 1866 had been a melancholy, soul-searching one for Martha McWhirter anyway. Two of her children had died. Then she placed her brother in the burying ground. The good woman was stricken with guilt, fearful that God had lost his patience with her foolishness, like giving birth to a dozen children.

He had finally gotten around to chastising her and her sins, then taking them all away again. Martha swore she would live a life cleansed by the Holy Word and decided that she could only get next to Godliness by not sleeping next to a man.

That left George to wrinkle his own blankets. That left George celibate. He made out the best he could by not making out at all. Belton felt sorry for George McWhirter, the outcast, the husband of a wife in exile.

George felt sorry for Belton. Martha was out in the downtown streets spreading the gospel. She was the prophetess, and she found a host of believers, all women, to no one's surprise, all willing to step forward and join her "True Church Colony," all anxious to free themselves from human bondage, which meant they could cut out sex even if they didn't have a headache, a right and a privilege they had never found in the Methodist Church.

"Martha's a fanatic," George was told.

"She only a victim of delusion," he answered.

Belton was full of victims. George wasn't the only one who had to go home at night to an empty bed. Men get cranky in an empty bed.

"We need love," they told their wives.

"God is love."

"Sleep with me," the husbands pleaded.

"You aren't sanctified."

"Then we'll get sanctified," the husbands said in a spirit of compromise.

"Then you won't need sex," the women explained.

"Sanctification be damned."

The men cursed and stomped and gnashed their teeth, all, that is, except George McWhirter, and he did the best he could to understand what he definitely did not understand.

"What you got here," Texas Ranger Big Foot Wallace told good old George McWhirter, "is a real poser."

"A what?"

"You can't fight women," the ranger said.

"I can't."

"And you can't fight religion."

"I don't know how."

"There just ain't one damn, cotton-picking thing you can do about the sanctified sisters of Belton, Texas, and that poses a problem you just can't solve." Big Foot Wallace turned and slowly walked away.

"Where are you going?"

Big Foot squared his broad shoulders. "Where the women ain't so religious, and sanctification ain't a dirty word," he said, which didn't seem like such a bad idea at all.

A few of the men packed up and headed South for Central America, hoping that shame and consternation wouldn't follow them that far. Others filed for a divorce as soon as the courthouse opened. Some got drunk, and others merely slept with a bottle, which was better than sleeping alone.

George McWhirter stayed at home. He was the patient one. He stood firmly by his wife, even kept the children clothed and fed while she strutted off to those prayer vigils,

held twice a week down at the Methodist Church until the Methodist Church finally locked the door and told the sisters to find their sanctification someplace else, which they did, proclaiming that their suspicions had finally been confirmed. Methodists had never had anything in common with the sanctified or the sanctimonious, which they had every right to be.

"You ought to kick her out," George was told.

"She's my wife," he said. "I'm afraid I still love her. She's a real good woman, you know.

"She's a loon."

He couldn't argue with that.

Martha would stand before her flock, spread her arms like an angel trying to fly, and tell those devout, God-fearing disciples of hers, "I have advised wives to live with their husbands when they could, but there is no sense in obeying a drunken husband. If a husband should go to a wife and ask her for his sake, for the sake of her children, and the peace of society to surrender her belief in sanctification as we teach it, I should say for her to do no such thing. For wouldn't that be giving up our religion?"

The sisters stood firm. One, however, was pitched out into the streets, and she promptly ran to the prophetess herself. "I've got sanctification," she said.

"You do indeed."

"But I don't have a home."

George McWhirter, good old George, took her in, even paid her eight dollars a month to help Martha do a little work around the house. She shared his food and shared his wealth and shared his roof above her head when the rains came and the wind howled. But she wouldn't share his bed either, not that he ever asked.

Sister Johnson stood by stoically as one of her most constant problems ended. Brother Johnson, blessed be to the Lord, sighed, took one last breath, rolled his eyes once or twice, and gave up the ghost, which caused her another, more immediate problem. He left her two thousand dollars' worth of life insurance, an inheritance from his membership in the Knights of Honor Lodge. Sister Johnson, blessed be to the Lord, refused it. "I can't take the money," she told the court. "It was left to me by the unsanctified earnings of an unsanctified man."

Her brother did not hesitate. As soon as he tracked down a judge, he had her tried for lunacy. A Bell County jury didn't hesitate either. The twelve good men promptly shipped Sister Johnson off to an insane asylum in Austin. The brother, being unsanctified and pretty damn proud of it, saw nothing at all wrong with spending two thousand dollars of unsanctified money on himself, which he did.

For a time, the husbands fought back with the only weapon they had – hard core sanctions. They took their hard-earned salaries and kept the dollars all to themselves. Their philosophy was simple. No sex, no money." To their chagrin, the sanctified sisters did quite well without either one.

The sisters – there being about thirty of them now – began pooling their butter and egg money. A school teacher brought in her life savings, all twenty dollars of it. Good old Sister Johnson was finally released from the asylum, and she strutted home with ninety dollars she had made as a seamstress behind those locked doors. The sisters took in washing and ironing since their husbands needed their clothes washed and ironed, chopped fire wood, and even hired out as maids in the finer homes around town.

Martha McWhirter sold the milk from her five Jersey cows and tucked it away in the True Church Colony. George tried to give her money, all that she wanted, but Martha would not take it. He didn't even ask for sex in return. She refused it anyway. But she did feel obligated to pray for his wretched and unsanctified soul.

On Tuesdays, the women – at least those who had received the blessed "second blessing" – all gathered together at Sister Henry's to do their weekly laundry. Brother Henry wasn't pleased, but then, Brother Henry had grown cranky sleeping in an empty bed.

He came storming into the house, pushing and shoving, throwing boards at anyone who didn't move fast enough. His wife didn't, and she fell, bleeding from a gash in her head. As the *Gainesville Advance* reported, "Mrs. McWhirter and three other female members of the Sanctification band in Belton have been fined $20 each for occupying Mr. Henry's premises as a laundry to raise funds for the Lord. Mrs. Henry and her daughter left their home after the trial and will cast their lot with the band instead of with ungodly Henry."

Ungodly Henry died a few weeks later. The dirt had not even settled on his grave when the sisters moved into his home, establishing a boarding house that, one day, would become a prosperous hotel.

In 1880, a couple of brothers from Scotland came to town, looked around, liked what they saw, pressed their Bibles hard against their hearts, said a prayer or two, and moved right in with the sisters. God forbid. It did not look good at all, not with those hairy-legged foreigners eating and sleeping in the midst of all those women.

"There's nothing wrong with it at all," Martha McWhirter piously declared.

"It's scandalous," the town whispered.

Martha McWhirter merely smiled as she had always imagined a saint would smile, and said, "They're sanctified, too."

The town laughed, and there was no humor in the laughter. The rumors leaked out and ran like rainwater in the streets. Gossip was as ugly as homemade sin and almost as plentiful. Belton grieved, then it soured. *You can't fight women*, Big Foot Wallace had said. And you can't fight religion. Belton, however, searched the scriptures day and night and finally decided that there was nothing in the Bible that said they couldn't roll up their sleeves and beat the living daylights out of two itinerant Scotsmen.

The Scotsmen hid in the McWhirter house. They found sanctification a thin veil to hide behind. Amidst a winter chill in the street outside, a crowd gathered and became an unruly mob. At midnight, they demanded that the grievous Scotsmen be brought out onto the porch. The only guards were frightened women and good old George McWhirter.

Calmly, he stepped out into the night. He was only one man, and he wasn't even sanctified. But he would do what he could to protect his wife. A gun fired, then another. A bullet slammed into the door beside George. It did not hit him, but the mob did. George fell beneath their feet as the angry and frustrated men of Belton battled their way into the house. Three men were almost beaten to death that night. Two Scotsmen, and, of course, good old George.

Belton knew what to do with those hair-legged old boys who came from afar. The Scotsmen were promptly hauled into court, judged to be insane, and dragged off to the asylum in Austin. The decision had been an easy one. Four doctors examined the wide-eyed Scotsmen. Four doctors agreed on their insanity. Four doctors had wives who were sanctificationists.

The superintendent at the asylum was aghast, among other things. "I'm going to release you," he told the Scotsmen. "You don't belong here."

The brothers nodded in agreement.

"However," said, the superintendent, "you'll have to promise not to go back to Belton."

"But we are going back," protested the brothers.

The superintendent shrugged. "Then I was wrong," he admitted. "You boys are crazy as hell."

Back home, George McWhirter was worried, standing in the front yard of his house and looking up into an evening sky, the color of molten lead, as dear, sanctified Martha stepped gingerly out onto the roof of their porch.

The crowd hooted. It yelled obscenities. And men passed a bottle. But then, that's why Martha McWhirter was standing on the roof in the first place.

She had grown tired of being ridiculed. The time had come to demonstrate her religious faith. She was going to prove, beyond the shadow of a doubt, that she belonged to the Lord and that the Lord kept His hand on those who belonged to him.

"I will jump," Martha McWhirter announced to all who could hear her, "and I will not fall. Even if, perchance I do fall, it won't hurt me. For I have faith, and I believe, and I have heard the voice of God."

Belton could not wait.

George was sick to his stomach.

Martha McWhirter had stepped out of the second-story dormer window, dressed in a long, flowing white robe, clutching two turkey-wing feather dusters. She stared straight ahead, a smile of triumph lighting up her dour face.

She paused.

And the crowd grew silent.

She prayed.

And the faithful prayed with her.

Martha McWhirter leaped out over the banister of the porch, a goddess in flight, crowned by a halo of fading sunlight, an angel with a broken wing, gliding with the grace known only to a sack of cement.

Only George, good old George, was left to console her, hold her, and gently care for Martha's two cracked ribs and the fractures she suffered in both legs. George had always been there when she needed him. George didn't laugh at her. George loved her.

But, at last, even he walked away as well. He had supported her. He had defended her. He had provided a refuge for homeless sisters, and George never complained. But the night Martha brought home a male convert, good old George rebelled. He had finally had enough.

He lived in the same town with her, but, for two years, he did not see Martha or want to see her. He always made sure to go where she wasn't, and, after a while, he didn't bother to go at all.

George McWhirter lay dying, and he was alone, and his thoughts were on Martha. He had done what he could for her. He had carefully written his last will and testament, bequeathing his wife twenty thousand dollars, declaring his faith in her integrity, confirming his conviction that she would do justice to all of their children.

One last time, he wanted to see her. With dimming eyes, he kept looking at the door of his little room above the mercantile store. Where was she? Surely, Martha had heard of his illness and the seriousness of it. Surely, she would come. Surely, he would be able to gaze upon her face again.

After all, George was devoted to her. She knew it. She would come. He lay back in that empty bed of his and waited. George smiled. Martha would come. He strained hard to hear the faint sound of her footsteps on the stairway.

Across town, Martha, too, was alone. She had told her followers that morning: "I'll go see George if I receive a divine revelation from God telling me I ought to go." Now she sat in an empty room, listening to the stillness, awaiting the revelation, looking for a sign.

It never came.

She never left the room.

Martha McWhirter heard that the funeral went about as well as could be expected, and she took the twenty thousand dollars to a bank, hoping that God in His infinite mercy and wisdom, would sanctify it and never doubting for a minute that He would.

On the Fringe of Flight

THE REVEREND BURRELL CANNON stood on the edge of an open pasture and listened to the wind antagonize the tall brittle pines that rose up from the forest behind him. He loved the winds, and, yet, he hated them. They were free, and he wasn't. They went where they wanted to go, and Brother Burrell Cannon couldn't even get himself unstuck from the red clay farmland that kept the pines and Pittsburg, Texas, glued together.

He watched the sun and the moon share the same afternoon sky, and he hugged a black, well-worn, tear-stained copy of the Good Book tightly against his chest, staring up toward the far heavens that tempted him and taunted him and dared him to rise above the clouds. He was destined to go there. He was sure of it. And he wasn't willing to wait for Judgment Day either. He would worry about the resurrection later.

For Brother Burrell Cannon, the clouds didn't seem so far away anymore, and the good reverend knew that he and he alone could reach out and touch them. He would defy the winds. He would fly because God intended for man to fly. At least, God, in His infinite wisdom, meant for Brother Burrell Cannon to soar above the pines. He was the anointed one, the chosen one. Thus it had been written if he had to write it himself.

Late one night, as candlelight flickered upon the wrinkled pages of the Good Book, the East Texas preacher stumbled across the blueprint for flight tucked away in the lyrical, mystical incantations of Ezekiel, where it had lain hidden for thousands of years.

God had locked it away Himself, waiting for the right man at the right time in the right place to finally unearth its Biblical secret. Maybe old Ezekiel had been having visions, or maybe he had actually caught sight of the future. Brother Burrell Cannon didn't know. He only realized that on a dark Texas night, he had seen the light, and it shone squarely on him. Those cursed winds would never shackle him to the ground again.

The good reverend turned to the book of Ezekiel and gazed once more upon the phrases that had inspired the mechanical eccentricities of his soul. He studied closely the passage about the whirlwind that came out of the north, a great cloud of smoke and fire, and of the four living creatures that were supported by wings and wheels.

Brother Burrell Cannon read aloud: *The appearance of the wheels and their work was like unto the color of a beryl: and the four had one likeness and their appearance and their work was as it were a wheel in the middle of a wheel ... And when the living creatures went, the wheels went with them, and when the living creatures were lifted up from the earth, the wheels were lifted up from the earth ... And under the firmament were their wings.*

The good reverend sat back and stared into the darkness of the night. The revelation was as bright as the candle that burned gently before him.

God had spoken.

Brother Burrell Cannon had caught a faint glimpse of the man who had glimpsed the future, and the secret of the ages burned into his mind as clearly and as surely as if God had handed him a blueprint and said, "Build it, and the earth shall loosen you, and you, among all mankind, shall fly." If he were God, that's what he would have said.

Brother Burrell Cannon knew that at last he stood on the fringes of flight. The Good Book was his master plan and his workbook. It was perhaps the hundredth time that he had waded his way through the mystifying prophecy of Ezekiel. He knew the words by heart now. They had become clearer, and so had his destiny. With metal and tools, he would make a whirlwind of smoke and fire, one supported by wings and wheels, one that would carry living creatures within it.

Brother Burrell Cannon would fly, no doubt about it.

It's just that he wouldn't be spending so much time in the pulpit of the Baptist Church anymore. God had finally led him to the machine shop where he belonged, and he prayed for strength, wisdom, perseverance, spiritual guidance and a lot of money. He prayed hardest about the money.

The good reverend walked boldly into a room where the pillars of Pittsburg sat waiting for him. He was a big man with a strong voice. The Baptists liked the way he preached, and the leaders of the little town trusted anyone who could keep them pushed away from the burning gates of hell – although Brother Burrell had been acting kind of strange lately.

"I need twenty thousand dollars," he told them.

"What for?"

"To build a manufacturing plant."

"What for?"

"For the Ezekiel Airship Company."

Now he was talking kind of strange as well.

The pillars of Pittsburg paused, frowned, and raised their respective eyebrows to different heights. Perhaps they hadn't heard the preacher's words correctly. Perhaps they had misunderstood. After all, the windows were open, and the wagons were making a lot of noise in the street outside, and the summer insects were humming louder than unusual. At last, one of the businessmen asked in hushed, measured tones, "Just what are you planning on doing, Brother Burrell?"

"I'm going to fly."

Nobody laughed. The good reverend, they saw, was dead solid serious. His eyes were afire. He believed in the scriptures, and nobody laughed at the scriptures. Maybe he could fly. The people of Pittsburg were certainly willing to buy stock for $25 a share in the Ezekiel Airship Company to find out. The plot thickened when Brother Burrell Cannon talked P.O. Thorsell into cleaning out the second floor of his foundry so he would have a place to work.

Slowly, the odd, skeletal flying machine began taking shape. The preacher read the Good Book, then read it again, searching for clues that he could incorporate into his design. Night would usually catch him in the shop, but it seldom talked him into going home. He was a man obsessed, some thought he might be possessed, and Pittsburg hung onto every prayer, every curious sound that drifted down from the open window of P.W. Thorsell's foundry.

A year later, as summer stained the red clay farmland with sweat but no rain, the good reverend dragged his airship out to the street, piece by piece, and began putting it back together again down by the railroad tracks. It was the only way he could haul the mystical contraption of Ezekiel through a narrow doorway on the second floor. It didn't look like much. But then, nobody knew what a flying machine was supposed to look like anyway. So the crowd applauded and thanked God that somebody else was going to ride it up above the pines while their feet remained firmly on solid ground.

"He's a mad man," said the cynics.

"He's wasted his time," said the non-believers.

"He's wasted our money," said the worried.

"I'll just wait for the rapture," said the religious.

Brother Burrell Cannon loaded his blessed contraption onto a railroad flatcar and headed toward St. Louis where a group of high-dollar investors waited to see him defy the winds.

Unfortunately, the winds caught up with him first.

Just outside of Texarkana, a sudden tornado ripped down the tracks and tossed the flimsy little craft off the rails and into the pines, leaving it torn and tattered and in assorted broken pieces.

The good reverend, however, did not quit on God, himself, or the winds. He would not be able to build a new airship. He had run out of money, and Pittsburg had run out of money, and most everyone had run out of patience. So Brother Burrell Cannon patched up the disjointed remains of his airship and kept on moving toward St. Louis.

The investors had read all about the prophecy, and they watched a cumbersome old motor generate eighty horsepower, spitting fire and smoke and sounding a whole lot like a whirlwind rushing out of the north.

The wings and the wheels in the middle of wheels were all in place, and, lo and behold, Brother Burrell Cannon coaxed it off the ground.

He would have flown, too, some said, if the damned old telegraph pole hadn't gotten in his way, if the wires hadn't snatched him back to earth again.

The good reverend lost altitude, and the investors lost interest.

The flying machine and his last bankable dollar hit rock bottom about the same time.

A dejected Burrell Cannon journeyed home in shame. Maybe he had been wrong. Maybe God did not intend for man to reach for the clouds after all. Like the airship he left behind, he was broken and beaten.

A year later, on the sands of Kitty Hawk, North Carolina, a pair of brothers named Wright crawled into a flying machine with wings and wheels in the middle of wheels, and they did defy the winds.

They flew.

Not far.

And not particularly high.

But they flew.

It was so simple, Brother Burrell Cannon decided as he walked among the pines and silently cursed the winds as only a preacher could. They both had their chances, the good reverend and Ezekiel, and they had failed.

God had anointed another.

Coming Home to the Ghosts

HE CAME BACK to the pine forests and red clay hills of East Texas to bury the ghosts that had trailed after him every waking hour, and mostly when he was asleep, for the past forty-six years, seven months, and sixteen days.

He had not lost track of the time.

He could never forget the moment.

He heard the cries even now.

Time and space, and mostly the miles, had not dimmed them.

His muscles jerked slightly, and he felt far older than he was as he drove down crooked little highway 323 from Overton to New London. He dreaded what he would find. About the time he left one dying little town, he reached the other.

The afternoon was quiet and gray, much as it had been forty-six years, seven months, and sixteen days ago.

Skies overcast.

It looked like rain.

His was the only car on the road.

It had once been so different.

The name on his paycheck had been Travis Flowers, but a lot of names were lost, misplaced, thrown away, and forgotten in the oilfield. He had taken the train to East Texas in the autumn of 1933, trying desperately to escape the Great Depression, on his way to anyplace that had a job and paid him enough to buy all of the white bread, bologna, and cigarettes he wanted.

They were drilling oil wells in East Texas.

And Travis could drill oil wells.

Never had.

But he knew he could.

Travis had worked his way from roustabout to roughneck long before the spring of 1937, and he had married once, lost a baby, and then put his wife on a bus back home to Holly Springs, Mississippi.

He thought she would come back.

She never did, and, after a while, her letters, if there were any, no longer found their way to either the oilfield or Overton.

He parked beside the New London School. He thought he would never see it again. It looked so bright, so new. Not even the past forty-seven years had been able to age it or stain the bricks. Travis shook his head. The last time he saw it, the school lay in ruin.

And still he heard the cries.

The rubble was gone.

The cries had not left him.

The afternoon of March 17, 1937, had been unusually cold, and a slate gray sky promised rain. The well was in. The flow had been controlled. The slush pit was full. Not much left for Travis Flowers to do but pack up his tools and go on home.

The time had clicked down to three-thirty. He knew. He had checked his watch. Didn't know why, but he had checked it all the same. Inside the school, just beyond the clearing in the pines, children were beginning to line up in their classrooms, waiting for the final bell to dismiss them.

Thirteen minutes.

That was all they needed.

Such a short time.

It became eternity.

As Travis Flowers leaned against the rig on the platform, while he was rolling a cigarette in the mist, the school exploded.

Suddenly.

And without warning.

For years, he later learned, the school had been heated by raw natural gas, piped straight from the oilfield. No one knew why, but a leak began spilling fumes into a darkened basement. No one could smell it. No one knew it was there. And no one would ever know for sure what ignited it.

That's what hurt worse.

Plain and simple, no one knew.

But for one frightening, grieving moment, Travis witnessed the sky before him turn black with smoke and debris and ragged bricks tumbling to the ground. The day became a shroud of leaded gray, and the walls of the school came tumbling down.

Travis knew the sound must have been deafening, but all he heard was silence.

Nothing.

The day was ending.

The world was ending.

In silence.

Then came the cries.

And he would never be the same again.

Travis Flowers was one of the first to reach the burned-out hull of a school dead and dying. He heard someone say, "There was a spark, a flash, and then it was gone."

All gone.

Around him, almost three hundred students and teachers lay beneath mounds of rubble. Like Travis Flowers, oilfield workers were leaving their jobs and rushing to the pile of twisted metal and shattered bricks.

Some were searching for their own children.

Others were simply searching for life, any sign of it.

Travis could hear men cursing.

And praying.

And one was no different from the other.

The shattered walls of New London became a wailing wall.

He pushed away metal and wood and bricks and carried child after child to an Ideal Bread truck. The driver had thrown the loaves onto the ground and turned his truck into a rescue vehicle.

Bodies were limp and broken.

He hugged them.

He held them tightly.

He kissed them.

He brushed dirt and blood from their faces.

Only the ones crying had hope, and so few of them were crying.

Day became night, and night turned to morning, and Travis no longer felt a rain that soaked the darkness. He was too tired to lift another brick, but still he stayed, crawling through the debris, praying that another life remained and he could find it.

Mothers stood hollow-eyed in the cold rain, hoping that missing sons or daughters, listed among the living, would still be alive.

Tired workers knew that at any minute they might roll aside a stone and look upon the lifeless body of their own child.

In the sparse light of an early day, Travis stumbled across a blackboard, and upon it, in a childish scrawl, someone had written the lesson of the day: "Oil and Natural Gas are East Texas' greatest mineral blessing. Without them this school would not be here, and none of us would be here learning our lessons."

Travis erased the words with his sleeve, and the rain washed away the chalk dust. Around him was a hurt that would not heal.

Forty-seven years, seven months, and sixteen days later, he walked across the campus and watched the children at play.

He was surrounded by laughter.

All he heard were the cries.

The sun cut sharply through the pines.

All he felt was the rain.

Travis Flowers had come back to the pine forests and red clay hills of East Texas to bury the ghosts of his past.

Forty-seven years, seven months, and sixteen days later, he drove away at dark.

He was not alone.

The ghosts rode with him.

And the muted silence of the cries was almost more than he could stand, and they sounded a lot like his own.

Pearls of Wisdom

WILL TEAL COULDN'T believe that Caddo was mad at him, but it must have been. He had heard the sacred Indian tales about the night a great spirit appeared before the chieftain, warning him that "the earth will heave and sink, and it will rain for many nights – and water will come upon the lands."

Will Teal had even read the words of a wrinkled old Indian who claimed to have been an eyewitness to the night a troubled and trembling quake tore open the grounds beneath his feet: *Once there was a prairie where we hunted the buffalo. But that was before the earth had chills and fever and shook. In the night, the village sank. Then the water rolled over our ground, and we fled to the hills.*

Will Teal knew the feeling. He was on his feet and scrambling for the hills himself. So the earth had had a tough bout with fever and chills, he thought as the water reached out to suck the mud and scum away from his boots. Will Teal reached out and grabbed the trunk of a young pine sapling, frantically holding on as the lake swamped everything, man and beast, in its path.

Damned if it wasn't happening again.

On a bright morning, three years earlier, as the mist danced lightly around the cypress knees and Lily pads of Caddo Lake, Will Teal and Tom Allen rowed their wooden Jon boat slowly away from the sleeping streets of Potter's Point. Neither spoke. Neither had anything to say.

Fishing had long ceased to be a pleasure; it was work in the year of 1909. The men casually eased their way along the trotlines that stretched beneath the Spanish moss of the bayou, checking the hooks, putting new bait on the empty ones, using the soft white flesh of the mussels that lived in the warm, shallow waters of Caddo.

The day began slow, then lost ground. Late in the afternoon, Will Teal gingerly sliced away the outer edge of a mussel's shell, inserted his knife point and quickly pried the shell apart. It was an old practice, one that had become a habit, done without thinking or looking.

For once, fate reached down and tapped Will Teal on a weary shoulder, and he glanced down at the mussel in his hand. Lying there in the tender, waxy flesh – no bigger than the eraser on a No. 2 pencil – was a pearl.

At least, it looked like a pearl, although Teal wasn't quite sure what he had found or what it was doing amongst the lily pads and beneath the calm, shallow waters of Potter's Point.

The two men, curiosity nagging at their common sense, mailed the small gem to Dr. Owens, a buyer of precious stones up in Newport, Arkansas. At first, they were feeling on the near side of euphoric, then merely hopeful, and finally just a little on the lame and embarrassing end of foolish.

Doc Owens, however, wired back, "I'm on my way to Caddo Lake to set up a purchasing agency to handle as many pearls as can be found."

Potter's Point had been nailed together out of pine logs, just a shelter and a refuge for the fishermen and hunters and farmers who had cast their lots upon those soggy East Texas bayous. Overnight, it exploded into a boom town.

Wagons and buggies and hacks came rumbling down the dusty roads to Britt's Gap, Alligator Bayou, Towhead, Perch Gap and Little Green Break. Those muddy banks were lined with digging, clawing, dirt-grabbing fortune hunters who crawled on hands and knees into the mossy, tepid water with a mother-of-pearl gleam in their eyes.

More than two dozen camps quickly sprang up amidst the cypress knees. A tent city of 500 new souls was whipped by the winds that swept the leaves atop a pin oak ridge, and the canvas cracked and popped like gunfire, but no one cared about anything but the sounds of mussels belching pearls.

Fishermen no longer ran their trotlines, and farmers forgot about their crops, leaving them for the sun to sap and the bugs to consume, and the bugs had never had a healthier summer.

The hunters called each other *hogs*, and they would tie one end of a rope around their waists and latch the other end to a boot, splashing around in the shallow water, easing their bare feet along the lake floor, picking up mussels between their toes and finally tossing them onto the boat that trailed peacefully behind them.

Back on the shoreline, their women waited eagerly with vats of boiling water, old hoe files, and butcher knives, prying the shells open and digging out white pearls from washboard mussels, pink pearls from white-eye mussels, and wine pearls from buttermilk mussels.

Buyers from across the country rode without wasting time or changing horses down into the heavily-timbered bayous around Potter's Point, setting up shop beneath the shade of pine thickets and clutching leather satchels filled with money.

They bought pearls as soon as they were dredged out of the water – one or a handful; it didn't make any difference – offering silver, gold, greenbacks, or whatever would spend in the country stores of Britt's Gap and Alligator Bayou.

As soon as a *hog* uncovered a shiny, white gem, he would holler, "Pearl!" And the bidding began before he could catch his breath or wipe the mud from the grin off his face.

Some of the pearls sold for a hundred dollars. A few brought as much as six hundred dollars. A fisherman could be a pauper at breakfast and an aristocrat by the time he sopped up his last meal of the day.

Sachihiko Ona Murata, who had walked off his job as a cook on a drilling rig, rolled up his sleeves and plunged into Caddo. The roughnecks had sadly shaken their heads and ridiculed him. They were still laughing, but not nearly as hard, when he pawned off one of his pearls for $1,500.

The gems brought as much money and were more plentiful than oil, and not nearly as deep or as hard to find.

Will Teal and Tom Allen weren't selfish. There were enough pearls down beneath Caddo to make them all rich. They weren't even worried about the secret being smuggled out of the pine thickets. The wealth that lay under their bare feet would be theirs for the taking forever, and there weren't any calendars large enough to hold forever.

The search for pearls lasted three years.

Then one morning, without any threat or warning, the gates and locks on the old dam in Mooringsport, Louisiana, were removed and the dam raised. Flood waters came rushing madly into Potter's Point, chasing them all to the high ground and burying the mussels in bayous far too deep to hunt.

Will Teal, clutching the young pine, looked down at the rising lake. Caddo had given, and it had taken away. Maybe the earth didn't have fever and chills this time, but Will Teal knew that he was shaking as badly as a stray dog afflicted with malaria.

He would have felt like giving up, but he had saved his trotline and, if nothing else, the fish in those churning waters would keep a hungry man from going hungry.

He pulled his last pearl from his shirt pocket and couldn't figure out why in the world anybody would pay so much money for something so small. It didn't glitter, glare, or glow in the dark. It just lay there in the palm of his hand.

If Will Teal had seen one lying among the rock pebbles, he would have just walked on past. He pitched the pearl into Caddo and watched it sink down into dark waters where not even a probing sunlight could find it.

A pearl was like a lot of things in life, he thought. Men fought over them, women swooned over them, and one was never enough.

Sins of the Father

HE WAS OLD and grizzled, but not nearly as old and grizzled as he looked in the courtroom.

He wore rumpled suits. His shirt was frayed. His tie was almost always out of style and out of date.

And he hated losing. Lord, he hated to lose.

Mister Rayford was what they called him, and they always called him if they were in trouble, and if they were in trouble, Mister Rayford was the man they wanted by their side when the law was against them. He had, some said, the wisest legal mind in fourteen counties. Never named the counties. Didn't have to.

Mister Rayford never handled divorces.

Didn't like divorces.

Thought a man and woman should stay married and endure the consequences if they were foolish enough to get married in the first place.

But if one killed the other, Mister Rayford was the man who would stand and argue for their lives.

He kept most of them free and on the streets.

Didn't care if they were innocent.

Didn't care if they were guilty.

The fee I charge them, he always said, is punishment enough.

His son followed Mister Rayford footsteps, and they led him to law school and then to the courtroom.

Practiced in Dallas. Did well. Earned a pretty good reputation.

Called his daddy with the news.

"I'm coming home," he said.

"Why?" Mister Rayford asked.

"I want to practice law in the same town you do."

"Can't afford a partner," Mister Rayford said.

"Don't want to be your partner."

"This town's not big enough for another good defense attorney," Mister Rayford said.

"Don't plan to defend anyone," the young man said.

Silence. Mister Rayford was puzzled.

"I want to prosecute," the young man said. "I'm going to work for the district attorney."

More silence. Mister Rayford sadly shook his head.

"Don't do that, son," he said.

"Why not?"

"You and I will have to face each other in court."

"We'll both enjoy it," the young man said. "Old school against New School."

Mister Rayford heard a chuckle. It turned into laugher.

"The whole town will get a kick out of it," the young man said.

"Don't do it," Mister Rayford said again. His voice was soft. "For your sake and for my sake, don't do it."

"Too late," the young man said. "I've already accepted the job."

A month passed. That's all. And the inevitable happened.

Mister Rayford sat in the courtroom across from his son.

The boy looked dapper.

New suit.

No wrinkles.

New shirt.

Freshly pressed.

New tie.

And he had every loose end in the case neatly tied up.

He had done his homework.

The facts were on his side.

The young man couldn't lose.

He presented his case, clearly and concisely.

Mister Rayford slumped in the chair. Every word from the prosecutor hammered another nail in his client's coffin.

Mister Rayford did not present any witnesses.

He did not offer any evidence that might acquit his client.

He had none.

There were no character witnesses.

His client had no redeeming qualities.

Mister Rayford was proud of the job his son had done. He loved his son dearly.

But he hated losing.

Lord, he hating losing.

Mister Rayford stood and walked slowly toward the jurors. He knew them all. Hard workers. Farmers. Truck drivers. Teachers. They were his friends. He could not let them down. It was not a good year when he lost a case.

He said, "I hope you listened to every word my son told you. He is eloquent. He makes a fine speech. He makes a fine lawyer."

Mister Rayford paused. He jammed both hands into his pants pockets and leaned against the rail, his back to the jurors as though he was afraid to face them.

"But let me tell you one thing," Mister Rayford continued. "I've studied the case thoroughly, and I know one fact for sure, and it's the one fact you need to know, too. My son was lying to you. Every word he spoke, though eloquent he was, was a bald-faced lie."

Mister Rayford turned to face the jury. His voice bristled.

"I was there when that boy was born," he said. "I watched him grow up. I heard the first words to ever come out of his mouth. The boy was lying then, and he's lying still. The boy just can't help himself."

Mister Rayford sat down and looked as though he might cry.

By mid-afternoon, his client was a free man and on the streets.

By quitting time, his son had resigned.

By nightfall, the young man was driving back to Dallas.

Mister Rayford grinned over a chicken fried steak and bowl of turnip greens.

That's where the boy belonged anyway, he knew. The boy was a damn good lawyer.

But he would never learn to lie as well as his daddy did.

A Few Kind Words about Possums

THE PROFESSOR HIT town, then dodged before it could hit him back. He hitched up his faded blue overalls with all the grace, dignity pomp, and aplomb of a razorback hog in heat, and he preached out loud. Mercy, how he preached out loud.

The professor scratched at a short white beard that was strung up around his face like barbed wire that had been shaved with a pair of fence cutters. And he was a floater and a promoter, which, after all, is what the professor did best.

"The professor's got a silver tongue," said his intrepid partner, Dr. Richard Potter.

"He's that good?" I asked.

"Have you seen the price of silver lately?"

I shrugged. Dr. Potter frowned. And the professor cleared his throat.

"He won't talk long," whispered Dr. Potter.

"Why not?"

"On account of his throat."

"Is it sore?"

"He's afraid of getting it cut."

I frowned. Dr. Potter shrugged. And the professor wiped the pith off his helmet.

His name was Jack S. "Spot" Baird, but back in his hometown, he was known simply as good old Jack S.

"He hangs out here in Gilmer," said Dr. Potter confidentially.

"Why'd they cut him down?"

"Dr. Potter shrugged.

I shrugged.

And the professor sniffed at the pot he was holding. It was the aluminum kind. Spot Baird was the renowned, self-appointed, self-anointed, genuine Professor of Possumology, a title he held with pride, as though anyone else would want it. He knew more than anyone else cared to know or hoped to ever find out about possums, and Spot Baird just might have been one of the world's last authentic, honest-to-goodness gourmet chefs of possum and yams.

He had been cooking one for four years.

"Why doesn't he serve it?" I asked Dr. Potter.

"You can still tell what it is."

"So?"

"I'm not for sure the possum is dead yet."

"What makes you think that."

"The flies won't land on it."'

The professor turned to a little girl in a red dress and asked, "Which side of the possum has the most hair?"

She didn't know.

"The outside," he said, and people marveled at his knowledge and wisdom.

The professor would have made a slick snake oil salesman. He could probably could have been a carnival barker, maybe even a circuit-riding, pass-the-hat tent revivalist. Instead, Spot Baird had become the chief mouthpiece for the biggest minority group of them all.

"Nobody really understands the possum," he mourned. "Most people just think the possum is born dead by the side of the road, and that's not true at all."

"What are they good for?" I asked.

"Fertilizer."

He paused and nodded toward Dr. Richard Potter, his director of research and taste deflector down at the Spot Baird Possum works in Rhonesboro, just outside of Gilmer, but not nearly far enough.

The good doctor rose and straightened his tie, which was a pretty good trick since he wasn't wearing one at the time, and he explained, "We have scientifically tested high-nitrogen possum fertilizer on geraniums planted in clay pots. And after five long weeks of being constantly soaked with that reconstituted, recycled, homogenized, pelletized fertilizer, the geraniums remained the same size."

He reverently removed his hat.

"But the clay pots had grown four times as large as they had been," he said.

The proud potentate of possumology pointed out, with a certain amount of anthropological aplomb, that the opossum, as it is properly called, was the only surviving pouched mammal in the Americas. He said, "It has fifty teeth, more than any other living creature, with the possible exception of Jimmy Carter."

Why is the little critter called an opossum?" I asked.

"I believed it was probably named by an Irishman," Dr. Potter said.

The professor shook his head. "No," he interrupted," I think it happened when some East Texas hillbilly came home one night after a hard day's hunting. Mama hillbilly probably was expecting a deer or a wild turkey. But when she looked in the old man's hunting bag, all she could say was, 'Oh, possum.' At least that's always been my theory."

He's entitled to one. But no more than one. For years, or longer, Spot Baird and Dr. Potter had been out sermonizing on the culinary glory of the boiled, braised, basted or baked possum.

"It's a memory food," explained the doctor.

"Once you eat a possum, you'll never forget it," said the professor.

"It tastes a little like caviar."

"Very little."

He burped. "The possum," he said," is one of the world's great travelers."

Dr. Potter nodded. "Just take a bite," he said. "A little possum goes a long, long way."

Carefully, the professor unrolled a wrinkled paper chart, especially developed for supermarkets, and upon it he had diagrammed the choicest cuts of East Texas hybrid possum meat. There was the curloin, the tail. The strip possaloin. The P-bone steak. The possbelly. The possham. And, of course, the possabaloney.

He opened his aluminum pot and lifted out the twisted, remains of a boiled possum, all prepared for Sunday dinner, scrawny and hollow-eyed, dripped with grease and arthritis.

"It's just as good as it looks," said Dr. Potter.

"It sorta takes your breath way," said the professor.

A lady gagged. "Is that really a possum?" she asked.

"Madam," said the professor politely, "if it's not a possum, then what in the world could it be?"

"Thrown out, if we're lucky."

"It's better if you eat only the white meat," explained Dr. Potter in a comforting voice.

"How do you get the white meat?"

"We usually use Clorox."

Both men highly recommended that you smoke the possum to give it a better flavor. "We've cooked some with half hickory and some using half ash," Spot Baird confided, "and everybody says that the half ash possum is much more delectable."

His possum recipe is a simple one. He said:

"Get one five to six-pound possum, dressed with most of the fat removed from the carcass. Wash and bake six Number one East Texas yams, length wise. Obtain a half cup of ribbon cane syrup, bring it to a boil, and use for basting the possum while it is being baked in a 350-degree oven. Obtain a white oak board about twelve inches wide, eighteen inches long and one inch thick. Place the possum on the center of the board and surround it with yam halves prepared earlier. Place in a 350-degree oven for two hours, then remove the possum from the oven. Take the freshly cooked possum to the nearest garbage can, throw it in, eat the yams, and pick your teeth with what's left of the board."

Until several years earlier, Jack S. Baird and Richard Potter were businessmen, solid pillars of the Gilmer community. But they decided to do what they could to help promote the October Yamboree, the town's tribute to the sweet potato, and they realized that, in the deep piney woods of rural East Texas, possum and taters had long been a traditional dish, a staple during times both good and bad. Possums had graced many a table during the Great Depression, and when the Great Depression left, it left the possums behind.

So Baird and Potter became traveling missionaries, elucidating what they knew about the possum and making up the rest. The professor carried a buckeye at all times. "It's a petrified possum egg," he would explain in case anybody cared and, sometimes, somebody even did. He and the good doctor always drank peach soda water, never wine, with their possum meals, and they constantly kept their eyes open for any prehistoric trace of the dinopossaumasaur.

"Some think he's extinct," said the good doctor. "We don't."

"What's your theory?" I wanted to know.

"We just believe he's playing possum."

The Professor took his responsibility seriously. It was his simple goal in life to put the possum within reach of everyone. It had not been long since he mailed a possum to the governor's mansion in Austin, Texas. By return mail, he received word that the state's chief executive would not touch a possum with a ten-foot pole.

Spot Baird never hesitated. With as much dignity and grandiosity as he could stuff in an anonymous cardboard box, he promptly sent the governor an eleven-foot pole.

The Man in the box

BEN HAD GONE to spy on the old man in the box.

He was nine, scrawny, with brown hair that always needed a trim. He wore navy blue shorts, a white tee shirt, and the oil roads had burned a hole in his tennis shoes. He lived in the country at the end of an oil road.

For boys living deep in the thickets of East Texas, spying on the old man in the box was a rite of passage.

Who is he?

Don't know.

Where did he come from?

No one ever said.

He guessed no one knew.

Does he have a name?

Daddy met him once.

Daddy said he called himself John Kelly.

Didn't talk a lot. Hunted a little. Fished when he was hungry. Planted a garden every spring. Mostly tomatoes. Mostly new potatoes.

Mostly he kept to himself.

Maybe John Kelly was an outlaw. That's what the boys in town said. Maybe he was running from something. Maybe he was hiding from the law.

Some heard he was an army deserter. Some said he had abandoned his wife. Some said he killed his wife.

And he lived by himself in a little one-room log cabin at the end of a dirt road, down by the edge of the creek. The boys called it a box. It sure looked like a box.

Ben only knew one thing as he moved through the pine forest and out across a meadow thick with bull nettle thorns and beggar lice. John Kelly was a man to be feared. See him coming, run the other way.

There was a boy ten years ago who went to spy on John Kelly, and nobody ever saw him again. Ben asked his daddy about it. His daddy just laughed and kept on reading the newspaper.

One by one that summer, the boys had gone out to see if they could get a quick glimpse of the old man.

They walked into the woods.

They ran home.

Never before had they come so close to death. They were sure of it. Louis said he didn't sleep for a week. Nightmares kept him awake. Nightmares were real. He awoke in the morning with fever and sweats.

And now it was Ben's turn. He had been walking for an hour or most of the day.

The afternoon was sultry. The sky was turning dark. Ben heard the rumble of thunder to the west. Lightning crackled across the top of the pines.

He knew he should turn back. He knew he should go home. But the boys would laugh at him and call him yellow.

What's the matter, Ben? That's what they would say. *Afraid to look at old John Kelly?*

The rain caught him in the far corner of Jacob's Meadow. It came down in sheets. The day turned as dark as the clouds. Ben huddled beneath an aging oak, chilled and blinded by the rain.

The thunder rattled the trees and pounded the ground around him, and he could smell the lightning, and he thought it smelled like brimstone although he had never smelled brimstone before.

The old man reached down from the rain and took Ben in his arms. He was a mountain of a man. In the distance, the boy heard the creek running with white water. A door opened, and man and boy walked inside the cabin.

It was a box. The box was dry.

Old John Kelly placed the boy in a chair and slumped down in a rocker.

Ben glanced around the room. He saw nothing but books. From floor to ceiling, the room was lined with books, old and dusty.

"Have you read them all?" Ben asked.

"At least twice and some more." John Kelly's voice was soft and gentle.

"How long you been living here?" The boy glanced quickly toward the door in case he had to run for his life.

"Since the war."

"Which war?"

"Does it matter?"

It didn't.

"Why don't you ever come to town?" Ben asked. He wiped the drops of rain from his face.

"Don't need to." John Kelly grinned. He pointed to his books. "I got all my friends right here."

"There's nobody here."

"My friends, they live in the books."

"But they're not real."

"To me they are."

"People in town, they talk about you," Ben said.

John Kelly shrugged. "I'm sure they do."

"They think you're crazy."

John Kelly laughed. "They may be right," he said.

"They think you're hiding something."

"I am."

"What?"

"Myself."

"Why?"

"I've been to war, and I've seen men die," John Kelly said. "I've been in love, and I've broken a heart or two, and I have had mine broken a time or two. I was always worrying about where I was going and how I was going to get there" He smiled. "I don't worry about that anymore," he said.

"Why not?"

"I pick up a book and can go anywhere in the world," he said, "and I never have to leave home. I read about death, but nobody ever dies. I can fall in love, and she never walks out on me, and she's always here whenever I open the book again."

"Don't you ever get lonely?"

"Sometimes."

"What do you do then?"

"Sometimes it rains, and, on good days, I find somebody wanting to come in out of the rain, and we sit where it's dry and talk a spell. It helps me know all's right with the world I left."

Outside the rain died away. Thunder faded. Lightning no longer lit the sky.

"Can I come back?" Ben asked

"Sure, but I may not be here."

"Where will you be?"

"In a book somewhere." Old John Kelly grinned. "You can always find me in a book."

Requiem for the Tamale Lady

MARIA HOUSTON SELDOM smiled anymore or had any reason to. The pain had wiped the smiles away and left her to trudge the streets of Longview alone, peddling her tamales just as she had back when oil lay new upon the ground and before her boys had run away for the last time.

She missed them. She always would. And Maria hated those boys for leaving her but forgave them even though she knew in her heart that they would never be coming back again. She felt old but really wasn't. Her shoulders were stooped, and those wrinkles in her face matched the ones in her faded yellow dress.

Some laughed at her and took her for granted. But they bought her hot tamales, so Maria ignored them and simply faded into the shadows when they were gone. The sun could not find Maria Houston. She wouldn't let it. And nobody ever looked for long into the dark, empty eyes that couldn't cry anymore.

At night, Maria would lay upon her small bunk in a tarpaper shack and try to remember her growing up days down in Chihuahua, Mexico. They seemed so far away, the fragment of a dream that splintered. She had been the daughter of aristocracy. Her wants had been many and her needs few. And Maria had wanted John Houston, a mining engineer who had come to dig his fortune out of those stubborn Mexican mountains. He was young, and some said he was handsome and quite dashing.

Maria smiled a lot in those days, and she promised herself John Houston would not journey back to American soil without her. He didn't. And the engineer led his bride back to his home on the Texas coast.

She was used to the best, and that's what he would give her.

Maria gave him sons, four of them, and the couple adopted two more young brothers whose parents had died and left them abandoned on the streets without a home. Maria Houston was never happier than when she was with her boys, and she always kept them close to her. They were her strength. They were life itself, at least the best part of it.

Maria didn't really mind when her wayfaring husband ventured again into the mountains of Mexico. After all, he was searching for wealth. After all, he believed that it lay somewhere deep within the hidden ridges of Chihuahua, and it was waiting for him, and John Houston vowed to remain in Mexico until he found it.

He stayed the rest of his life.

Late one afternoon, Maria heard a knock on her door. She opened it, and a stranger brought the news she never thought she would hear.

"I have word about your husband," he said.

"What's wrong?"

"He got caught up in the Madero Revolution. He was riding on a train when terrorists dynamited it."

"Is he hurt?"

"He is dead."

Maria Houston turned to face life without the support and comfort of a husband. She had plenty of money, she thought. It was quickly gone. And all she had left to cling to were her boys. For Maria, they were enough. They worked together, and they worked hard, to scrape up enough money to put food in their bellies and a mattress beneath their tired backs at night.

The good life lay shuttered behind them, and Maria Houston roamed the streets, day after day, selling hot tamales from her cart. She had lost her dignity, but she kept her pride, and she refused any help that anyone offered.

"Me and my boys, we'll get by," she said.

Sometimes she smiled. Mostly she didn't. The boys fought in school, angry over snide remarks they heard about the tamale lady, and nobody ridiculed their mama, not when they were around. She had given them her pride, if nothing else.

Maria never worried about the faded shirts or patched trousers that the boys wore. But she saw their black eyes and split lips, and it hurt. Yet, it gave her the strength to go on. She needed them. God, how she needed them. And Maria prayed that they would be with her forever and she knew her prayers were selfish, and she hoped that the Good Lord would forgive her and answer them anyway.

But, alas, World War II raged across Europe. And the Army took her boys away from their tarpaper home and scattered them on foreign soil. All six of them volunteered as soon as the bullets started flying even though the youngest had to lie about his age in order to crawl his way into the trenches of Germany. He even went AWOL from his unit just so he could find his brothers and fight beside them again. He was used to it.

Maria watched them leave, somewhat proud, somewhat sad, and somewhat bitter. And she waited patiently for their return, peddling her hot tamales, wrapped in corn shucks, throughout the oilfield and army camps that stretched from Texas to Arkansas. She became a common sight, pushing her little cart through the mud, telling anyone who would listen about her boys who had run off to fight the big war.

"They're coming back soon," she would say.

"When?"

"When the fighting's over."

"And what are you going to do then?"

Maria paused behind a fragile smile and answered softly, "I'm gonna laugh again."

The fighting stopped. And Maria looked eagerly each day for the boys in uniform to come marching home again to her doorstep.

The soldier who stood at Maria's door was a stranger.

Again. A stranger.

She was frightened the moment she saw him.

"I regret to inform you," he said solemnly, "that your sons have been killed in action."

"All of them?"

"That is the information I have," he said.

"Gone?"

He nodded. "Each of your sons was covered by a ten-thousand-dollar insurance policy," the stranger in uniform said. "I'll help you fill out the applications for the money that is due you."

Maria shook her head. "No," she replied, her voice low and firm. "I did not sell my boys to the government. The government can buy guns and ammunition and beef to eat. But it cannot buy my boys."

She turned away and, as the darkness of a late afternoon threaded its way down the ragged cracks in the sidewalk, she followed her pushcart, as she always did, down toward the empty end of a lonely street.

Someone stopped her to buy a hot tamale.

"Not today," she whispered.

"Why not?"

"I've lost them," she said.

"That's impossible."

"No."

"But your cart is full of tamales," he said.

"Boys," she said and walked slowly away. "I lost my boys."

I NEVER FORGOT the tamale lady and her boys.

War had separated them.

They would never be all together again.

Her heart had a hole that time could not fill.

Her grief was the grief of many.

She cried until there were no more tears.

My hometown felt deeply about the plight of a mother who had fallen as far as she could go into the depths of hopeless despair.

She did not cry alone.

We did not know her, but we cried with her, which is what small towns in East Texas did when tragedy struck and left gold stars nailed on the doors of those whose World War II sons had been lost forever in lands they had never known or seen before.

She made her living during the 1930s and 1940s pushing a cart through down the back streets of the oilfield peddling hot tamales.

Hard work.

She never complained.

She had her boys.

She kept them clothed and fed.

They marched off to war.

None came home.

They all died so far away.

And she was alone.

I heard my mother tell the story often, and she cried when she told it. Those who heard the story cried when they heard it.

It was the saddest story any of us had ever known.

I grew up haunted by a mother who had so little and lost so much.

We grow up and forget a lot.

I could not forget her.

Many years ago, I wrote her story in my weekly column of *Westward Magazine*, the Sunday Supplement of the *Dallas Times Herald.*

The story ran.

I shoved it aside.

There was always another column to write.

The phone rang one afternoon. I heard a strange voice on the other end of the line, which wasn't particularly unusual. When you write regularly for newspapers or magazines, you field a lot of phone calls and hear a lot of strange voices.

"Hello," I said.

"I'm not dead," he said.

Silence.

I wasn't for sure what to say.

"I didn't die," he said.

"I'm glad," I said, sounding probably as confused as I was.

"You said I died," he said. The voice was not hostile. It was friendly but tinged with sadness. He continued, "My mother was Maria Houston, the tamale lady. I was one of the brothers. There were six of us. We all did go to war. Five of my brothers did die. I was the only one to come home."

"I never knew," I said.

"Most did think we were all dead," he said. "When rumors get started, you can't stop them, not even with the facts. I Just wanted to thank you for the story you wrote about mama. She was a lovely woman who suffered much, and you treated her with the respect she deserved. I just wanted you to know the truth."

Silence.

Finally, "Welcome home," I said.

"Thank you," he said.

He hung up.

Then war had sent her home one of the missing pieces.

It was only one.

It would be enough

Nobody's Above the Law

RODEO IS A rough sport.

Wild horses.

Tough bulls.

Crazy men.

They say they are as rugged, as tough as the animals.

I prefer crazy.

Down in Huntsville, in another day, there was no event rougher than the Texas than the Prison Rodeo.

It began during the 1930s and was known as the wildest show on earth. For convicts, the rodeo became the one bright light of entertainment slipping the past the dark clouds of cell blocks, chain gangs, death row, and the Great Depression.

For a month during the fall, they became cowboys.

Some had never seen a horse before.

They saddled up bucking broncs.

Or they rode bareback.

Mostly they didn't ride at all.

They ached for weeks.

The broken bones took longer to heal.

Nobody cared.

Some of the convicts had never been closer to a bull than a second-hand sirloin steak, yet they crawled on the backs of brahmas with stars in their eyes and saw even more stars when they hit the ground.

Stay in the saddle for eight seconds.

That's all it took.

Eight seconds were an eternity.

They walked into the arena chewing tobacco.

They walked out chewing dirt.

Big name country stars always came to perform, singers like Ernest Tubb, Johnny Cash, Willie Nelson, and Dolly Parton.

But the inmates furnished their own entertainment, too.

The most popular was Juanita Phillips.

She always stole the show.

She danced a little.

She sang a little.

Everybody knew her better by her stage name: Candy Barr.

On the far side of the walls, she had danced at the club owned by Jack Ruby.

Ruby shot Lee Harvey Oswald.

Lee Harvey shot the President, or so they said.

Candy Barr was everybody's sweetheart, even when she wore clothes.

I told you it was a crazy place.

During one fateful autumn, a pair of convicts sauntered through the arena, trying to appear inconspicuous, wearing stolen clothes, holding their heads high, and hoping they looked as though they belonged among the great unwashed with tickets in their pockets.

They glanced uneasily up at the crowd. On some years, it would number a hundred thousand.

Amidst the corn dogs, popcorn, and cotton candy was the tumult.

And the shouting.

And mostly confusion.

The two convicts grinned.

The planets were aligned just right.

It would be a perfect time to escape.

They had spent months hatching their plan.

An ex-wife had stolen the clothes and smuggled them behind the walls.

She would be waiting outside with a car.

She might not be an ex-wife for long.

The plan could not fail.

They were sure of it.

The two convicts slowly and casually worked their way into the crowd. It was easy to get lost or at least misplaced in that many people, all shoving elbow to elbow onto the rodeo grounds.

The they abruptly cut away from the masses and the multitudes and moved behind the arena.

They made their way to the barbed wire fence surrounding the grounds.

They glanced both ways.

No one was around.

Or so they thought.

They were crawling through the barbed wires when they heard the man's voice.

It was loud.

It was deadly.

It sounded like thunder.

They looked up and saw a prison guard marching across the yard, his shotgun dangling loosely in his hands.

He had a scowl on his face.

He was not a happy man.

The guard waved the shotgun in the faces of both convicts.

His voice was cold.

It was devoid of humor.

He scolded them – two grown men – for trying to sneak into the prison rodeo without paying.

They should be ashamed of themselves.

If they couldn't afford a ticket they could just turn around and go back home.

He didn't care.

But one thing was for certain. He was not about to allow them on the rodeo grounds.

The guard grinned.

It was a sardonic grin.

He placed his shotgun on his shoulder.

And he promptly threw them out.

"Don't come back," he barked.

The men smiled and walked away.

Good riddance, he thought.

Nobody was above the law.

The Great American Hero

IF THERE WAS a neon sign out front with at least two letters burned out, if there were at least a dozen pickup trucks of varying shapes, sizes, colors, makes, and models, with a required number of dents, bunched together on a dirt or gravel parking lot, and if the wailing, heartbroken sounds of a honkytonk troubadour cut through the night and reached the highway, I knew I had found a genuine, down-home, home-grown, old-fashioned Texas beer joint.

They were all the same. Small. Frame. Peeling paint. Gone through too many storms outside and just about as many inside. Tucked alongside a back road. Far enough away from town for the kickers to do whatever it was they wanted to do. Close enough to town for an ambulance to arrive when needed and in a hurry.

Same beer.

Same waitresses. At least, they all looked alike. Tall. Blonde. Eyelashes too long. Lipstick too red. Legs never quite long enough. There was only one difference in them as far as I could see. Some wore tight jeans, and some tight short shorts, preferably patched with denim.

Same tattoos.

Same smiles.

Same jeans.

Same boots.

Same peanut shells on the floor.

Same jukebox, all pouring out an assortment of literary short stories about drinking and fighting, living and dying, love lost and love found and love thrown away.

The lines in a Texas jukebox song could be classic.

"I'm gonna put a bar in my car so I can drive myself to drink."

"Her woman's intuition told here I was in to wishin' she would leave."

"I can't get over her until the grass grow over me.'

"Drop kick me, Jesus, through the goal post of life."

"I gave her a ring, and she gave me the finger."

If a man sat alone, he was there to drink.

If a woman was sitting alone, she had come to dance.

No names, proper or otherwise, were required.

We were in the Rambling Rose late one night in the Hill Country, somewhere on a crooked road between Comfort and Welfare. The beer was flowing and never stale, the jukebox had put cheating to four-four time. And a woman sat alone waiting for her heart to be broken by a rancher, cowboy, truck driver, or stranger just passing through.

An old cowboy sat at the far end of the bar.

He had been worn down by hard work and hard times. His face was wrinkled. His eyes had faded. He was a good five inches short of being six feet tall. He was lanky, not much more than a tanned hide stretched over a satchel of bones.

A cowboy hat sat back on his head. It was obvious that, too many times, he had spit tobacco into the wind and walked into it.

His boots were caked with mud and a little cow dung. The boots were made from bull hide. No ostrich or rattlesnake or anything else exotic had ever touched his feet.

He barely looked up when the stranger walked through the door.

A big man. Broad shoulders. Thick chest. Well over six feet tall. He was a man who had muscles in places where I didn't have places. He wore wind pants, a muscle shirt, and penny loafers. He said he was from Houston. He was a big city boy and wanted everybody in the bar to know it.

The stranger had already been drinking, probably the hard stuff. Now he wanted a bottle of beer. No. Wait a minute. "Bring two," he said. The first one wouldn't last nearly long enough. "And keep the rest of them cold."

He laughed. It was a surly laugh.

He hadn't seen the girls.

He was too busy looking in the mirror.

He grinned at himself.

He winked.

Now, I have always noticed that there are basically four kinds of drunks.

Those who turn quiet.

Those who turn loud.

Those who want to kiss somebody.

And those who want to hit somebody.

The stranger was a mean drunk. He was looking for a fight.

After a half-dozen beers, he turned around, leaned his big frame against the bar, and, in a loud voice, announced, "I can whip anybody in this whole damn place."

Nobody moved.

Nobody said a word.

He yelled, "I can whip anybody in this whole damn county."

Nobody moved.

Nobody said a word.

The stranger looked around, wiped the beer and spittle from his mouth, and yelled even louder, "I can whip anybody this whole damn state."

Nobody said a word.

The old cowboy stood up.

He ambled across the broken peanut shells on the beer joint floor and walked up to the stranger. His back was bent. His shoulders were sagging. He tipped his hat farther back on his head.

The stranger folded his arms in defiance.

The muscles in his arms looked even bigger.

He smirked.

The old cowboy didn't say a word.

He reached in his pocket, pulled out a Case pocketknife, opened it as quickly as a rattlesnake might strike, reached up, and, with the flick of his hand, cut off a piece of the stranger's ear.

"Out here," the old man said softly, "we like to mark you tough sons of bitches."

He ambled back to the bar.

By the time he sat down, the tires on the stranger's car were already whining, spinning gravel, and pointed back to Houston.

The old cowboy put a dollar on the bar.

The lady handed him a cold beer.

She winked.

She left the dollar where it lay.

Home to Die

GEORGIO SAW FEAR in his father's eyes as he sat beside the campfire on Houston Creek, or maybe it was sadness. The old man had come to Texas searching for a home. But he had only found a place to stay for a while, and his time was running out. His eyes had turned as gray as his hair, and a thick white beard hid the wrinkles on his face, and he didn't laugh much anymore.

Georgio knew that his father had seen the end time and had suddenly felt like a stranger upon the land that bore his crops and fed his children. The old man wasn't afraid of dying. Georgio was sure of it. There was a time to be born and a time to die. His father had known it all his life. The old man was not afraid of the devil himself and had always said hell was just a place to cool off from one of those Texas summers that sapped the soil and fried his vegetables on the vine.

A month earlier, he had come to Georgio, his first born, about sundown as the frogs began to complain down along the Elm Fork of the Trinity River. "I'm dying," he said softly.

Georgio had tried to protest, but his father wouldn't listen. It's all right, the old man said, He had expected to die someday anyway. His years had already been long enough, and they had been good and bad but mostly better than he probably deserved.

Georgio nodded.

His father looked out across the gently rolling plains as he had done for the past forty-six years. He knew them well. But they didn't belong to him. Not really. They had kept him alive and their dirt had stuck beneath his fingernails, and their rocks had dulled his plow. But they were foreign to him, and he wanted to go back home. Lately the old man had been thinking a lot about the home of his childhood.

"I want you to make me a promise, Georgio," he said firmly.

"What, papa?"

"Don't let me die here. I want to be buried in the earth of my fathers. Carry me back to Italy, to sunny Italy, before I die.'

"It's a long way, papa."

"Promise me, Georgio."

"Yes, papa."

The old man kissed his children and grandchildren goodbye, placed a handful of wildflowers on the grave of his wife who had left him so many years ago, and climbed into the oxcart. For a moment, Georgio thought he saw a faint smile tug at the corners of his father's mouth, and he heard the old man whisper, "Italy."

He seemed stronger than before, and the gray cloud had faded from his eyes.

"Italy."

The old man could not wait to touch the soil of homeland and let it hold him close forever.

The journey turned southward, and the oxen were headed toward the port of Galveston. There, Georgio knew, he would a find a ship to carry his father home. For the first few days, the old man spoke loudly and often of his years on a farm outside of Rome, of his family and his mother who wept and refused to see him the morning he sailed away to seek his fortune in a new land of promise. He wondered if he would be able to find any of his kin and if they remembered him or had even heard of him. Maybe he was just an outcast and would come home and no one would care.

He had told his mother that someday he would return as a wealthy man to walk with dignity and respect down the road outside their farm home. The old man sighed. He was only returning to die. But maybe someone would carry his coffin with dignity and respect down the old road. He suddenly felt very tired. The miles were exacting a heavy price. He grew weak, then silent, and the gray cloud found its way back to his eyes.

He sat staring at the campfire on Houston Creek, chilled even though the night was warm, alone even though Georgio sat beside him. "Are we going to get there?" he asked his son.

"Yes, papa."

The old man closed his eyes, and Georgio thought the old man had drifted off to sleep. He pulled the blanket tighter around his father's shoulders and threw another dried oak limb onto the fire. He, too, was tired. It had rained early that morning, warm and gentle but enough to turn the black land into a quagmire. It had slowed the old cart to a crawl and drained the strength from his oxen.

Beyond the trees, Robert Aycock sat in the dim candlelight of a house that served as both a grocery store and a post office for the settlers scattered along Houston Creek. He was a perplexed man. Around him were the makings of a good town, and all it needed was a name. He was having a hard time finding one.

Most of his neighbors wanted to call the hamlet Houston since they all believed old Sam Houston had once camped out along the creek that wound among their farms.

So Robert Aycock, being the postmaster, had applied for the name, but, alas, the post office rejected it. Texas already had a Houston, the letter said, and one was more than enough.

Aycock was too frustrated to sleep, and he heard someone knocking on his door. He opened it and saw a frightened Georgio.

"My father's extremely ill," the young man said. "Can I bring him inside?"

Robert Aycock rushed with him back to the oxcart and helped carry the old man into the darkness of a bedroom. The hot air was stifling.

For days, Georgio sat beside his father and held his hand, waiting to see those gray eyes open again. On a Thursday morning, Robert Aycock walked into the room as the old man eased out of his coma and turned his head toward the window, watching as sunlight streaked across the prairie. His voice was faint and drifting.

"Italy," he said softly. "Sunny Italy."

Aycock saw Georgio close his eyes and wrestle with his conscience before speaking. Then the young man answered, "Yes, papa. It is Italy."

The old man smiled broadly and tightly grasped Georgio's hand. "Thank you, son," he whispered.

That afternoon, Georgio borrowed a shovel and dug his father's grave beneath a live oak on the banks of Houston Creek. He grieved, but not for his father's death. "I lied to him," the young man told Robert Aycock. The old man had depended on his son to return him to Italy, and Georgio had failed. Then he had lied. It would be a burden and a sin that he would have to shoulder for the rest of his life.

Aycock shook his head. "You did your best," he said, "and I'll make sure you didn't lie to your father."

That night in March of 1880, he sat down and wrote the Post Office Department a letter. His hamlet at last had a name.

It was then, as it is now, the only town in America called Italy.

Godmother in the Desert

MAGGY SMITH HAD all she wanted, which was not nearly as much as she needed, and the Mexicans who waded across the Rio Grande regarded her as a godmother and sometimes as a god herself. When the children were hungry, she fed them whether she ate at all, and often she smuggled them the first, and probably the last, stick of hard candy they would ever have.

When they were sick, Maggy Smith gave them comfort, wiped the grit away from shriveled, fevered little faces while concocting a syrup from sliced onions that had been smothered with sugar and left to stand overnight in the cool air funneling out of Boquillas Canyon. It may not have cured many. But then, it didn't kill anybody, and that made Maggy Smith a saint in the volcanic creases of the desert.

Once a young Mexican vaquero had swallowed too much tequila and argued loudly and heatedly with another man who had also soaked his innards with too much tequila and *cerveza.*

Words weren't enough.

A gunshot was.

The young Mexican fell amongst the *sotol* and maguey plants, lying still in the dust and the tumbleweeds that brushed against his face.

A friend rode twelve miles for help, taking the only trail he knew, the one that led toward the Chisos Mountains, down the embankments of dry arroyos, through the stands of dying mesquite, and across the river to Maggy Smith's place.

When she finally found the vaquero, he was pale from the loss of blood that had stained the sand around him.

Was he dying?

She didn't know.

Maybe it was too late to save him at all.

She didn't care.

Maggy Smith loaded the young vaquero in the backseat of her 1940 automobile and cut out across the desert floor toward the nearest hospital she could find. It rose up on the near side of Fort Stockton, more than a hundred and fifty miles away.

The doctor examined the vaquero and had only one basic question. "Does he have any money?"

"No."

"Does he have a family?"

"I don't know." Maggy Smith paused, looked around the sanitary white walls of the emergency room, and asked, "Will he live?"

The doctor shrugged. "Who'll pay for his treatment?" he asked.

Maggy Smith reached for her purse.

The vaquero lived, but it cost her five hundred dollars. She never complained. That wasn't Maggy Smith's way.

One morning after a high wind had torn the shingles loose from her roof, she found the young vaquero perched on top of her store, hammering them back in place.

He hadn't forgotten his scar.

He would never forget her.

He didn't need to speak English to say *thank you.*

It was always said that Maggy Smith lived off the Mexicans, but she took care of them. She had come to the abandoned spa of Hot Springs in the early 1940s and took over an old rundown trading post that had been nailed together down below Tornillo Creek back in 1928.

The Indians had once used the steaming hot water to ease the soreness from their bodies. The Mexicans had sworn for years that the springs could heal and restore energy to a weary soul, and that's what most of them had.

They worked hard, earned little, and were buried young in the parched earth. But they laughed a lot and danced a lot and always came to Maggy Smith's store on Monday morning, the day when the mail finally arrived. For most, Maggy Smith lived just beyond the end of the world. For those peons, her store was the beginning.

It was late in the afternoon, and the shadows had swarmed like purple sage over Tornillo Flats when she looked up and saw the wagon barreling down a road that horse hooves had chiseled out of the sand and rock.

A young man was pushing the horses at a feverish pace, and his wife lay at his side. Maggy Smith could hear her cries of pain long before the wagon rolled to a stop beside her front door.

The woman, her face glazed with sweat and agony, was obviously in the final stages of a hard, unmerciful labor. The baby was on its way, and she had done everything she could to prevent birth until she reached the general store.

Old, ragged cotton stockings had been filled with stones and tied tightly around her swollen body, just below her breasts and across her hips – chains that kept the child locked firmly into her womb.

The woman was cold, even though heat shimmered up from the cactus floor beneath her. She was scared. The pain wracked a pretty face that was twisted and gaunt and no longer pretty. She turned her head and saw Maggy Smith walking quickly toward her, and she smiled through clenched teeth, wiping the sweat and dust away from her face.

She hurt. The pain was that of a twisted knife.

But Maggy Smith was there.

She was not frightened anymore.

Maggy gently removed the cotton stocking chain and carried the woman to the bed of her pickup truck. The ride to a doctor in Marathon would be rough, and the woman's husband held her against his chest to keep the chuck holes and the rocks from jarring her as the truck bounced madly through the sand and cactus flats. Maggy Smith only hoped that the old pickup would hold together and the baby would wait another eighty miles.

The truck cooperated.

The baby didn't.

At the top of a hill, she heard the kind of scream that she had heard so many times before, and she knew it was useless to drive any farther. There beside the banks of a dry creek bed, with night only a faint promise of sundown, Maggy Smith rolled up her sleeves and helped another kicking, squalling life find its way into an empty world. She handed the child to his pale father and washed the woman's tired face with the drinking water from her canteen.

"A mother needs to be beautiful when her little boy sees her for the first time," she said softly.

The woman smiled.

The baby didn't stop crying until it lay its wet little head up snugly against the woman's face, no longer twisted, no longer gaunt, a face as pretty as Maggy Smith had ever seen before. And the mother cried alone.

Late that night, Maggy Smith searched through an old trunk and found some baby clothes for the infant to wear. It had come naked into the world, all right. Maggy would make sure it didn't have to go home that way.

Five years later, she was startled one afternoon when a small boy dragged a squealing pig to Maggy Smith's feet. "Mama said to give it to you," he said.

"Why would she do a thing like that?"

"It's her birthday."

Maggy Smith laughed softly. "Then I should give something to her," she told the little boy.

"You already did."

"What?"

"Me."

He was still grinning, sucking on a stick of hard candy, when the wagon that brought him to the mineral waters of Hot Springs rolled back across the Rio Grande and on toward the dry arroyos of home.

Confessions of a Soiled Soul

THE RANCHER WITH sun-faded eyes saw them coming across the desert flats, two lost and miserable souls who were trying to scrape by the best they could with what they had, which was two dollars shy of a dollar and a half.

One spoke English quite well. The other rarely spoke at all. They worked from dawn to dusk, usually later, finding shelter at night down in a ramshackle line shack that had been patched together before the turn of the century, back when grass was stirrup high and cattle ran wild in stray herds along the Rio Grande.

Those unforgiving days of the dust bowl in the 1880s wasted the prairie, water holes dried up, and, one old cowboy recalled, the alkali in rivers was so strong it could take the skin off the tongues of any animals that tried to drink from their tepid pools.

It was not a good time to be a cattleman in the Trans-Pecos of Texas. Perhaps no time ever was. One rancher, who felt like giving up, wrote: "A few good years are followed by more lean years, which eat up everything the good years have made, and then some."

The Big Bend became a no-man's land, a country for lost souls. And miserable ones. The land, the rancher with sun-faded eyes sometimes swore, was cursed. He knew. He had cursed it a lot.

The earth demanded everything he had. It gave so little in return. But the rancher with sun-faded eyes dug in his heels and stayed, even when others had quit and left for greener pastures. Maybe they would find better stretches of grazing land. Maybe not.

The rancher with sun-faded eyes watched the two vaqueros riding his way, and they were closer now, and the sun was sprinkling its last rays among the mesquite branches. Their clothes were old and coated with a month's worth of dust, and their dark faces were as coarse as a cracked saddle horn. Their black eyes mirrored the emptiness of their souls. Lost. And miserable. They were good hands. They did what they were told and seldom complained, not loud and not in English anyway.

Other cowboys were earning a hundred dollars a month and barely surviving from payday to payday. The vaqueros drew forty dollars a month and were sending money home, back across the border, back where life was meager and children came into the world hungry and left as old men and women the same way.

The fortunate ones found their way to ranchers who asked no questions and paid them forty dollars a month. They became the richest of the poor.

The vaquero who spoke English dismounted and sauntered over to his boss. "I have to go to town," he said.

"I can't let you."

"But it's Saturday night."

"That's why I can't let you. You got work to do tomorrow, and I don't want you in town raisin' hell an' gettin' drunk an' forgettin' how to get on back here before daylight."

The vaquero held his head high. "I need to see a priest," he said softly.

"A priest ain't got no use for you unless you're gettin' married or buried."

"I have to make my confession."

"What the hell for?"

"It is the way of our church."

The rancher frowned and spit into the ashen dust that held his boots. Damn, he thought. He couldn't let them go gallivanting off into town. He needed them, even on Sunday. Cattle didn't take Sunday off. Neither could they.

Yet, he was a God-fearing man. He did understand the ways of the church, even though he hadn't darkened its doorway for years. He did his praying out in the pasture where, he hoped, it would do him some good. He and God didn't have anything in common down by the altar. Out on the grasslands, they worked pretty good together.

"I'll tell you what," the rancher with the sun-faded eyes said at last. "You just plan on stayin' around here and workin', an' I'll see the priest for you. I got to go into town anyway."

Now it was the vaquero's turn to frown. "You can't do that."

"Why not?"

"Our prayers of confession are personal ones. They are very important to us. No one can do it for us."

"Sure, I can." The rancher had a grin in his sun-faded eyes. "Me an' the priest are pretty thick. I been knowin' him for years." He paused, reached for a cigar, then continued, "You just tell me what you want to confess about, an' I'll work it out with the priest, an' he can work it out with the Good Lord, and you won't have a damn thing to worry about."

"You sure the church allows it?"

"You only got two people to worry about. Me and the priest. We'll take care of everything, and the Good Lord can get rid of your sins before I get back."

The vaquero sighed and reverently removed his hat. His eyes were cast down to the ground, and his words were barely audible."

"Last week, I drank too much whiskey and got drunk," he said.

"That's all right," the rancher bellowed. "God's not gonna hold it against a man for bein' thirsty. I'll take care of it."

"An' I shot Renaldo because I wanted Renaldo's wife."

"Now that's gonna take some doin'," the rancher said. "The Good Lord don't like it much when you start whittlin' off some of his commandments. But, don't worry, I'll take care of it."

"An' I took Renaldo's wife to bed with me."

The rancher arched an eyebrow, grinned as he shook his head, and said, "The Good Lord's got more on his mind than what you do behind the locked doors of your own home."

"It was Renaldo's home."

"The Lord probably don't even know where Renaldo lived. Not too many people do down here." The rancher with the sun-faded eyes grinned again, and the air was filled with the acrid smoke of his two-bit cigar.

The vaquero took a deep breath and continued, "I stole a bag of cornmeal down at the trading post."

"That ain't nothin'."

"An' I got in a fight with my sister's husband."

"He probably had a good fight comin' to him."

The vaquero closed his eyes, held his breath, and cupped his hands repentantly beneath his chin. "An' last night," he said weakly, "me and Lupe were hungry, and we butchered one of your calves."

The rancher's grin vanished, and his eyes turned cold, and he felt his hands tremble as anger boiled up from deep inside of him.

"You did what?"

"We killed one of your calves to feed ourselves. An', of course, Renaldo's wife had to eat, too."

The rancher with sun-faded eyes threw his cigar into the dust and crushed it with the heel of his boot. He could not believe what he had just heard. His cattle were the only way he had to make a decent living, and now his own cowboys, good cowboys at that, were stealing from him.

He said nothing for a moment. He gazed across a barren landscape. Shadows crawling from the mountains were the color of purple.

Then he spoke, and his words were as hot as the smoldering end of a branding iron. "You know you shouldn't have done it," he snapped.

"Yes, sir."

"What you did was wrong," the rancher said. "Dead wrong."

"Yes, sir."

"It's against the damn law. The law's law and my law both."

"Yes, sir."

The rancher's voice became as soft as a whisper. "If I wasn't representing Jesus Christ," he said, "I'd kill both you no-count, good-for-nothin' sons of bitches."

He turned abruptly and walked away in the shadows of the night as they reached out to cover the prairie with shame. By daybreak, he was in town, knocking on the church's front door, doing what he could to save from a burning hell the souls of two lost and miserable vaqueros.

They would learn all about purgatory when he got back to the ranch.

An Afternoon with Emily

JAKE CAME TO the church on a Sunday morning when heat was running through the canyons as though it had been blown from the back doors of hell.

He was lost.

He was trapped by a harsh desert land.

The creeks were dry.

The mountains were chiseled from rock, their canyons a prison wall.

The lizards had thorns.

His car had shuddered to a stop two hours and eight minutes back down a dirt road.

The motor had coughed one last time.

Only steam was curling up out of the radiator.

Jake figured he had two choices.

He could die of thirst sitting on the hood of his car.

Or he could die walking down the dirt road.

He looked around him.

Only the lizards lived in the desert.

The desert wanted no one else.

The narrow little road led him to an aging sign on a weathered post that said T*erlingua.*

An arrow pointed to the left.

He saw a cluster of houses.

They were made from adobe. They were empty. Their floors were dirt.

The winds had blown their roofs away.

He walked to a general store.

At least a sign hanging crookedly above the doorway said that's what it was.

The one street through town lay on the far side of a cemetery.

Jake walked among the graves.

Wooden crosses.

Wooden markers.

Names carved on rock.

When the quicksilver mines played out, rocks were all that remained.

Some were lined with veins of quartz.

Jake pushed on the door. It was locked.

He looked through the window. The room was dark.

A web hung on the windowsill. Even the spiders were gone.

On the crest of a hill, atop the boulders, beyond the cactus, sat an old church.

Jake began trudging up the slope and waited for the birds to sing.

Silence.

Jake saw the old man before he reached the church. He was sitting on a wooden bench, watching the sunlight paint the red slopes and shadows hide the canyons of the mountains.

His hair was white.

His skin was burnished leather.

His jeans were faded, his boots scuffed, the red and white checked shirt missing a button. A straw hat shaded his face.

He hadn't shaved in a while. The old man was as lean and as bent as a fence post when he stood.

"You lost?" he asked.

"Car used up all its water."

The old man nodded. "Happens a lot out here."

"When will the general store open?"

"When old Nathan rises from the dead."

'He been dead long?"

"Died in '78."

Jake sat down beside the man. "What do you do for water around here?"

"We got a creek," the old man said, "and a pile of empty buckets."

"I may steal one of the buckets."

The old man grinned. "You wouldn't be the first."

Jake's gaze shifted back to the ruins of downtown Terlingua. "What brought you to this godforsaken little place?" he asked.

"A girl." The grin turned to a gentle smile. "Name's Emily. Pretty as a sunset, and I see a lot of sunsets."

"You find her."

"This is a far as she got."

"Why didn't you leave?"

"She didn't want to go."

"And you stayed with her."

The smile on his face widened. “I told you,” the old man repeated. ”Pretty as a sunset.”

“You ever get lonesome? Jake asked.

“Not me.”

“It’s a lonesome looking country.

The old man’s smile faded. “I go to church,” he said.

“I got the Good Book,” he said.

“And I spend my afternoons with Emily.”

Jake shook the old man’s hand and walked away.

Looking for a bucket.

Looking for a creek.

The bucket was easier to find.

Jake was kneeling alongside Terlingua creek when he glanced up and saw the old man leave the church, stumble down the hillside, and wander among the wooden crosses.

One was new.

White.

Freshly painted.

A straight-backed chair had been placed beside the grave.

The old man sat down.

Jake would have stopped to say goodbye. but that would have been impolite, he decided.

He left with his bucket of water.

He left the old man alone.

He left the old man to spend an afternoon with Emily.

Border Justice

BUCK NEWSOME FEARED the Lord Almighty, but nobody else, and he had no use at all for the man in the fancy robe who preached God's word in a tongue he could not understand. Newsome didn't read the Good Book much, but he knew that, if he wasn't sorely mistaken, one of God's words surely had something to do with compassion, and the man in the fancy robes either didn't know it, had forgotten it, or just didn't give a damn anymore, and by gawd, it was about time he did.

Buck Newsome stomped – with red face and cool, lethal eyes – alongside the dirt and trash of a South Texas sidewalk, a border patrolman who had grown tired of kicking hungry illegal aliens back beyond the Rio Grande. He didn't mind removing them to their homeland. Hell, that was his job. He just hated to see them go home with their bellies as empty as their hopes.

Newsome glanced back at the old woman and the boy who toddled along after him. They owned nothing and were wearing the only possessions they had. The old woman's dress, a collection of patches and rags, dragged the ground, and the boy rolled his eyes and slobbered. His jeans were torn and hadn't been washed since he put them on for the first time. He was barefoot, the bottom of his feet as tough and scarred as shoe leather. She was worn out, and he was mentally retarded, and together they had fled Mexico, escaping to the land of promises where even an old woman and her backward grandson could find work and pennies to buy their bread.

That was the promise.

Buck Newsome knew better.

The old woman had crawled to the foot of the church and prayed. She prayed all night and all week. At first, she prayed for a job, then a roof over her head, then food for her grandson, and finally she just prayed that God would end her misery. God may have heard her. Buck Newsome came along and answered that prayer.

In the year of '51, he had seen the banjo-bellied, cigar-smoking, high-rolling farmers of the Rio Grande Valley sneak wetbacks across the border, work them hard for weeks, then frantically call the Border Patrol to arrest them as illegal aliens. No passport. No visa. No papers of citizenship. It was easier to send the wetbacks home than pay them.

And there was always another unfortunate and unsuspecting soul wading the river to take their place at the bottom of a ladder with no rungs. Some he carried back across the Rio Grande and set free, whether they knew it or not. Some he buried in dry ground. No name. No age. No next of kin. He simply laid them away with a short scripture among the weeds and never amidst the flowers.

Somewhere in the church, if he wasn't sorely mistaken, the man in the fancy robe was blessing souls in a tongue that Newsome could not understand and forgiving sins and washing them away in hundred-dollar bills. And the farmers were all singing *Jesus Loves Me*, but not the wetbacks in the field.

Newsome had found the old woman and the slobbering twelve-year-old that morning, sitting alone in a back alley of Edinburg. They had left San Luis Potosi and ridden on a crowded bus until she ran out of money. Then they had walked the crooked road for nine days, searching for salvation just north of the river.

All she wanted was a job. But no one was hiring an old woman with a mentally retarded grandson who slobbered on himself, and she could not leave him because she was all he had. They sat down in the night and were waiting to die together, although the grandson did not know it. The boy didn't know anything except that he was hungry, and he devoured the cheese, crackers, and sardines that Newsome dropped in his lap.

And now, by gawd, Buck Newsome was dead set on teaching the man in the fancy robe about compassion if he had to do with the blunt end of a rusted shovel. He banged on the cathedral door, and a lovely young lady opened it.

"I want to see the padre," Newsome told her.

"He's in the gym doing his morning exercises," she answered.

"We'll wait."

Minutes later, the sweating Irish padre swaggered into the room, red-haired and hairy-chested, his fat belly – usually hidden by a fancy robe – hanging out over a pair of silk boxing trunks.

"Why are you here?" he asked.

"This woman and her grandson need help," Newsome replied as softly as his brusque voice could manage. "If I'm not sorely mistaken, they are of the same religious faith that you are, and I thought you might be able to help them.

The padre nodded.

The woman, crying, fell to her knees and kissed his hand, and he blessed her. She had never expected to be so close to someone so holy.

"She doesn't need her soul blessed," Newsome said, biting off his words like tobacco and spitting them in the padre's face. "She needs her belly full of groceries."

"We don't have the money to give everyone who knocks on our door," the padre said.

"I thought the Good Lord said to feed the poor."

"He had better resources than we do."

"So you're gonna let her and the boy walk away hungry."

"We're here for lost souls."

"But not hungry ones."

"I'm sorry."

Buck Newsome narrowed his eyes and folded his arms in defiance. "I take the poor ones across the border every day and turn them loose," he said. "My orders are to stand there and make sure none of them come back."

"How can you keep them out?"

Newsome grinned. "The Good Lord gave you a Bible. He gave me a pistol."

"We both have our jobs to do."

"I'm taking a bunch over this morning," Newsome said. "I suggest you be packed and ready to leave in, say, fifteen minutes or so. You can preach to them all the way home."

The color drained from the Padre's face. "You can't do that to me."

"I can deport pretty much who I damn well please."

"That would be a grave mistake."

"It's a mistake I can live with," Newsome said.

"I'll have your badge," the padre said.

"Probably," Newsome said with a nonchalant shrug. "But, if I'm not sorely mistaken, you'll have to get back across the river first."

"The river's not that wide."

"I'll be waiting," Newsome said. His grin was a scar and devoid of humor.

The padre frowned and looked hard at the patrolman. He blinked.

Newsome knew he would.

"I can spare her ten dollars," the padre said at last.

"Not enough."

The padre paced the room. He was sweating again. He had no problem dealing with the devil. But Buck Newsome frightened him. God may have been the judge. But Newsome was the law. God only condemned mankind. Buck Newsome carried a gun.

"How much is enough?" he asked.

"If I'm not sorely mistaken," Newsome said, "it'll take about a hundred to keep them bed and get them back to their village."

From his safe, the padre hesitantly and gingerly removed a cigar box filled with hundred-dollar bills. Newsome pried one of the bills loose and handed it to the old woman.

A tear touched her eye. She was rich. Maybe not forever. But for a day, she was rich.

Newsome turned to the padre and said, "May the good lord take a liking to you. I don't."

Late that afternoon, he loaded the old woman and the boy in his pickup truck, carried them down to the bridge at Hidalgo, and pointed them south toward home. A bus would pick them up before sundown. Newsome thought for a moment he saw her smile. But maybe he was sorely mistaken. Maybe it was only indigestion. That happened sometime when a full belly had never been full before.

The Last Belle of Tascosa

FRENCHY STUMBLED UP the buffalo grass slope to the top of the hill where the winds of November blew gently through her hair and sang away the sadness of the night. The wind was her only companion, the only neighbor who had not moved away from Tascosa and left her to face the icy chill of winter alone.

Mack did not want to desert her, but he had no choice, and she had expected to see him long before the winds of November had led her again through the buffalo grass to the hillside where no one walked much anymore.

Frenchy had gone to sleep many nights, hoping to be at his side when she awoke the next morning. But Mack was never there, and she had not felt his touch for almost twenty-seven years, and she knew just how dreadful those winters could be without his arms to keep her warm. She smiled as she whispered his name, and Frenchy knelt among the buffalo grass as the wind sang across the hilltop and upon his barren grave.

She had ridden into the Texas Panhandle back when it was wilder and a good deal louder, and a woman could earn herself a good living if she knew how to shuffle cards at the gaming tables of Mobeetie, and Frenchy did. To Mack McCormick, she was his good luck charm, and he never seemed to lose when she stood and kept her eyes upon the hands that he was dealt.

Frenchy was tall, and some swore she was a beauty, and the trunks in her bedroom were packed with satin shoes and colorful plumes that decorated the fancy dancing dresses she never wore anymore. No one knew her past. No one knew her name. Mack simply called her Frenchy, though he had no idea what bloodlines ran through her veins, and she vowed within the sanctity of a saloon one night that "no one will ever find out who I am."

Her daddy had caught her dancing on the frayed stage of a burlesque theater, some whispered. Maybe. And he pulled her off and beat her, and she left on the next stagecoach out of town. That's what they said anyway. Frenchy only smiled.

She ran off with a no-good man, which could have been any man west of no-man's land, and he abandoned her, others swore. They said she was just too ashamed to ever go back home and face her grieving family again. Thus, she had to become a dance hall girl to keep from starving to death in a hard land where few cared if she starved to death, no matter how pretty she was or wasn't. Talk was cheap. Some thought that she was, too.

But Frenchy didn't really mind. She had what she needed most. She had a man, and Mack McCormick - gambler, hunter, and freight hauler - gave her the last and most important possession he had – himself – for better or worse, and Frenchy was used to having the worse that life offered. The lovers had ambled down to the saloon in Tascosa one night, and Scotty Wilson, the justice of the peace when he wasn't pouring whiskey and tending bar, made an honest woman out of Frenchy and a husband out of Mack.

McCormick promptly built his wife a two-room home out of adobe down close to his livery stable, and Frenchy found it plenty big enough to hang the marriage license on the wall. It gave her honor. It gave her self-respect. She could hold her head high with dignity when she walked down the mud streets of Tascosa, dubbed by the cowboys who drank its whiskey and dealt its crooked cards as the "Prodigal Queen of the Panhandle." Many of them figured that the title could just as easily be applied to Frenchy as well. Perhaps.

But as she once told a friend, "Mack and I talked over the fact that we had both lived on the somewhat seamy side of life. But he took my hands in his, and we vowed to stick to each other and to Tascosa. And that's what I aim to do."

It was on a chilled October day in 1912 that Mack left her. He had been planning to ride away on a hunting trip. But death took him instead. And Frenchy buried her man amidst the buffalo grass on top of a little, wind-bothered hill.

No one else came to mourn his passing, and Frenchy trudged slowly back to a town that was choking on barbed wire and in the final throes of death itself. By 1920, the population of Tascosa had dwindled down to one. Only Frenchy McCormick remained. She had her milk cow and her garden, and from the doorway of her adobe home, she could see the white stone marker rising up out of the buffalo grass, and she knew she had a promise to keep.

The years treated her unkindly, and time began to erode the ruins of Tascosa. Buildings crumbled around her. Weeds erased the old streets where she and Mack had walked in the moonlight. Dust storms swept over the Llano Estacado like a plague. Blizzards ranted and raved, and weeks, then months, would pass before Frenchy saw another living soul. No one ever came to stay for very long in Tascosa. Drifters were either lost or just passing through. Sometimes they only came to gaze with sadness or curiosity upon the crazy lady who had stayed behind in a world that had gone from ashes to ashes, from dust to dust.

Her milk cow died. The drought robbed her vegetable garden. A rattlesnake bite poisoned her dog. County workers brought her coal for the stove and kerosene for her lamp. They worried that one day the adobe shack would simply give out and fall down around her.

"You should leave," they told her.

Frenchy did not answer. She only smiled and looked up toward the hill and the white stone marker. There was no reason for her to go. There was no place for her to go. Frenchy was where she belonged, with the town that gave her a husband and near the man who had given her love and respect, and provided her all that she had, which wasn't much, but more than she had ever had before. He was waiting for her. He had been waiting for so long.

"Do you have a family we can get in touch with? the county workers asked.

Maybe. Maybe not.

"No one knows who I am," was all Frenchy would ever say. "And I'll never tell."

She had her secrets, and she kept them as profoundly as she kept her vows. A passer-by did drive her to church one morning in Channing, but Frenchy, her head bowed, unable to pray and unable to remember why she had any reason to pray, adamantly refused to enter such a holy place.

"It might be out of place for me to go into the Lord's home," she whispered softly.

"He knows who you are."

"Then he's the only one."

"He doesn't hold grudges."

"I been told he don't forget either."

During his sermon, the minister glanced toward the window, and he saw an old lady's wrinkled face pressed tightly against the glass. He raised his Bible and gently motioned for her to come inside, but the face faded away, and he never saw it again.

At last, on a bitter January day in 1941, Frenchy McCormick didn't keep Mack waiting any longer. The kerosene of her lamp had finally burned out for good. A Catholic priest said that her love and devotion to her husband surely atoned for any unrepented sins that might have trailed Frenchy to her grave, and strangers buried her beside Mack, beneath the buffalo grass where the wind in the shadows sang away the sadness of a town that was no more and the last resident it would ever have.

A Friend Unexpected

THE BELLS AWOKE Arthur Daniels, and he thought for a moment that he was probably dead, and it wouldn't have surprised him at all. But slowly his head cleared, and the fog faded away from the edge of his eyes, and Arthur Daniels climbed off the mattress that was only costing him fifty cents a night but was dreadfully overpriced at that.

His bare feet touched the floor of an old walk-up hotel, and he shuffled toward a window that had been stuck closed with paint years ago. The paint faded away. The window was still stuck. Arthur Daniels brushed back the dust from a cracked pane and looked out over a backstreet of Matador.

And at the far end, the bells were playing a song he had never heard before. But then, Arthur Daniels couldn't remember much of anything he had ever heard in church, except the commandments against lying and stealing and killing, and he had at least managed to keep from breaking one of them.

The morning was as gray as the town below him, and for once Arthur felt like maybe he belonged for a change. Matador might never be home, but it was someplace to linger for a while, and no one had tried to run him out of town, at least not yet. Of course, the day wasn't over. It had barely begun.

Arthur Daniels had spent his whole life on the move, not quite sure of where he was going, not quite sure if he had ever gotten there. As a young man, he had begun picking cotton in those black delta fields of Mississippi, and the rows stretched out before him as though they would never end. Maybe they didn't. Arthur just followed them day after day, month after month, he and the boll weevils, and he looked around one morning and found himself a long way from home and a stranger to everyone but himself.

The cotton wilted, the winter winds slung ice in his face, and Arthur turned back toward the house that held the fires and the laughter of his family. That had been twenty-two years ago, and he hadn't quite made it back yet, although he never quit trying. The road, a week earlier, had stopped at the edge of Matador, and so did Arthur Daniels.

He smiled as he listened to the bells and was glad he had awakened early enough to hear them. He guessed cotton had led him astray.

Or maybe it was the war. Both had beaten him and left him alone and sometimes even lonely, and Arthur found that he had just about as much in common with strangers as he did with friends. Neither paid a lot of attention to him, but Arthur Daniels didn't mind. He made it just fine and always found something to eat whether he was hungry or not, and he almost always was.

Arthur wasn't proud. He dug postholes until his hands were raw. He chopped kindling, and the blisters became calluses, and his hands were as tough and as wrinkled as uncured leather. He dug a well or two out in the Llano Estacado, the land of the backshade folks, out where water was only a promise, and men could die of thirst before they ever ran across a stream, sometimes clear, usually stagnant and the color of mud.

It was life.

It was death.

Too often, the old timers swore, those tepid pools were either too thick to drink or too thin to plow or so old that even the vultures had lost interest in them.

Arthur chased cattle, sometimes on foot and sometimes on a horse, and he always found a job as easily as he lost it. He was never fired. It's just that one day he would not be around anymore. A boss hated to see a hand like Arthur Daniels walk away. He didn't say much. He never got in anybody's way. He seemed to prefer those chores that he could do by himself, the ones that nobody else would take. Arthur definitely liked to be alone. He wasn't close to anyone.

He had been. Once there had been people that he liked to be with and drink with and laugh with. Why, Arthur had stood up as the best man at George's wedding. He and Sam had started a small grocery store together down just west of New Orleans. They threw a party to announce its grand opening, and Arthur let the wine mix with his politics, and he even proclaimed his candidacy for mayor if the little town needed one.

His friends thought Arthur Daniels just might have actually won. But the war cut the campaign short, and Arthur buried George at Shiloh. He left Sam lying on a hillside at Vicksburg, as the green of the grass turned brown beneath the stains of wasted life.

Arthur never bothered to get close enough to shake hands with anyone again. He was a loner because he couldn't bear ever saying goodbye again.

He didn't need friends. Or maybe he did, and maybe there were none of them left.

Arthur Daniels eased out into the Matador Sunday morning and glanced at the little chapel down at the end of the street, white and proper, its aged paint blistered and peeling. Men in pressed suits and ladies in alabaster dresses had crowded around the doorway, and children played chase between the buggies.

Arthur looked down at his own clothes. His pants were wrinkled, and dirt had been ground into the fabric. There was a patch just below the left knee where the jackass had kicked him, and his boots were as cracked as the windows in his cramped little room. He needed a shave, but he usually did, and Arthur felt like whistling, and usually he didn't. He slapped the dust from his shirt, tried to remember what color it had been before the last creek washing, and walked slowly toward the ringing of the bells.

Every eye watched as the gaunt man with a nose as crooked as a pick axe, found an empty seat on the back pew. No one spoke. Men frowned. Women looked quickly away. Children whispered, and one giggled, and a mother began to softly pray.

Arthur Daniels was an outsider, an unfamiliar face in a town that never took the time to trust an unfamiliar face. Arthur picked up a hymnal but did not sing. He stared ahead and hoped to hear the bells again. He had heard such bells before on a Sunday in Vicksburg until a sniper's bullet silenced the hands that rang them.

The minister piled brimstone in front of his congregation, then set it afire. He spoke of a man who walked as a stranger among men, of a man who had been rejected and persecuted and spit upon. As the service drew to a close, the minister raised his arms and said loudly, "If there are any Christians in the crowd today, please stand and testify for Jesus."

No one stood. The timid seldom do.

Arthur raised an eyebrow and sadly shook his head.

"Isn't there a single Christian here?" the preacher asked loudly. "Nobody here who loves Jesus? If there is, will he please rise and give a soul-stirring testimony for Christ?"

Arthur looked around. No one was standing. He slowly rose from his back-pew seat.

"Bless you, brother," the minister said. "Please tell us your experience. What do you know of Jesus?"

Arthur Daniels shrugged his slumped shoulders. "I don't know anything about him," he said softly. "You told me more this morning than I had ever heard before. Me and this Jesus fella aren't really acquainted at all. But I'll tell you one thing, preacher. I'd stand up for any man that ain't got no more friends than he does."

Heads were bowed, and they said someone prayed, and someone sang. But no one saw Arthur Daniels walk away on the morning that the man in the ragged clothes softly and tenderly condemned them all.

The Ballad of Carnation Milk

SHE LOOKED OUT across a vast, windswept prairie, scarred only by the hoof prints of rangy, longhorn cattle and the boot prints of those cowboys who worked them. A harsh, unforgiving sun blistered the ground at her feet, the oppressive silence around her broken by the mournful bawling of a stray calf in search of the mother herd.

It was a day like any day and all days on the Panhandle ranch, lonely and filled to the brim with heat, dust, and solitude that worked its way into her skin like a thorn. She might see a familiar face before sundown, but she hadn't seen one for weeks now, none, at least, except the old crippled cowhand who did odd jobs out around the barn.

He kept the troughs full of tepid water, hauled hay out to the feeding grounds once early and once late, and tossed the dried manure into piles to burn. A horse had thrown him on the drive north to Kansas more than two decades ago, leaving his legs twisted and his back crooked.

His long days in the saddle had come to a painful end, and he grimaced with each step he took, but still he kept working and grimacing as long as he had a bedroll in the bunkhouse and a spare plate at the table.

The rancher's wife talked to herself in the shank of a summer afternoon. It wasn't much of a conversation, mostly about the weather and the tomatoes drying up on the vine outside her plank and mud-chinked house, but it kept the lonely silence from stifling her.

She could, of course, have talked to the crippled old cowboy, but he punctuated most of his sentences with an emphatic damn or hell, or worse, and the rancher's wife, being a Bible-reading, God-fearing woman, decided that she just might have a better chance at earning eternal life without his salty words ringing in her ears and probably condemning her poor, miserable soul to someplace even hotter and more blasphemous than West

Texas, if there was such a place, and Preacher Armstrong swore there was most every Wednesday night and twice on Sundays.

An uncompromising drought was strangling the ranchlands. As a distant neighbor had told her, "I owned a ranch and ran some cattle, but the last two summers have made a hired man out of me." For years, he and the banker had owned the land, and now the banker had it all and had no idea what to do with it. The same drought that broke men had been known to break a few banks as well. As her neighbor had said before riding away, "I came out here fifty years ago with only sixty-five cents and asthma. And I still got the asthma."

She looked out across the prairie one final time. There were no faraway dust clouds that might signal riders on their way back home, nothing more than an occasional whirling dervish rising up to outrun the wind. Her husband and a sparse band of trail hands had been gone since the middle of July, rounding up a dwindling herd of cattle scattered north of the Canadian River, its banks cracked with mud and thick with alkali dust. "When are you coming home?" she had asked.

"When I get back," he had answered.

"That could be a long time."

"Time's about all I got left."

The rancher's wife glanced up at a searing sky, wiped the sweat off her face, and stepped back into the cooling shadows of her house. "Oh, well," she thought, "we're one day closer to rain than we've ever been before."

As darkness draped the land, she thumbed through a worn magazine, reading as the flickering flames from a kerosene lamp cast a strange assortment of shapes across the bare walls. She was intrigued with page forty-three, the one carrying an advertisement for some new-fangled product called, of all things, canned milk.

It would revolutionize the ranching wife's kitchen, the ad said, graciously omitting the fact that cowboy artist Charles Russell had once pulled a can of Eagle Brand from a cook's shelf, tasted it, and remarked, "It must have come from that bird on the label. It's a cinch it never flowed from any animal with horns."

The rancher's wife wasn't particularly interested in the product. She knew that cowboys had a vehement dislike for milk and cream, especially in their coffee. Her husband didn't mind herding cattle, but he certainly had no intention of drinking their milk. He never minded his breath smelling of whiskey and tobacco, but he certainly didn't want it smelling like that of a young calf.

No, what fascinated the rancher's wife was the promise that she just might win a prize if, perchance, she submitted the best jingle about Carnation milk. Chances were she wouldn't, of course. But in a life filled with loneliness and drudgery, it was the only promise that the rancher's wife had been given in a long time.

She sat down that night and carefully wrote:

"Carnation milk, best in the lan'.

Comes to the table in a little red can."

She smiled with approval, placed her poem in an envelope, and eagerly waited for the night to pass. She had not been this excited in a long time. She re-worked the two lines over in her head time and again, but, for the life of her, she could not think of any way to improve them.

As the first rays of a new day spilled shadows across the barn, the rancher's wife summoned the crippled old cowboy and gave him a hot cup of coffee, which he usually had to brew himself if he wanted any, and the crippled old cowboy always did. She handed him the envelope, along with explicit instructions: "Hitch up the buckboard and ride to the nearest post office in Amarillo. Mail the letter, and don't waste time wandering around the backcountry, looking for stray cattle."

She would throw hay to the herd for him, and the manure didn't have to burn until tomorrow. The crippled old cowboy nodded without a word and began leading a pair of matched jackasses out of their stalls.

If he hurried, he thought, he just might make it on back home by dark. Then again, if the Amarillo whiskey was wet, and it generally was, it might be daybreak, tomorrow or even the next day before he got a good look at the ranch again.

The rancher's wife was only interested in making sure her letter was mailed, not seeing his face again. He only knew a few certainties in life, and that was one of them. He would have bet on it, but he'd lost his money and his cards in the same game.

The rancher's wife sat on the front porch day after day, waiting to hear whether or not the prize would be coming her way. She had never considered herself a poet, but, for the life of her, she couldn't figure out how anyone could have written a jingle any better than the one she sent to Carnation.

The days dragged wearily into weeks, then months.

Her husband and his cowhands had returned. A few more strays were in the near pasture. The grasses had turned dry, the hay brittle. A man who owned the water rights to his land was worthless if the water was gone, and the river was no longer wet enough to make a good mound of mud.

And finally, the letter from Carnation Milk arrived at her doorstep. With trembling hands, she tore it open it and read: "We're sorry, but we cannot use your poem. We're afraid that it is unfit to print."

The rancher's wife grew angry, then bewildered, and finally confused. There was nothing unfit about her poem. She was sure of it. Suddenly, suspicion began to worm its way into her confusion. She stormed out to the barn and found the crippled old cowboy striking a match to a pile of dried manure.

She was blunt and direct. "Did you do anything to my jingle before you mailed it?" she demanded to know.

Her face was flushed beneath his whiskers. He grinned a shy, slow grin. Her boiling gaze melted, then erased it. "Well, ma 'am," he said, "I took the liberty of reading your little poem and figured it was too short. I knowed how important it was for you to win that little old prize, so I figured I could add a verse and make it a might better."

"Then what in creation did you write?"

"Oh, I just gave it a little more punch."

"And what'd it say?"

The crippled old cowboy took a deep breath and recited in a ragged voice:

"Carnation milk, best in the lan'.
Comes to the table in a little red can.
"No teats to pull, no hay to pitch.
"Jes' punch a hole in the sonofabitch."

The rancher's wife would have cried, but when drought crept across the land, water was too precious to waste even as tears upon her face.

Last Dance for Christmas

EDGAR WAS TIRED of being alone. He shouldn't have been. He should have been used to it. After all, he saw a lot more cattle than he did men, and he never had much to say even when standing in a crowd, and too many people standing in the same place made him nervous anyway.

Edgar Davis held one scripture dear to his heart, the one that said: "Blessed is the man who has nothing to say and cannot be persuaded to say it." Maybe it wasn't in the Bible. Edgar didn't know anymore. He only knew that it would have been a sin to leave the verse out, and he remembered his daddy quoting those words long ago with the same reverence he used for the Sermon on the Mount.

His daddy had also told him, "The bigger the mouth, the better it looks when it's shut." Edgar didn't figure that was in the Bible either, but it was damn good advice, and he would have given it to somebody, except there was nobody else. He was simply alone and tired of being that way.

Edgar lay back into the rumpled bunk of his line shack and listened to the wind try and wedge its way between the cracks in the gray, weathered cabin, stuck back amidst a clump of mesquite that bent low across the Caprock.

He had been there for two months and didn't mind at all until December came rolling out of the Panhandle with frost on its breath. During the day, he was busy enough, chasing down Swenson cattle that had drifted too far from the winter grazing range. But it was those nights that tormented Edgar, those hours when he had too much time on his hands and nothing he could do with it. He even missed George. And he never really liked George in the first place.

It had been a wet, chilled November afternoon when the two cowboys came riding back to the line shack that held their grub and whiskey. They kept their dirty clothes on to keep from messing up the floor, and they draped yellow slickers over their shoulders to push back the sleet and rain.

George shivered. "These danged old slickers ain't too warm," he growled.

"No," Edgar answered. "If I had two of the damned things on, I'd probably freeze to death."

Late that night, they heard the howl of a hungry beast echo across the barren West Texas countryside.

"Wolf," George said quietly.

"Coyote," Edgar replied.

The next morning, just after daylight had sneaked in beneath the slate-colored clouds, George, without a word, packed his grub and whiskey in leather bags, walked silently out to his horse, and slung them across the saddle horn.

"Where you goin'?" Edgar asked.

"Away."

"Why?"

"You argue too damn much." George lit a cigarette, bowed his head into the winds, and rode into a wind with frozen mist around the edges.

Edgar slumped across the wooden bed, shook the dirt from his ragged quilt, and pulled the wrinkled covers tightly around his shoulders. He wasn't sleepy. He was only cold. His stomach was complaining, something about food or lack of it. Edgar wouldn't have minded eating if the fire had already been lit, and the wood wasn't buried beneath the drifting snow. He chewed tobacco instead and hoped it would ease the dull ache of hunger pains in winter.

Edgar looked up and counted three thousand, six hundred, and twenty-two bullet holes in the ceiling, put there by another bored cowboy during another boring December. He had spent his nights shooting at bugs and spiders that crawled out of the rotten wood, and he had hit about as many as he missed.

Edgar looked at the shelves around the shack. He could either kill time reading labels on the baking powder cans, or he could thumb through that old patent medicine pamphlet again. Edgar grinned as he remembered what an old friend had once told him after a season in a line shack: "I read about them patent medicines so often, I was convinced I had the symptoms of seven different maladies, all of them said to be fatal."

Darkness moved inside the room, and Edgar at last climbed out of his bunk, shoved his hat into a broken window pane to shut out the wind, and kicked snow off the kindling that lay just outside the back door. He rubbed the numbness out of his hands and rolled the dough for his sourdough biscuits with a whiskey bottle. He would sleep that night on a full stomach after all.

The days dragged fitfully on, and loneliness began to nag Edgar like a bad cold that wouldn't go away. He rounded up wayward Swenson cattle, mended a broken barbed wire fence or two, and late one night even added a dozen bullet holes to those three thousand, six hundred, and twenty-two in the ceiling, trying to gun down a runaway cockroach that was better at running away than Edgar was at aiming his pistol.

On a blustery December afternoon, Edgar Davis nailed the door shut on his line shack and rode off toward Anson and down to that big barn just outside of town where the ranchers and their wives, and especially their daughters, were gathering to dance away the troubles of an awkward year. They celebrated because it may have been bad wasn't nearly as bad as it could have been.

Edgar drifted in with the crowd but didn't say much since too many people always eroded his nerves and made him feel like the splintered end of a broken bottle. He was content to just watch, standing in the shadows back behind the hay bales, tapping his foot to the rhythm of a hoedown fiddle. He drank a little whiskey and smiled at the ladies but was much too bashful to let any of them see him.

He would have struck up a conversation, but Edgar Davis couldn't think of anything to say. It had been a long time between words, a long time since he had said anything to anybody, except, of course, arguing too much during that cold night with George. Edgar thought it was a coyote. Hell, it might have been a wolf after all. Edgar had cursed at a cow or two, and he did berate a rattlesnake in the woodshed one morning before he shot him. But those vocal outbursts didn't count as conversation. Not really, they didn't.

Edgar couldn't take his eyes off the Harper girl. She was young and soft, and she laughed a lot, and her long skirt was only a flash of blue and white gingham as it swirled to the music in the glow of the yellow lantern lights. Long skirts. That's all he had ever seen west of the Caprock, and Edgar grinned as he thought of the dance hall girl who had performed off-key up in Dodge one night at the end of a three-month cattle drive.

She had awed and amazed him in that little bitty get up she was wearing. It was the first time that Edgar ever realized that women did indeed have legs beneath those long skirts, and, for the life of him, he couldn't imagine why in the world women, at least the tall, slender ones, wanted to keep them hidden.

The Harper girl must have thought Edgar was grinning at her because she smiled back, and he finished his glass of whiskey and didn't taste any of it at all. His head was clear, but his mind wasn't. The snow slacked off outside and finally stopped about the same time the fiddler did. The lanterns dimmed, and the ranchers all began their long journey home.

Edgar Davis watched them go, waiting around the barn until he couldn't hear their voices in the distance. Then he began walking toward the doorway, as alone as he had always been. Near the entrance, Edgar spotted a pair of rubber boots that some lady in her haste had left behind. The name inside indicated they had come from the Harper Ranch. Edgar smiled and didn't feel so lonesome anymore.

The next morning, he dug around beneath his bunk and found some clean clothes. He washed his hair amidst the ice in the stock tank and let the cold wind dry it as he rode twenty miles to the Harpers' front door.

He knocked and came face to face with the young girl who looked so soft and laughed a lot. "Ma 'am," he said as earnestly as he could, "I believe you left this rubber boot at the dance last night. So I brought it to you."

Her eyes widened with surprise. "Why, thank you," she replied. "But I had two boots."

Edgar looked shyly away and shoved his nervous hands into the hip pockets of his faded Levi trousers. "Yes, ma 'am," he said. "And I'll bring you the other one tomorrow."

Her smile told him she would be waiting, and he told her on their wedding day that he had ridden all the way home wishing to God she had been a centipede.

Home for Good

SHE WOULD NEVER forget their first Valentine's Day together. He was a senior in high school, and she was a year younger. He had invited her to a dance, and it wasn't just an ordinary, after school, Friday night sock hop with a jukebox throbbing in the far corner of the gym. This time, there would be a real six-piece dance band, maybe a violin for a waltz or two and surely a saxophone, and a revolving chandelier that sent reflected light spinning around the walls like a handful of thrown diamonds.

"What'll I wear?" she asked.

"Wear the red dress," he said. "It'll match this."

And he handed her a single red rose. He pulled a small box from his pocket, opened it, and awkwardly handed her a gold-chain necklace with a single black stone.

"It's garnet," he said.

She smiled.

It was probably glass, she thought.

But she wore it as though it had been part of the Crown Jewels.

She would never forget their first Valentine's Day together after the wedding. He was employed as an automobile mechanic, worked steady, had long hours, and made pretty good money for a young man. And she was talking about going on to college and, perhaps, becoming a teacher.

She liked small children.

She wanted one of her own.

"It can wait," he said. "Don't rush life. It passes fast enough as it is."

She smiled.

And he called a restaurant to make reservations. Not a drive-in this time, but a genuine restaurant with white tablecloths and maybe a lit candle. There might even be a glass of wine.

"What'll I wear?" she asked.

"Wear the red dress," he said.

He handed her a single red rose, and she fastened the black garnet necklace around her neck.

She didn't wear it a lot.

But she wore it when the moment counted. And Valentine's Day always counted.

By now, she no longer wondered whether or not the garnet was glass.

It was hers.

And he was hers.

And life was just about as good as it could get.

She would never forget their last Valentine's Day together. He was a sergeant in the army, worked on tanks, never saw any action, had ventured into Germany only once, and was home on leave.

Another year, and he would be home for good.

The big war was nearing an end. That's what all of the newspapers said. Germany had crumbled and been left in ruin. A bomb had devastated Japan. And the bands were all playing *When Johnny Comes Marching Home Again.*

Maybe the band would play it tonight.

"What'll I wear?" she asked.

"Wear the red dress," he said.

He handed her a single red rose, and she smiled as she began looking through her jewelry box for the black garnet necklace. He liked it best, which meant she would wear it every time he was home.

The months never passed quickly enough. The agony and loneliness of being separated from him had begun to wear on her frayed nerves. Long days. Empty nights. Too many empty nights. She sighed. Now they would finally be together again. On Valentine's Day as it should be. Valentine's Day was special for her. He was coming home, and she was on her way to meet him.

She stepped into the red dress.

It wasn't quite as red as it had been. But that didn't matter.

It fit a little tighter than it once had. He wouldn't mind. He loved the red dress.

She slipped the black garnet necklace around her neck and walked out the door. The sun was as bright as she had ever seen it. She checked her nails. They were as red as the dress. She stopped long enough to pick a single red rose from the garden.

The day grew warm in a hurry. Summers were like that.

She sat and waited and forced a smile.

The words she heard had been perfect. They were all about duty and honor and devotion and love. They sounded just like him.

She clasped the Bible tightly as the rifles fired.

Three times in unison.

Twenty-one shots.

She had not counted them. She knew there would be twenty-one. Her body jerked slightly with each discharge of the rifles.

The last notes on a trumpet faded into the distance, and a young man smartly dressed, younger than she, placed a folded American flag on her lap.

He saluted.

She tried to smile.

It was stifled by a tear.

The soldier backed away, and she stood to reach out and touch the love of her life.

All she felt was the warm wood of a mahogany casket.

They would never be apart again, she thought.

At last, he was home.

And this time, he was home for good.

The Plot for Jesse

HE WAS JUST a little fella back then, barely seven, and lost within the grit and glitter of the Alabama-Mississippi State Fair, his mind awash with the spectacles he was supposed to see and the scandals he wasn't.

Dempsey Biggs looked around and couldn't believe his eyes, and he believed everything that stretched out before him – naked belly buttons hiding behind frayed feathers and freaks that couldn't have been born but were and shouldn't have been. The boy's senses, in that year of our Lord 1907, ran wild, then rampant, then out of sight.

Dempsey Biggs elbowed his way to the edge of a sweating crowd and glanced up into the face of a somber man with cutting eyes who never smiled. The man, his face blurred by a heavy mustache, spoke softly, but his words were as clear as the ring of a hammer against a blacksmith's anvil.

He stared down from his wooden platform and swore, "My brother's a living man."

One farmer gasped.

Another spit.

A holy woman prayed.

"I could produce him today," the man with the cutting eyes said. "I could bring him out here and show every one of you that my brother is alive if the law would just guarantee his immunity."

"Who is that man?" Dempsey Biggs asked the tall Delta farmer standing beside him.

"Frank James."

"Who's he talking about?"

"Jesse."

"But Jesse's dead."

For a moment, the man with the cutting eyes almost smiled.

Twenty-nine years later, Biggs was standing in his hometown streets in downtown Wichita Falls, Texas, when a respected gentleman, John T. Young, stopped beside him, his face white, his expression confused.

"Did you see where J. Frank Dalton is in town, putting on a show over at the Princess Theater?" he asked.

Biggs nodded.

"He came to my office this afternoon and called me by name," Young continued. "And he reminisced a while about the time in 1879 when he and his brother rode by our farm up in Missouri. They hung around just long enough to eat mama's supper and sleep on a hay loft out in the barn. J. Frank Dalton remembered it all."

"So?"

"He's not J. Frank Dalton."

"Then who is he?"

"Jesse James."

"But Jesse's dead."

John Young told Dempsey Biggs the strange tale that the white-haired old man with the white beard had passed on to him that day just before the doors opened down at the Princess Theater.

Late one April afternoon in 1882, the James boys, along with Bob Ford, rode slowly into St. Joseph, Missouri. In town, they knew, was a two-bit outlaw named Charley Bigelow who had robbed a few banks and a few trains and who whispered to the victims that he was Jesse James. He even bore a strong resemblance to the outlaw.

"If he can steal good cash money as Jesse," Frank said softly, "he can die as Jesse."

And so he did.

That night, according to J. Frank Dalton, the James boys met with Missouri Governor Tom Crittenden, who had offered a $10,000 reward for the celebrated outlaw – dead or alive.

The next day, Jesse hid in the closet while Bob Ford brought Charley Bigelow into the house. While Bigelow stood alone and looked at pictures of fine Kentucky racehorses on the wall, Bob Ford shot him down, then swaggered into the streets and bragged, "I just shot Jesse James."

Jesse quickly put on Bigelow's blood-drenched coat and lay on the floor while Frank dragged the dead man away. The curious ran inside and stared – some with grief and some with relief – at Jesse's still body. Some shouted, and some cried.

And when the room was empty again, the James boys stuffed Charley Bigelow into a wooden crate and nailed it shut.

At first, Jesse 's mother gazed down at the face of death and said, "Gentlemen, this is not my son." But later, when she realized that the grave would be Jesse's only chance to escape justice, she had the crate buried in her front yard to keep prying eyes from ever learning her secret and his truth.

The governor handed Bob Ford the $10,000 reward. Bob handed half of it back. In the choir, his face hidden by the shadows, Jesse James sang at his own funeral. He served as one of his own pallbearers. Then as he rode south toward for South America. Bob Ford was pardoned. Frank James surrendered to the governor, was tried, and acquitted. For $5,000, it seems, all of their sins were washed away.

That was the tale J. Frank Dalton spun, the tale that reached the ears of Dempsey Biggs. He never forgot it.

That afternoon, Jim Marlowe, who had married the sister of Frank and Jesse James, stormed into the Princess Theater to prove that J. Frank Dalton was a dastardly fraud.

"You know a fella named Jim Marlowe?" he yelled.

"I guess I ought to," Dalton said. "He's my brother-in-law. How're the folks, Jim?"

In the mid 1980s, Dempsey Biggs moved to Granbury, Texas, and he learned of a 104-year-old man who had died and been buried in the city cemetery in 1951.

According to police records, Jesse James had seven bullet wounds, a rope burn around his neck, a fingertip that had been damaged by an exploding gun, and the scars of burns on his feet.

So had the old man who had come to Granbury nine days before his death.

"What was his name?" Biggs asked.

"J. Frank Dalton."

Dempsey smiled reverently. "Well," he said. "I guess Jesse's finally dead."

He checked with the courthouse records and pulled the old man's death certificate. It agreed with him. The name was typed and easy to read.

No smears.

No smudges.

Jesse James was what it said.

Dempsey Biggs nodded and walked down to the burying ground to pay his final respects. Jesse James, at last, was at peace a long way from home and nowhere near a bank.

A Message for Daddy

HIS WAS NOT a great story.
His was not a story anyone would remember.
But everyone has a story.
And each is a thread in the fabric of mankind.

HE WAS SITTING alone in the park when I saw him.
Don't know how old he was, or how young.
Didn't matter.
He was a stranger in town.
I knew.
It was a small town.
I didn't know all of the names.
I did know the faces.
And his was a new one.
"Driving though?" I asked.
"Walking."
"Where are you from?"
"Back East."
"Where you headed?"
"Out West."
"Got a job?"
He shook his head.
"Going to see my daddy," he said.
"If you're close, I can drive you the rest of the way," I said.
"Arizona."
He wasn't close.
"It's gonna take you a while," I said.
"I got time."

"How about your daddy?"

"He's not going anywhere."

He pulled a faded snapshot out of his shirt pocket, handed it to me, and I was looking into the face of a soldier boy.

He couldn't have been older than twenty.

He was smiling.

He had a firm jaw.

He had determined eyes.

He had one stripe on his sleeve.

"Which war?" I asked.

"Vietnam."

"He came home?"

"In a box." The young man shrugged. "I never knew him."

"Where is he buried?"

"Cottonwood."

"Was that his home?"

"That's where his mama lived."

"How about his wife."

"She cashed his checks and gave me a picture."

"She ever talk about him?"

"She cried a lot."

"You go to Cottonwood often?" I asked.

He gazed out across the town square.

"Never been."

"I guess it's about time."

"I've got something to tell him," the young man said.

"It must be important," I said.

"It is."

He stood, and for the first time I saw him smile.

"It's taken me a long time," he said.

I nodded.

"Nobody said I could do it."

I nodded again.

"I graduated from college this month."

His was a sad smile.

"Daddy would like to know," he said.

He began walking across the square, headed for the highway.

In the distance, I saw a lot of eighteen-wheelers rolling west.

Twelve minutes later, I saw one of them stop.

Peace At last

HE WAS MAD when he left.
But then, Chester was usually mad.
He left on a train.
He didn't look back.
The little town was home for many.
It had never been home for him.
It didn't know he was gone.
The house was empty.
That's all.
Chester grew up behind the bus station.
He lived in a shotgun house.
His mama worked two jobs.
She was a waitress.
She was a maid.
She was hardly ever in the house.
But she kept cold bologna sandwiches on the table.
Cold bologna.
And mayonnaise.
Chester was a child of Cross Plains.
He didn't belong, and he knew it.
His friends wore boots.
He had tennis shoes.
His friends drove cars.
Chester walked.
His friends ate steak.
He did what he could with cold bologna.
One day he awoke, and it had happened.
He no longer had any friends.

They left town.

He was stuck behind the bus station.

They were in college.

He was changing tires at Fred's service station.

He watched his mama take her last breath.

She was a good woman, the minister said.

Heart wore out, the doctor said.

The county buried her.

Chester stood beside her grave, Chester and the minister.

A psalm.

A prayer.

Amen.

Chester was alone.

Goodbye, he said to his mama.

Goodbye, he said to them all.

He walked to the depot and bought a one-way ticket.

Uncle Sam wanted him.

No one else did.

He was mad at the town.

He was mad at life.

If he had a gun, he would kill somebody.

The Army gave him a gun.

They shipped him to a place the newspaper called Southeast Asia.

They shipped him to a place his sergeant called Da Nang.

They shipped him to hell.

A year later they shipped him home.

He carried a bullet in his chest, limped from shrapnel in his leg, and wore a Silver Star on his chest.

The Medal of Honor came later.

He had survived the day he was supposed to die.

He had eleven men with him.

If necessary, he would die for them.

He went where no man should go.

The bullets hit him.

They didn't stop him.

One man alone.

One man still mad.

One man with a gun.

When night fell, the fighting had stopped.

It was so quiet.

Chester listened.

He heard nothing.

He thought his was dead.

Eleven men carried him out of the valley.
A train carried him home.
The wounds hurt.
But they healed.
His leg was crooked.
But he could stand straight.
The whole town was waiting when Chester stepped from the train.
Cross Plains had a hero.
Cross Plains couldn't wait to honor him.
The Mayor planned a parade.
Flags flew on every street corner.
The band played.
The crowd cheered.
The Mayor made a speech.
He looked around for Chester.
Where was Chester?
Chester was down at the corner café, eating a cold bologna sandwich.
He saw the parade pass by.
He ordered another Coke.
He smiled at the waitress.
She winked at him.
He remembered her from eighth-grade social studies.
She had been the third girl from the left in the second row.
She had freckles then.
Chester smiled again.
He had left his anger in hell.
Chester wasn't mad anymore.

Who Pulled the Trigger?

BURIED SOMEWHERE THE pages of every book of fiction and non-fiction alike is a mystery, a scene of intrigue, an unexpected moment of tension or confrontation that jars the reader's imagination, veils a character with a mask of uncertainty, and provides the story with another rich layer of doubt and apprehension.

And everybody loves a mystery.

Why not?

Life itself is made up of doubt, uncertainty, intrigue, and, on more than one occasion, a little mystery. At least you stumble across a fork in the road and have no idea whether to turn left, right, or go straight. And, regardless of your decision, you have no idea what the consequences may be.

I was writing Gamble in the Devil's Chalk *about the battle for oil during the Giddings boom of the 1970s. And out of the blue, before I even knew he was around, here came Jim Dobos.*

Jim Dobos lived in a little shotgun house beside the railroad tracks near Old Dime Box in central Texas. He had been born into hard times and never left. The badge on his shirt made him a constable. The badge made him important, and he liked it when he swaggered down the street and everyone in town knew he was important.

Jim Dobos was a big man, broad shoulders, weighing almost two hundred and fifty pounds, and he was a man who carried a pistol for one reason. He wanted a cause or a reason to use it.

Down in Burleson County, he and a friend leased a thousand acres simply because there was an oil boom going on, and one sucker had as much of a chance getting rich as the next guy. He and his partner knew absolutely nothing about the science of drilling and completing a well, so they brought in a third partner, and he was pro in the oil game, as slick as a slush pit when a gusher reached up to touch the sky.

A few months and a dozen or so wells later, Jim Dobos and his partners sold the wells, the leases, and the reserves for fifty-three million dollars.

Money would make Jim Dobos a miserable man.

The constable made a brave effort to change his lifestyle. He had always been poor, and now he had money, and he could not figure out how to spend it all. Not wisely anyway. He retired his badge. He stayed in the oil business. He bought a six-passenger Aerospace CL helicopter. He hired a Vietnam marine veteran to fly it.

The copter would skim along two hundred feet above the ground with Dobos leaning out of the side and shooting running coyotes with a .357 Magnum pistol. He would hit them right below the left ear. He was known in the oilfield as the damndest shot any of them had ever seen.

Jim Dobos loved poker. He loved sports. Mostly, Jim Dobos loved to bet on them. He never met a bookie he didn't like. Jim Dobos had a reputation, and it wasn't sterling. He wasn't good about paying his bills or keeping tabs on his money, and bookies and oil operators had short memories when the invoices lingered too long on the wrong desk.

Dobos wasn't trying to shortchange anyone. He simply wanted to keep his money for as long as he could before losing his grasp and seeing it leave town in somebody else's hip pocket.

A dollar gone was generally not a dollar coming back. Bankruptcies had a tendency to follow in the wake of his business deals. Gambling debts were staggering. And after a while, he began having trouble finding partners or investors in the oilfield.

Get your money up front.

That was the warning.

Get it quick.

Jim Dobos could make it disappear.

Not even Dobos knew where it had gone.

By early autumn of 1991, the bottom had fallen out of the petroleum business. A barrel of oil was barely worth more than a barrel of spit. The oil patch was suffering. No one could see the light at the end of the tunnel. No one could find the tunnel.

Only a short, narrow bridge separated wealth from poverty, and it was crumbling. Oilmen who went to bed rich weren't sure they wanted to wake up the next morning and face another day of turmoil in the Austin Chalk.

At first, someone only saw the smoke pouring from the roof of a mobile home parked back behind the office of the Dobos Corporation on the outskirts of Old Dime Box. It was a Monday afternoon, and fires were a dime a dozen in the oil patch.

Firemen burst inside and found Jim Dobos lying across a bed. His mother, seventy-four-year-old Magdalene Kati Dobos, was seated in a living room recliner.

Both were quite dead.

During those first brief moments of the investigation, it was believed that mother and son had probably died tragically from smoke inhalation.

An autopsy told another story: gunshot wounds from a high-powered, .357 Magnum, the kind Dobos used to shoot down coyotes running two hundred feet below his helicopter.

The pistol lay near the body of Jim Dobos.

A representative from the State Fire Marshal's office determined that a liquid substance of some sort had been poured in a bedroom closet and ignited.

Texas Rangers privately suspected foul play.

The gossips around Giddings thought it was an odd and uncharacteristic way for Jim Dobos, the former constable of Precinct Six, to die.

Maybe he had crossed one man too many, they whispered.

Maybe he was involved with a bookie, who preferred to be paid on time, a bookie with a gun, a bookie who had access to the .357 of Jim Dobos.

Maybe a bad deal or a stolen deal in the oilfield had simply claimed another victim.

The former constable could count his friends on one hand.

His enemies were legion.

The Travis County Medical Examiner was not swayed by idle opinions or gossip.

Suicide, he ruled.

No note. No matter.

Bad health.

His mother was a victim of Parkinson's disease.

And Dobos had suffered a stroke or two. Jim Dobos, he reasoned, simply drove home one afternoon, set fire to a mobile home to destroy the final traces of his existence on earth, put his mother out of her considerable misery, lay down on the bed, jammed the muzzle of a pistol against his head, pulled the trigger, and splintered his skull.

For a split second, he knew what the coyotes felt.

A Quiet New Year's Morning

HE ROLLED OUT of bed the morning the calendar rolled over to a new year.

He glanced out the window and surveyed the landscape around his farm.

The year didn't look particularly new.

Nothing had changed.

It was snowing yesterday.

Snow was still coming down.

George looked at the clock.

It was six-twelve.

He waited a minute.

It was six-thirteen.

George smiled.

That's what he liked about time.

It was always changing.

Then again, maybe it wasn't.

Six-thirteen yesterday was no different from six-thirteen today.

Common sense said it had been twenty-four hours.

The clock didn't know the difference.

George poured a cup of coffee and walked out onto the weathered back steps.

A brisk wind slapped him hard across the face.

Snowflakes touched his eyelids.

A damp cold began to sink into his bones.

Just beyond the barn, the last star of night, or maybe it was the first star of morning, was hanging above a thicket of oaks.

A coyote howled.

A calf bawled.

A dog barked.

He heard an old pickup truck grinding its way down the road, its motor complaining about the cold.

Must be Henry, he thought.

Henry wanted breakfast.

Two eggs.

Buttered toast.

Burnt bacon.

And coffee.

His breakfast never changed.

Only one thing was for certain on the cold, snowy morning of a new year.

The Corner Café would be open.

Agnes had the coffee hot.

Agnes was cooking the eggs.

She knew how Henry liked them.

She knew Henry was on the way.

Henry owned the café.

He never had a holiday.

Farmers didn't take one.

And farmers were hungry.

George would have taken the road to town.

But George didn't farm anymore.

It was always too cold, he said.

Or too hot.

And he was too old.

And too tired, he said.

The government sent him his social security check.

He didn't drink as much coffee as he once did.

George was doing just fine.

The sound of the old pickup truck faded in the distance.

The snow kept falling.

The snow didn't make a sound.

He glanced at the clock again.

It was six-eighteen.

She would be pulling into his driveway in eight minutes.

She was never late.

And this morning, she might even be early.

He closed his eyes and could smell her perfume.

He figured it was Avon with a fancy name.

Dorothy Marie was right on time.

The Buick was new.

The day was new.

The year was new.

She had the kind of wicked and apologetic smile George had never seen before as she rolled down her window.

He walked through the snow toward her.

"I've had it," she said.

Dorothy Marie was not a happy woman.

"What's wrong?"

"I'm leaving Henry."

George quit smiling.

"He know it?"

"No."

"You didn't tell him?"

"I left him a note."

George had no idea what to say.

He waited for Dorothy Marie to climb out of the car.

She didn't.

He waited for her to her smile to turn warmer.

It was as cold as the snowflakes upon his cheeks.

"I'm leaving you, too," she said.

George folded his arms.

"At least you didn't send me a note."

"No."

"Why not?"

"I love you better than Henry."

George arched an eyebrow.

"I could go with you," he said.

"Can't."

"Why not?"

"Charlie wouldn't like it."

"Who's Charlie?"

"Does it matter?"

"Don't guess it does."

Dorothy Marie backed out of the driveway and headed west away from town.

George looked around.

He sighed.

He guessed it would be a new year after all.

Who's to Blame?

THE LAND HAD broken him.

It lured him West.

But that was a long time ago.

He was young.

He was blessed.

He was full of hope.

The land was full of promise.

And nothing stood in his way.

He stood morning after morning, year after year, and admired her beauty.

It was a good feeling.

He would never be alone again.

He.

And the land.

They belonged together.

Nothing would ever be able to separate them.

They grew older together.

They prospered.

They didn't have it all.

But they had all they needed.

Sun to warm the land.

Rain to wash the drought away.

Wind to turn the windmill blades and draw water from deep in the ground.

He loved the land.

The land defied him.

Times were hard.

Times were troubling.

They shook his faith from time to time.
They had not chased him away.
The land touched his heart.
Each sunrise told him he was one day closer to the promise than he had ever been before.
He held the land tight.
The land was eternal.
It would never leave him.
That's what he told himself.
It was a lie.
That was the mystery of life.
The land broke him.
The sun came and stayed.
It climbed higher.
It remained hotter.
The rains went elsewhere, didn't even spit when they said goodbye.
There was no wind to turn the blades of a windmill.
The water had dried up deep in the ground.
He was alone.
The land left him.
He sat in the silence and remembered the face of the land.
So young.
So soft.
Green eyes.
They were always laughing.
The laughter stopped.
Auburn hair.
It ruffled in the winds until the winds died.
It turned gray.
His life had turned ashen.
He knew the truth.
He hated the truth.
The land had not left him.
She had.
He watched the sun leave its final shadows scattered beneath the windmill.
He was alone.
She was gone.
It was easier to blame the land.

End of the Line

DARRELL MILLER COULDN'T sleep late at all on the morning someone must die.

He watched as the first fingers of daylight crawled across the dirty floor and chased the shadows out of his Uvalde jail cell.

And he thought about his wife who waited for him so far down the road in San Antonio. A judge had said she was nothing more than a common-law wife, but Darrell Miller had never needed a fancy-gilded piece of paper to make sure she belonged to him.

So they hadn't said, "I do."

They had done everything else they were supposed to do to consummate a marriage, and, besides, Darrell Miller loved her.

He missed her.

He swore to himself that he would see her before another night came to separate them again or forever.

Miller reached for the butcher knife that lay hidden beneath him, his reward for being a trusty.

Trusties had the opportunity to steal

Some didn't.

Darrell Miller did.

IN A BEXAR COUNTY jail cell, a woman watched another day slip behind the bars to taunt her with the freedom she might never have again.

She was lonely.

She was afraid.

She blamed Darrell Miller, and he didn't give a damn – never did, never would.

He was no good and the woman knew it.

But, for a time, he had been hers, and having something was always better than doing without, and the woman had done without most all of her life.

Maybe that's why she had taken the stolen credit card and bought so many clothes. For a few hours, she felt like a lady, a rich lady who was no longer ashamed of the dress on her back.

But she had no place to wear the new clothes in jail, and she cursed Darrell Miller, silently and aloud, and hoped the law had locked him so far away he would need a road map to find the front door.

DARRELL MILLER KEPT his eyes on the cell door and waited for the jailer to come and take him out for another day of hard work.

Miller grinned a wicked grin.

This was like no other day he had ever seen before.

There was a tinge of intoxication that ran through the blood in his veins, an awakening of the mind that seemed sharper, a lot less congested than usual.

For this was the day when someone must die.

Miller wrapped his long fingers around the butcher knife and glanced at the clock. It was ten minutes after six on the morning of March 4.

He had to get out.

His wife needed him.

Only months earlier, Darrell Miller had walked away from the Illinois State Penitentiary after serving six years for armed robbery.

His whole life had been wasted in a cell somewhere, always in trouble for theft, assault and battery, public intoxication, reckless driving or forgery.

If it was against the law, he had tried it.

If it was a sin, he had not yet repented.

Preachers had tried to save his wretched soul.

Preachers had tried to find redemption for him.

But he had learned the hardest of lesson of all years ago.

He wasn't confessing to anything.

Miller's probation officer had called it "irresponsible living," and Miller guessed it was probably as pretty reasonable explanation. But now, he faced life in prison.

The court said he was an habitual criminal.

He had a lot of life ahead of him.

Darrell Miller was only thirty-one.

He had to get out.

He couldn't take it.

Not anymore.

He figured his eleven-year-old son had been the only smart one in the family anyway.

His son had committed suicide.

He didn't have to run anymore.

Darrell Miller thought he could start over in Texas, escape his past. And he did all right until the winter night Miller barged into a Uvalde Pizza Hut waving a sawed-off shotgun.

He took the money.

He forced two women employees to disrobe.

Then he doused their clothes in hot water and ran.

Miller saw the humor in it

The law didn't.

Darrell Miller heard the jailer's footsteps coming down the hallway, loud and obnoxious the way jailers always walked, and he had heard a lot of them in the long and darkened hallways outside of his cells.

He knew it was time.

He had waited all night.

He wouldn't be waiting any longer.

Darrell Miller had a wife he wanted to see.

He missed her.

He had treated her badly, and it gnawed at his conscience.

He wanted to tell her he still loved her.

If nothing else, he still loved her, which meant it was the morning that someone would die.

Darrell Miler glanced up as John Johnson ambled slowly to the cell door and opened it. A moment later, he had the butcher knife jammed into the jailer's throat.

This was indeed the day someone would die, but it wouldn't be John Johnson.

Miller ordered him to unlock the cell of an illegal alien from Honduras, then grabbed the keys to the jailer's '68 Oldsmobile.

The clocked ticked off two minutes.

Then five.

Miller and the Honduran were gone.

San Antonio lay ahead of them.

And a wife was waiting.

Miller always said he would do anything for her.

Now, by the grace of God, he would prove it.

The new Uvalde jail hadn't stopped him.

Neither would the one in Bexar County.

Miller pulled his black cowboy hat down low over his eyes and barreled down the highway where someone must die.

Near Hondo, Richard Muennink sat in his truck by the side of the road, watching for a friend. A few minutes late, he was. That was all right. His friend was always late.

Darrell Miller and his butcher knife arrived first, and Muennink fled toward the pasture. The wild man with the butcher knife could have the truck for all he cared. He didn't want it anymore.

A few miles down the highway, Miller burst into the home of Elsie Lindeburg. She wasn't home. She was shopping. So the fugitive picked up a few loose dollars lying on the table and the keys to her truck.

The truck hadn't been empty.

A shotgun lay on the floor.

Miller grinned as he climbed into the cab and gunned the blue pickup hard and low to the road, headed eastward. The alien from Honduras was just along for the ride, having no better place to go and no other way to get there.

At twenty minutes past eleven o'clock on the morning of March 4, Texas Highway Patrolman Joe Cerney, a hot sun beating down from overhead, was keeping his eyes on the '62 Ford truck that eased up to a makeshift roadblock on the outskirts of Castroville.

He was looking for two escapees, but Cerney could see only a lone driver in the blue cab, wearing a black cowboy hat.

The trooper remembered the report he had read.

One part of it stuck in his mind.

Darrell Miller loved black cowboy hats.

He inched closer and caught a glimpse of the illegal alien from Honduras crouched in the floorboard.

A shotgun lay beside the man in the black hat.

"That's him," Cerney yelled, and the pickup rammed its way through the blockade.

Miller fought off patrol cars at eighty miles an hour as he battled his way toward San Antonio and the woman he loved, a wife who knew she would be much better off without him but loved him anyway.

Miller had no doubt about it.

Her face.

Her eyes.

Her touch.

They were all he remembered as Miller roared past Castroville. He thought he was going to make it, but Cerney abruptly tore off the Ford pickup's rear tire with a shotgun blast, and Miller spun to a stop in the front yard of Harold Bippert's farmhouse.

The fugitive jumped to the ground and leveled his shotgun at the troopers who were closing in around him.

"You're not going to take me alive," he warned.

Silence.

All anyone heard were the insects buzzing in their ears.

Darrell Miller's mouth curved into a smile.

He had known all along that this was the day when someone must die.

He just didn't know who it would be.

Now he did.

And he felt better about it.

The uncertainty was gone.

His mind was clear.

It was all so simple, so reasonable.

After all, he had been reading the Bible in his cell, and he had even asked the Good Lord to forgive him, and if a man had to die it might as well be when his sins were all washed away.

Darrell Miller turned the shotgun toward his face.

He fired once.

The troopers could not have stopped Miller without killing him.

He saved their conscience.

He saved them the trouble.

On a day that the plain wooden casket of Darrell Miller was lowered into the warm Uvalde dirt, the 290th District Court in San Antonio acquitted his wife.

She didn't bother to go to his funeral.

She didn't hear the Assembly of God minister say softly, "God is his judge now."

But she knew that Darrell Miller had been his own jury.

One vote had been taken.

The verdict was unanimous.

Confessional in a Greyhound Bus

LEE WALBURN WAS the genius behind Atlanta Weekly Magazine and best editor I ever knew. He called me out of the blue one afternoon and asked, "How long has it been since you've ridden a bus?"

"At least twenty years," I said. "Maybe longer."

"Want to ride another one?'

"Why?"

"I bet you think a bus has passengers."

"Most of them do."

"You're wrong," he said. "Busses are packed with stories. Take a ride through the South on one and find out how many of them you can find."

I caught a Greyhound in Dallas, and it pulled out for Atlanta by way of Memphis while the sun was trying to make up its mind whether to end the day or drag out another few minutes of daylight. Busses don't travel in straight lines. I sat down and looked around. I was surrounded by strange faces, sad faces, lonely faces. They had miles to go but none would travel far enough to escape the troubles that clung to them like shadows dancing in the street lights above them.

What else were they to do? I let them tell me their stories

Strangers on a Bus

I FOUND HER when I wasn't looking for her, and after I found her, I wondered why anyone would ever let her go. She is perfection in a gingham dress.

She is seated alone in the back of a Greyhound bus, watching the tall buildings of Dallas slip slowly away into the slums.

She shudders.

It is a hard life outside, down on the sidewalks, littered with trash, back in the alleys where no one dared go after dark.

It had been her life.

The homeless with their carts.

Drug dealers with their switchblades.

Homes without windows.

Children without fathers.

A tear moistens the corner of her eye.

She silently whispers goodbye.

There is nothing to hold her now.

She will never be free, perhaps.

But she is has left Dallas behind.

Can't go back.

Won't go back.

What about tomorrow?

It's only another day but in another town, and if trouble didn't climb on the bus with her, she may be free at last.

Good riddance.

Good riddance to them all.

She is a small woman, her pale features framed by ruffled curls the color of a November sunset.

Her wrinkled maroon dress is two years out of date, and she is five years north of being beautiful.

She turns and smiles, and the five years fade away.

I sit down beside her.

"Do you mind?" I ask.

She doesn't.

We ride in silence for a minute or two, then I take a chance and ask, "You on vacation?"

"No."

"Going home?"

"Dallas was my home."

"Got a job somewhere?" I ask.

"I've got a bus ticket," she says.

"Be gone long?"

"It's one way."

She loses her smile and glances quickly out the window.

I glance at her left hand.

The ring is small, the diamond was just a dot of cut glass.

She's married.

I shrug.

"Your husband coming to join you?" I ask.

It is none of my business.

But I'm curious.

Writers almost always are.

Curiosity is a disease for which there is no cure.

"He's dead," she says.

"I'm sorry."

"No reason to be sorry." This time, she is the one who shrugged. "I was his wife in Dallas," she tells me. "He had another wife in Santa Fe."

"He get caught?"

"Cheating men always get caught."

"I guess he had a decision to make." I'm scribbling notes.

I wait for her to stop me.

She doesn't.

"He made the wrong one," she says.

"How's that?"

"He chose me."

The little lady sighs. She bites her lip and needs another patch of lipstick.

"He came home and begged me to forgive him," she says.

"Did you?"

"No."

"Did he go back to her?"

"He killed off a bottle of gin, packed up his clothes, and walked out the door, carrying a two-dollar cardboard suitcase. He wasn't walking none too straight."

"Last time you see him?"

"The next time I saw him, he was dead." She laughs softly. It has a somber tone. "A dark-haired woman in a green pants suit was waiting for him outside my door."

The little lady paused.

She watched the moon slip behind a cloud.

Both were hanging low in the sky.

"She shot him three times."

"Murder?"

"That's what the police would call it."

"And what do you call it?" I ask.

"Justifiable."

"Did you call the police?"

The little lady shakes her head.

"Why not?"

"She stuffed him in the trunk of her car and drove off."

"Did you report the crime?"

"No."

"You should have."

"I didn't know her name."

The little lady cocks her head and smiles at me. "Why are you asking so many questions?" she wants to know.

"I'm a writer."

"So?"

"I'm looking for a story."

"You like mine?"

"It has all of the ingredients," I say. "Love. Cheating, Heartbreak. Getting drunk. Dying. Of course there's a little mystery thrown in."

"You could write about me," she says.

"I could."

"You think I would make a good novel?" she asks.

"I don't know about a novel," I say, "but you're a damn fine country song."

A Soap Opera on Wheels

THE BIG GREYHOUND BUS chases after a Friday night, bouncing eastward and catching it early, a rolling soap opera stuffed with dried tears and broken promises, possessing little hope and dreams that come and go as quickly as a falling star.

The little man with the limp and funny accent has no hand.

A Vietnamese woman is afraid to sleep. She sometimes wakes up screaming, and she can't escape the nightmare of her past when her eyes are closed.

A basketball player sits alone. He's not used to being without a friend, but he pallbearers laid his friend away.

A shy blonde huddles up front behind the driver where she's safe and no one can harass her or, God forbid, do even worse.

One young lady wears a T-shirt with the slogan: "On the eighth day, God created Harley Davidson."

She had kissed a man goodbye at the bus stop door in Dallas, long and tender, and he had clung to the smell of her cheap perfume longer after the eastbound bus carried her away from his long and empty arms.

"There was a man I could fall in love with," she tells me as she settles back in her seat.

"Known him long?" I ask.

"Met him somewhere between a ham sandwich and the apple pie," she says. "That's not long."

"True love doesn't take long."

"My heart has lied to me before."

"Do you think he'll call you?"

"I doubt it."

"Why not?"

"I didn't tell him where I was going."

"He has your name, doesn't he?"

She shrugs.

"He has a name."

"But not your real one?"

"Not even my mama knows my real one."

She stares out the window.

The stars will be out soon.

But not soon enough.

Another young honey wears a "Love Those Jugs" T-Shirt, and she slumps back into her seat, rolls her eyes, and sighs loudly.

"Damn," she says, "he really thinks I'm coming back to him."

"Is that what you promised?" I ask.

"That's what he assumed."

"What did you promise him?"

"A divorce."

"Why would you do that?"

"He spends a lot of time at the shooting range."

"A lot of men do."

"I was the target," she says.

The shy blonde almost snickers, and she would have if she hadn't been a lady.

Three women.

All alone.

One in love.

One is despair.

One afraid.

Their yesterdays are filled with secrets.

Their tomorrows are saturated with the unknown.

They are running from one and toward the other.

Maybe they'll find hope.

Maybe they'll find a reason to be happy.

Then again, they might not even find Saturday.

The bus ambles into the late afternoon dipping past dip signs and pine trees and strips of rubber tires that trucks have left behind, lying useless and crippled by the side of the road.

Ahead, somewhere at the far end of a highway that has no shortest distance between two points, waits Atlanta. A night will pass, then a day, before the big old Greyhound finds it.

The bus is always in a hurry, yet it takes its own time about locating a getting-off place to empty its load of tired and wrinkled humanity, and it's never empty, and it never stops for long, and it has no pity at all for the restless souls who are either running toward troubles or away from them.

It only shares the highway with them for short snatches of time.

The faces are always different.

The problems are mostly the same.

As we grind on past a no-passing sign, no one knows if any of us will ever pass that way again.

Looking for Love

THE LITTLE MAN with the limp and funny accent gazes out on a countryside he's never seen before. When someone stares at the space where his left hand should be, he quickly pulls a black glove over the red, raw skin and hopes the curious eyes won't bother to look his way again.

He's in a foreign land.

But the stares are just as cruel back home in Paris, France.

He hears the muffled laughter behind him, and he frowns.

Perhaps the laughter wouldn't seem so depressing if he understood the language better.

Perhaps it's only a joke.

Perhaps he's the joke.

The little man with the limp and funny accent wraps his tweed jacket tighter around his shoulders and tries to comb the hair that refuses to lie across a scalp left bare by the flames on an Algerian battlefield.

He hates laughter.

He doesn't trust it.

No one ever laughed at Jean Marc Lavie when he was a hero.

But that was back in 1961 when he was a pilot in the French Air Force. Jean Marc had flown into Southern Algeria that morning, banking sharply and storming down on the machine gun nest.

He reached for the trigger that would fire his rockets.

"But before I shoot, the machine gun shoots me, and my plane is riddled with bullets."

"Did you crash?" I want to know.

"The plane explodes." He shrugs. "I know immediately the war for me is over. I know I am dead."

It wasn't his day to die.

Dying may have been easier.

All Jean Marc remembers is the burning petrol splashing across his hand, his head, and his leg.

He can still feel it.

The acrid scent of burning flesh, his own, has never left him.

Jean Marc was unconscious by the time his observer dragged him from the wreckage.

He did not hear the explosion when the flame touched those four rockets still strapped to a crumpled wing.

Nor did he know that a helicopter finally came to haul him back from the dead and the dying.

The darkness had been his grave.

Jean Marc Lavie would lie in a coma for three months, his legs broken in ten places. During the next four years, he would undergo thirty-four operations as surgeons fought desperately to make his skin grow on a body ravaged by fire.

Slowly it did.

And slowly he recovered.

"The skin of my chest is on my hand," he says. "And the skin of my belly is on my head."

Jean Marc pauses.

"So when a woman rubs my hand, she's rubbing my chest. And when she's touching my head, her fingers are massaging my belly."

He waits.

I laugh.

He does, too.

"I didn't make love for two years," Jean Marc says simply.

"The pain?" I ask.

"I was afraid I was ugly."

"What happened?"

"One night in a hospital, a nurse proved I wasn't ugly anymore."

We ride for a while in silence as the darkness crawls across the timbered landscape.

All we see are trees.

And shadows.

The shadows are in his mind.

"What do you think about the United States?" I ask him.

"I like your country," Jean Marc says. "But I don't love it." He shrugs. "The love I feel is for women."

"Have you found love?" I ask.

"Two times while I've been on the bus," he says.

"When did you get on the bus?"

"Phoenix." He pauses a moment, then adds, "One was nice, but she was serious. One was not so nice, but she was not so serious. I may go back and see her again."

"Where did she get off the bus?"

"El Paso."

"She live there?"

"She caught another bus," he says.

Jean Marc smiles.

He won't go back.

He won't look for her.

He won't find her.

It's simply the thought that counts.

Maybe he will find another who won't laugh at him, especially when it's dark, and he's afraid he's ugly again.

He likes the night.

The night whispers to him lies.

He's as handsome as he wants to be, and she is as sexy as she needs to be, in the night.

Luck Is on the Flip Side

THE BUS PULLS into Little Rock for a forty-minute dinner stop where we can order burgers, with or without mustard, and fries, with or without catsup, or indigestion to go.

The shy blonde shares her apple pie with the curly-haired stranger, and she has been blushing since Hot Springs when he asked her what perfume she had on, and she wasn't wearing any.

The four-year-old scatters another sack of potato chip crumbs although some make it to his stomach and some are hanging on his mouth.

Navy and Flat Feet go to war with a video game.

And Jean Marc Lavie is concerned because his bags aren't on the bus, and he's tired, and he wants to get off and spend the night in an Arkansas motel. It's essential that he have his suitcase. There is medicine inside, and he must take his medicine before breakfast. The pain of thirty-four operations is embedded deep in his eyes.

Billy Myers, behind the Greyhound counter, looks at the long line before him, and he doesn't want to waste his time on the little man with the limp and funny accent.

"Even if the ticket agent in Dallas checked the bags," he says, "there's no telling when they'll get around to putting them on a bus."

"But he said he would get them on."

"You should have taken them to the bus yourself."

"Please call Dallas and see about them."

His broken English is breaking up again.

"Can't," the Greyhound man says.

"Why not?"

"It wouldn't do you any good. The next bus to Little Rock has already left." Billy Myers shrugs. "Maybe your bags are on it."

He is gruff.

His voice is filled with gravel.

Jean Marc's eyes are pleading.

The Greyhound man is not concerned.

Lost bags.

Found bags.

Forgotten bags.

They happen all the time.

"Please call," says the man with the limp and funny accent. There is desperation in his voice.

Billy Myers rolls his eyes and dials Dallas. He says a few words, then hangs up.

"What did Dallas tell you," Jean Marc asks.

"He says he can't work the ticket counter and the baggage claim both. You'll just have to wait until the next bus gets in and see if your bags are on it."

"When does it arrive?"

"At two-forty-five in the morning."

"Does it have my suitcase for certain?"

"You'll know when the bus gets here."

"I'll come back then," Jean Marc says.

"Can't."

"Why not?"

"We're closed at two-forty-five in the morning."

Billy Myers turns his attention to another customer with real cash money in his hand.

At the newsstand, Love Those Jugs thumbs through the tabloids with headlines that scream: "How to Flatten Your Stomach," "Flush Out Body Fat," and "Amazing Miracles of New Holy Shroud."

She buys the one that promises "Life After Dead – Startling New Evidence," and shuffles back to the bus.

Sleep has finally tracked down the four-year-old.

Invaders from another galaxy have eaten all of Flat Feet's quarters.

The shy blonde has drifted back to the darkness that hides the middle of the bus, and the curly-haired stranger squeezes in beside her, the legs of his faded jeans pressed hard against her thighs.

He whispers and she giggles.

And she no longer worries about anybody harassing her or, God forbid, doing even worse.

"Hey," Love Those Jugs," asks Miss Harley Davidson, "do you believe in life after death?"

"Why?"

"It says here this woman remembers dying and waking up in a beautiful pace with lush, green grass and flowers all around and a bright blue sky overhead. And she actually talked to her granddaddy."

"I did that once."

"What?"

"Actually talked to my granddaddy."

Love Those Jugs turns with surprise. Her eyes are wide with excitement.

"You did?" she exclaims.

"Yeah," Miss Harley Davidson tells her. "He lives in Omaha."

"Was he dead?"

"My grandma sometimes wishes he was."

The lights are out.

The bus is dark, the color of pitch, and on the move again.

It smells of sweat, onions, garlic, and potato chip crumbs.

A woman sneezes.

A man groans.

I look for Jean Marc.

His seat is empty.

If his bags don't arrive with his medicine at two-forty-five, he may be spending the night in a hospital.

That's what he told me.

If his bags don't arrive with his medicine at two-forty-five, the Greyhound Bus Counter Agent may lying be in the bed next to his.

Jean Marc knows what the Greyhound man doesn't.

Jean Marc has just enough money left to buy a taxi ride, a motel room, and, if necessary, a second-hand gun.

All he needs is one bullet, he told me before we left, and he can steal one of those.

Say a Prayer to Jesus

FOR THE PAST sixteen miles, the basketball player has listened to Love Those Jugs quote passages from the two-bit tabloid about living and dying and what may or may not happen when there are no more breaths to take.

Personally, he doesn't know if there is life after death.

He only knows there is pain for those who survive, and he did.

The basketball player came to Dallas from West Virginia, and now he's headed home. It will be the first time in three years he's walked on the old rundown front porch that reminds him so much of the poverty he is trying to escape.

He didn't believe it would ever miss it or the bad side of a bad town, but he's homesick to see those he hasn't been around in a long time, the ones he's suddenly fears are being stalked by time and fate and circumstance.

Death does that to a man.

It makes him think sometimes, and it almost always makes him think of home.

It had been at nine o'clock on a sunny spring morning when the basketball player and a friend – a co-worker – had eased into a North Dallas intersection.

Bright day.

Bright sun.

Bright hopes.

An eighty-seven-year old man, trying hard to beat a yellow light, slammed into them before they had time to make it across.

"I saw him coming, and I saw he wasn't gonna stop," the basketball player says softly. "I yelled my friend's name, but he never had a chance to look."

Their car tumbled through the air for thirty-five feet, then struck a light pole.

It snapped and smashed into the basketball player's door, trapping them inside.

"I woke up," he remembers, "and I was wrapped with metal."

Sweat glistens on his ebony forehead.

"I prayed hard."

"God listens."

"I didn't pray hard enough."

"Was your friend still in the car?"

"He was lying beside me." The basketball player shakes his head.

When he closes his eyes, he sees the carnage again.

Every day.

Every night.

Awake.

Or asleep.

He sees it again.

The old man keeps coming.

He feels the car coming apart.

He hears the explosion.

It sounds like death.

"My friend, he was crying for help," the basketball player says, "and I couldn't move."

The basketball player pauses and stares out into the darkness of the night, passing just beyond the stains that fingerprints and hair oil have etched upon the window of the bus.

"His neck was broke." The basketball player's voice is hoarse, a whisper. "And I couldn't move."

Sirens screamed their mockery of a bright and sunny day.

Engines roared and whined.

Crow bars were ripping away the twisted metal.

His friend was loaded into an ambulance.

The emergency vehicle raced away.

The basketball player told his friend goodbye.

He would be all right.

They got him free.

They were having a hard time tearing the metal away from the basketball player.

Pain ricocheted through his body, needles driving through his chest and down into his legs.

"Am I all right?" he asked the paramedics.

"Why?"

"I can't move," he said.

He wondered if he would ever move again.

The basketball player was checked into the hospital, and his eyes searched the emergency room.

They were looking for the face of his friend.

His friend must be there somewhere.

So crowded.

So much pain.

What was happening?

To him.

To his friend.

Where was his friend?

The pain had departed his friend.

His friend had been checked into the morgue.

"He only had two real friends," the basketball player says. "Me … "

For a moment his voice leaves him.

"… and Jesus."

Outside, the closed and empty fireworks stands and bait shops are swallowed up by the night.

The headlights of the Greyhound bus glare off a "beer to go" sign, but no beer has either come or gone from the roofless, decaying building in years.

Nailed to the pines are boards scribbled with hand-painted messages: *Posted, No Hunting,* and *Jesus Is Coming.*

We slip through tiny, deserted-street hamlets that look as though The Good Lord may have already come back and overlooked them.

Or maybe He took them all and forgot to sweep the streets.

Memories are always hardest in the night.

On the Road to Salvation

MEMPHIS LOOMS JUST ahead. The puffy lady with the bright-eyed little girl stirs as the glow of city street lights spins through the bus. They sit amidst a tattered cluster of paper dolls as they have for three days, all the way from Los Angeles.

It's the puffy lady's fifth journey in the past eighteen months.

Her daddy needs her.

Doctors amputated his left leg, and she took the road to Atlanta.

They took off his right leg, and she returned to his side.

Pneumonia gripped his lungs, and she sat beside his bed to hold his hand.

A heart attack knocked him to his knees, and she rode three days and nights to pray for mercy and healing.

The last word the puffy lady received told of his passing.

A funeral awaits her but only if she and Greyhound can make it in time.

Three days seems like forever.

For her, it is.

"I just hope I can get there before they put him in the ground," she says.

"When is the funeral?"

"Yesterday." The puffy lady shrugs. "Maybe they waited for me.'

Maybe they should.

The bus eases into a bright new Greyhound depot, and Memphis – all around it – is ablaze with electronic gossip that lights up the night.

Down the street, a sign on the Ramada Inn warns: "Your arms are too short to box with God."

On the next corner, the Hotel Tennessee (Rates $12 and up, Stop and Come In) pales in a neon marquee that preaches: "God sent not his son into the world to condemn the world but that the world through him might be saved."

A lot who come to Hotel Tennessee are looking for salvation.

Not all of them have come to pray.

Redemption is just a kiss away.

A kiss leads to temptation.

Temptation leads to a twenty-dollar bill.

And a twenty-dollar bill leads to salvation.

Just beyond the taxi cabs, the Ellwest Adult Film Theater boasts about having full-color individual viewing booths with movies for every taste. It has live exotic shows on thirty screens, or so it says, including sexy dancers for twenty-five cents apiece.

Or, for a quarter, you can "call-a-doll" and talk to the girl of your choice, and maybe even find temptation.

Redemption.

Or salvation.

They're all for sale at the Hotel Tennessee.

All for a price.

Love is extra.

Love is fleeting.

There are no guarantees on love.

Inside the depot – a clean, well-lighted place – Flat Feet is being chased by Pac Man.

The four-year-old is trying to figure out how to coax a sack of potato chips out of the vending machine without wasting a coin, which he doesn't have.

Love Those Jugs is punching the Rolling Stones into a jukebox. She listens as they tell her it's "No Use Crying.'

The curly-haired stranger is digging in the pockets of his faded jeans for a quarter so he can check out the shy blonde's bio-rhythm.

Doesn't know what it.

Thinks it might be something good.

He's looking for a way to her heart.

He knows where it is.

Over there alongside temptation.

On the far side of redemption.

Begging for salvation.

But love at rates for twelve dollars and up at the Hotel Tennessee is a little steep, and the bus won't wait around forever.

He'll settle for a bio-rhythm and wonders what it will get him, if anything. After all, the machine guarantees that it offers a road map to help them both on a safer, better, more meaningful, and productive life.

And the curly-haired stranger is definitely in search of a better life.

The shy blonde only wants to know "when to act and when to proceed with caution," as the machine says, in case anybody tries to harass her or, God forbid, do even worse.

She's fine with a little temptation.

She doesn't need salvation.

The shy blonde was saved the night before she left home.

Faded Love and Faded Dreams

IN A CORNER seat of the Memphis bus depot – away from the crowd – sprawls a big man with a black beard and a black leather jacket and a black patch that proudly proclaims: *I'm 100 percent Gayhawk.*

He would look more at home on a motorcycle.

His bike's broke.

And Gayhawk is on his way to Chicago to pick up another engine.

He looks mean, a gargoyle with yellowed teeth.

His smile isn't.

"We're not gangsters," he tells me. "Why, back in Mississippi we even have Easter parties for the kiddies, and at Christmas we take gifts out to the elderly."

"What do they call you?" I ask.

He grins.

"Trouble Man," he says.

"You get in much trouble?"

"Sometimes I get into confusion with people," he says.

He's calm.

He's relaxed.

I feel braver than I did.

"Gayhawk is an unusual name for a motorcycle gang," I remark.

I hope his fists are as calm as his face.

He shrugs.

"People saw a bunch of guys always out riding together and got to thinking we was funny," the biker says, "so we just changed our name to Gayhawk. They may still think we're funny, but none of them laugh."

"Are there any girls in the club?"

"There used to be."

"What happened to them."

Gayhawk sighs and shakes his head.

He knows the truth.

Truth hurts.

His eyes soften.

"They're all home taking care of the babies," he says.

The bus leaves Memphis and midnight behind.

The puffy lady glances at her watch and places a tired hand around a little doll lying amongst the candy wrappers in the seat beside her.

The four-year-old is singing himself to sleep.

The curly-haired stranger escorts the shy blonde to an empty seat at the back of the bus where there is nothing to disturb them except the occasional flushing of the toilet.

Apparently, the bio-rhythm checked out all right for both of them.

She's kind of pleased that he wants to harass her.

And he, God forbid, wants to do even worse.

A dancing girl in a tight sweater – her alabaster skin unblemished by the sun – falls into her seat and quietly watches the screaming yellow and blue neon slide by outside her window.

Her black hair falls below her shoulders.

It is straight.

And her face is pale in the light of the moon.

She is tall with long legs.

A beauty mark highlights her high cheekbones.

It was made with a brush.

The neon is throbbing outside on streets that never grow dark beside a cluster of buildings that never close.

Their doors may be locked.

They aren't closed.

Within those honky-tonks – she told her mother they were clubs – she had sought her fame and fortune, finding neither, but growing up and growing bitter and growing tired of the dream.

It faded.

Then busted.

She hasn't dreamed in a while.

She is a dancer.

They want burlesque.

"I was offered two hundred dollars a day,' she says, "and they paid a hundred more if I went topless."

"What did you do?"

"I walked out."

"Why?"

"I'm a dancer," she says. "They weren't interested in my dancing."

She was just a country girl from South Georgia.

She was looking for the big time.

So were they.

The bigger, the better.

They wanted to judge her talent with a tape measure.

She could have done well.

Her dancing shoes are lying in her lap.

Somewhere on the road to Corinth, Mississippi, she opens the window and throws them out into the night.

Souls for Sale

FROM ALL OUTWARDLY appearances, Jesus stays busy in the Mississippi Delta. According to the signs stuck along the side of the road, He lives, heals, saves, loves, and is coming again.

Baptist Churches are everywhere.

Some are Free Will.

Some are Primitive.

And if the churches are big and modern with giant crosses or heavenly steeples that touch the sky, they are First Baptist.

I am reminded of the old southern story about the large church sitting on the downtown square with a flashing neon sign that said: *If you're tired of sin, come on in.*

Beneath it, some lady had written in wicked red lipstick: "And if you're not, call 462-9325.

Throughout the countryside, church marques – always lit – espouse such wisdom as *Do Not Be a Cloud because You Can Not Be a Star*, or *You Can't Live Wrong and Die Right*, or *Be Fishers of Men …You Catch 'em and He'll Clean 'em*, or *Never Give the Devil a Ride. He'll Always Want to Drive.*

Church signs, I guess, have replaced the Burma Shave signs on southern highways.

Across the aisle, the signs mean nothing to a Vietnamese woman whose past is riddled with despair. She moans in her sleep, and her eyes are jarred open. She shudders and glances around the bus and sees only the night staring back with eyes as hollow as her own.

It's quiet, the way it was on a December morning when she left her brother and caught the ten-thirty flight out of Saigon.

Don't worry, he said.

I'll be right behind you. Some loose ends have to be tied up first.

Always, there are the loose ends and red tape and money spent in dark alleys to strangers with dark faces and darker hearts.

He would come and join her in the states, he said, and she settled down and waited.

It wasn't a good life.

Then again, it wasn't particularly bad.

There were no bombs bursting upon the fields.

She no longer caught the smell of napalm in the winds.

The years passed.

And one night the telephone rang.

It was late.

It was dark.

It was that time of night when a ringing telephone never brings good news.

"Your brother is in a concentration camp," the voice said.

It was foreign to her.

It spoke with a thick accent.

"Send three thousand dollars," the voice said, "or you can forget about your brother."

"But I don't have three thousand dollars," she said.

"Get it."

"I can't."

"Too bad."

She never heard from him or her brother again.

When she sleeps, the Vietnamese woman dreams of a brother coming to her, begging and pleading for his life, the life she could not afford to buy.

It was an open market in Vietnam.

Souls bought.

Souls sold.

Lives in the balance.

Screams always awaken her.

They come from deep within her throat.

She slumps beside the window and watches as the darkness bleeds into morning.

The reflection staring back is her own.

She thinks it may be her brother.

"His eyes are closed," she tells me.

No.

She looks again.

"His eyes are missing," she says.

All I see are stalks of cotton in dry dirt.

A war did not end when the firing stopped. A war won't go away until the nightmares end, the war and the endless miles to Atlanta where Jesus lives, saves, and heal.

A Strange Road to Travel

THE BUS AGONIZES its way through the timbered clay of Mississippi that became the hills of North Alabama, making its stops in the strangest of places. Depots, sometimes, are at any corner where two or more are gathered together.

In Mayfair, Mississippi, it had been a Gulf Service Station, with Terry's Package Store in the rear, out of the way, maybe, but not out of sight.

The Holly Springs depot was wedged in between a farmer's headquarters and a bail bond office, which – on occasion – comes in handy for the hired hand who raises more hell than hominy.

The bus station at Sulligent, Alabama, is tucked away in Puckett's Discount Hardware Store.

And at Winfield, Greyhound loads them up from a Laundromat.

The South has its class.

It's not on the bus route.

The railroad man had climbed on board at Olive Branch, and he felt ashamed of himself, a little like a traitor, riding the bus when he was much more at home on the rails. He was on his way to pick up a train and guide it back to Memphis, grinning more than was usual as we rolled on through the ante-bellum streets of Holly Springs. It was a historic town, and he had the past on his mind.

"I got in a fight in a beer joint here one night," he says. "Kept me in jail till I paid my way out."

"What happened?"

"Don't remember."

"How did the fight get started?"

"Don't remember."

"Who won?"

"Don't remember."

"What'd it cost you to get out of jail?"

"Three hundred and twenty-six dollars and seventeen cents."

There are some things that a man never forgets, he says.

Money is one.

"What's the other?" I ask.

"Don't remember," he says

Along the highway are long driveways that lead to short houses with rabbits, boiled peanuts, and red worms for sale.

Antique stores have yards crammed and piled with rusty iron bedsteads, busted commodes, and a wooden Indian or two.

Women still hang their clothes out on the line to dry in the sun, and you can buy land for ninety-five dollars down.

In the fields are scattered houses, draped in kudzu, abandoned long ago as useless or worthless when the crops ran out.

They would probably be worth some money now if they only had doors or windows on them.

The kudzu has removed both.

It's a vine.

It's aggressive.

It took the South quicker than Sherman's army.

It covers houses.

It covers trees.

It covers fence posts.

If the cows don't keep moving, they'll be swallowed up as well.

The railroad man looks at me with a puzzled frown. "Some preachers say the world will be destroyed by fire," he says.

I nod.

I've heard them.

"Some preachers say it will be destroyed by great floods."

I nod again.

"But me?" The railroad man shrugs. "I'm betting on kudzu."

I'm not betting against him.

In the rural communities, diners have always opened under new management and will probably close the same way.

Bad food.

Bad service.

Bad reputation.

The diners never recover.

Chicken fried gristle is chicken fried gristle no matter how you cut it.

In some places, roller skating rinks are the only businesses in towns making money. Liquor in brown paper bags doesn't hurt them any.

An auto parts store boasts: "Prices are born here and raised elsewhere."

And a service station swears: "We have recessed prices on our inflated tires."

The bus has broken the crease that separates daylight from dark.

A woman stands on the corner of a small town and waves.

She waits for the bus to stop.

It doesn't.

Her smile fades.

Her shoulders sag.

"Why didn't you stop?" I ask the driver.

He grins.

"Wouldn't have done her any good," he says.

"Why not?"

"We'd have to stop again on down the road."

"Why?"

"That's Lillian," he says "She runs away once a week, and the police always come and stop me to get her back."

"She must really be lonely," I say.

"No," the bus driver responds. "Just think about."

"Think about what?" I wonder.

"She wants to ride the bus," he says. "She's not lonely. She's crazy."

The miles roll on forever.

And the stories never end.

Love in Never-Never Land

THE BACK OF the bus smells of smoke and sweat and dried urine, as though the innards of the Greyhound are running on the sixth day of a five-day deodorant pad.

Cigarette butts are scattered across a floor that has become sticky with spilled soda pop, and they stick to the bottom of your shoes if you walk up and down the aisle.

Some of the passengers are sleeping.

Some are writing letters they may never mail.

And kids with dirty clothes and ragged socks are climbing and playing across the seats, throwing potato chip crumbs and unaware they have no money, unaware that anyone does.

The four-year-old boy, with milk stains on his mouth, is singing, loud and off key. He doesn't know any words, and he has even less of a tune.

"Be quiet," his grandmother says.

He isn't.

"Do you want the bus driver to stop and put your out of the side of the road?" Her voice is a threat.

He presses his little nose to the window and watches the road speed past. He's tired of the road and the miles and the cramped space in a seat that's much harder today than it was yesterday.

"Yes," he says defiantly.

The old lady slaps his behind, then leans back and closes her eyes, apparently more interested in hearing him cry than sing.

In the back, two young men with close-cropped hair are headed in opposite directions on the same bus.

One is in the Navy, and it's not bad, he says, when there's no war going on.

The other was in the army.

But after six weeks, the Army sent him packing, said he had flat feet, said they didn't have any use for him anymore.

"I left Albany, Georgia," he says, "because I got tired of working in a cotton mill for four dollars an hour."

"Where are you going now?" I asked.

"Back to the cotton mill," he says.

"For four dollars an hour?"

"For whatever they'll pay me."

"We should have hitchhiked," complains Navy.

"Why?"

"If we'd a thumbed it, we'd probably be home by now."

"Maybe," agrees Flat Foot. "But you can sleep on a bus."

"So what?"

"Damn hard to sleep on the side of the road." He shrugs.

"You got a dollar?" Army asks.

"Yeah."

"They'll kill you for a dollar," he says.

It's mid-morning when the bus ride shudders to a stop in the Atlanta station.

Flat Feet is almost home.

The video games are free there.

He knows them all.

He never loses, he says.

"Games?" I ask.

"Quarters," he says.

Navy still has a long way to go.

Somewhere a ship is waiting.

But not a war.

He's at peace with himself and the world.

Across the aisle, the curly-haired stranger kisses the cheek of the shy blonde.

He waits for her to pull away.

She doesn't.

He smiles.

She blushes.

She knows what's on his mind.

She wonders if he'll harass her or, God forbid, do even worse.

The basketball player has a long wait for another bus.

He waits alone.

His friend should be with him.

He buried his friend.

And the railroad man is searching for a taxi.

Love Those Jugs welcomes sleep.

The Vietnamese woman keeps fighting it.

She doesn't want to sleep.

She doesn't want to scream.

Not again.

The puffy lady wonders if she's bound for a chapel or a fresh-dirt grave.

Is daddy already in the ground?

Did the family wait for her?

Or is she too late?

She's been too late all of her life.

The grandmother and the four-year-old look around to see if anyone has come to meet them.

No one has.

He's tired.

He's hungry.

He's not singing anymore.

In the back of the bus, the curly-haired stranger takes the shy blonde by the hands as she stands up in the aisle to leave.

The smile has crawled out of his eyes.

He's lonesome, and she isn't even gone.

"I don't have to go to North Carolina," he says.

"But you have a job there."

"I can get one here in Atlanta."

"Why?"

"That way I'd get to keep on seeing you," he says.

The shy blonde backs slowly away, easing her hand from his grasp.

"That wouldn't be real smart," she says.

"I can do it." The curly-haired stranger is pleading now.

"Yeah," she says and smiles an awkward smile. "But my husband would kill you."

She turns and walks away – and all of those who were together and were kept together behind the closed doors of a Greyhound bus – will never be together again.

The South

THE SOUTH IS sacred ground. Don't believe me? Just ask a southerner, but not unless you have a lot of time and nothing better to do than hear a story that may drift somewhere between truth and fiction. It may not have really happened that way, but it could have, and that's close enough for the storyteller.

The South believes that when God sent manna from Heaven, most of it was okra, and the rest was turnip greens. It fought a war, lost, doesn't forgive, doesn't forget. Why nobody would have ever heard about the war if Margaret Mitchell hadn't concocted Gone With the Wind, which, in the South, is considered the lost scriptures of the Old Testament.

The South invented country music, hog calling, moonshine stills, stock car racing, running for the roses, worm fiddling, frog gigging, and alligator wrestling. The South has its own set of rules. If you're not invited to the big social event of the year, you turn off the lights so folks will think you are among God's chosen few and are sipping champagne or bourbon with the movers and shakers of town. Nobody knows you aren't there. Their lights are off, too.

I am a card-carrying member of the hunkering and hankering society in the South and left my footprints on back roads that twist and wind through fields where cotton once grew. Ask someone his name or directions to the next town or the price of a barbecue pork or what he calls that old stripped-down car up on blocks, and he will tell you a story. Ask him the same question tomorrow, and the story will be better than the day before. I tell them just the way I heard them, maybe not the first time but the best time.

High Country Secrets

THE SUMMER TENNESSEE sun had baked the ground beneath Bob Duke's feet as he ambled out of the Great Smoky Mountains, following a winding dirt road that led him out of the high country and on toward Johnson City.

The dust on his face had turned to grime, and sweat cloaked his forehead. His throat was dry, his spittle tasted like dust, and the cardboard suitcase in his right hand felt as heavy as it had been all week. But then, it was always heavy when Bob Duke hadn't sold much, and the last seven days had been a total waste.

He was a drummer.

He was a peddler.

Nobody was buying.

Nobody in Lick Skillet or Loafer's Glory had any money to speak of, and Bob Duke was beginning to feel like the frazzled end of a misspent life. Maybe, he thought, all of the extra dimes and dollars had run downhill to Johnson City. That's what Bob Duke was hoping anyway.

But then, hope was about all a traveling salesman had when he found himself walking from place to place in the 1920s, trying to keep a full suitcase of wares, notions, and doodads from dragging the ground.

His legs were tired, his shoulders were slumping, and the white in his shirt had turned a pale shade of yellow. Bob Duke set the suitcase on the ground beside him and looked out across the timbered mountain ridge, turning a hazy shade of blue in the far distance.

He had no idea where he was.

He had no idea how much farther he had to walk before finding the city limits of Johnson City.

He had no idea what time it was.

He had traded his gold watch for a meal earlier in the week. The steak was tough, but it didn't matter. The gold watch wasn't gold anyway. Bob Duke certainly couldn't tell the time by looking at the sun, which dangled from a high sky like a worn gold dollar above his head.

In a pasture just beyond the fence line, he saw a farmer milking a lone dairy cow in the splintered shade of an oak tree. Duke walked to the edge of the barrow ditch and yelled, "Excuse me, sir."

The farmer barely turned his head. "You talking to me?" he asked.

"Yes, sir."

"What do you want, then?"

"Am I on the right road to Johnson City?"

"You'll get there if you keep following your feet."

"How far is it?"

"About thirty minutes if you don't wear out." A faint grin creased the farmer's face. "About half a day if you do," he said. "And if you get lost, you won't make it all."

"Any chance of getting lost?"

"The road knows where it's going." The farmer shrugged. "It's been there before."

Bob Duke wiped the grime away from his sunburnt eyes and asked, "Could you tell me what time it is?"

"Two-fifteen." The farmer had not hesitated.

Duke shrugged his weary shoulders and turned back toward the dirt road. The sun had not moved at all by the time he walked into the downtown streets of Johnson City. He glanced up at the clock on the courthouse wall. It said two forty-five.

A strange feeling began to work its way like a thorn into Bob Duke's mind. The farmer had been right. He had said the time was two-fifteen, and it had not taken Duke more than thirty minutes to reach town. The farmer had known what time it was, and he hadn't had a watch strapped either to his arm or dangling from a chain.

Duke was puzzled, then perplexed. He had traveled the high country of Appalachia for more than a year now, and he had long been amazed at the secrets of the mountain people.

A rainbow in the evening was a sure sign that fair weather would follow, or so they said. When the trees split their bark in winter, they knew it would be a dry, hot spring, and crickets singing in the house foretold of a long cold winter. When a baby boy was born in the wan of the moon, they swore, the next child would be a girl, or maybe it was the other way around. March held the fisherman's moon, and the hunter's moon hung in a November sky.

Now some farmer up on the side of the mountain could actually tell time without a watch.

How in the Good Lord's name did he do it? Was it the angle of the sun as it dangled in the sky? Was it the length of the shadow that fell away from the oak above his head? Was it the way the sunlight filtered through the leaves and struck the rock at his feet? Surely the birds didn't know, and the squirrels were barking about matters more serious than merely passing the time of day.

Mountain people did indeed have their secrets. Bob Duke knew he had to find out what this one was. He wouldn't be able to sleep or travel on unless he did. Duke hid his suitcase behind the trash cans in a back alley behind the mercantile store and headed back up the mountainside.

He found the farmer.

The farmer hadn't moved.

He was still milking his cow, or maybe it was another cow. But he had not moved.

"Excuse me, sir," Bob Duke yelled.

The farmer barely turned his head. "You talking to me?" he asked again.

"Yes, sir." Duke rolled up the pale yellow sleeves on his shirt and said loudly. "I don't know if you remember me, but I was up here a while back and asked you what time it was, and you told me, and you don't have a watch or anything. I was wondering if, perhaps, you could show me the secret of your mountain ways. I've always heard that mountain people can do things other folks can't do, and I'd like to be able to do it, too."

The farmer turned around to face him, pushing his straw hat back on his head, and scratching his chin. He started to grin, then thought better of it. "So you want to know how I can tell time."

"Yes, sir."

The farmer sighed. It had already been a long day. But then, most of his days were. "Then jump across that barrow ditch," he said.

Bob Duke leaped the ditch.

"Get down on your hands and knees and crawl under that barbed wire fence."

Bob Duke eased his way beneath the rusting barbs.

"Now come on over here beside this cow."

Bob Duke hurried across the barn lot.

"And sit down on this stool."

The farmer stood, and Bob Duke eased down onto the top of a wooden stool where the splinters had been worn down to a nub. The cow moved. Duke was too tired to be startled or care.

"Now put one hand on this teat," the farmer said.

Bob Duke did as he was told.

"And put the other hand on this teat."

Bob Duke reached for the other nipple and squeezed it."

"Now," said the farmer, "if you look over the hind end of that cow, you can see the clock on the courthouse wall in downtown Johnson City."

Bob Duke's shoulders sagged. His back ache. The muscles in his legs tightened. A cloud swallowed the sun. There was no shadow dangling from the oak limbs above his head and no touch of light reflecting off the rock beneath him.

Time marched on.

On the mountain, it stood still. Maybe it always had.

The walk down the mountain seemed a lot farther than the last time he made the trip.

Barter for the Bard

FOR ROBERT PORTERFIELD, it was like the last act of a bad play when the actors could not remember their lines, the curtain was hung up and wouldn't fall, and the audience had begun leaving sometime shortly after intermission. If it could go wrong, it had, and there was nothing that he could do about it.

The stage had gone dark.

The music had faded away.

The seats were as bare as the marquee.

Programs were left unprinted.

Poster sheets with his name and sometimes his picture on them had been scattered with the winds.

The footlights had dimmed, then gone out altogether.

The ticket window was nailed shut.

The cash register was twenty-three cents short of having a quarter.

An actor without a theater was an actor without a job. Porterfield had learned the lines of a comedy and was confronted with act one of a tragedy. He walked the streets of New York, but they were as dark as the stage, as cold as a critic's reviews, and were leading him nowhere. He had been there before. He wasn't looking forward to going back. Instead, Robert Porterfield went home.

By the time he was ten years old, Porterfield had already decided that someday he would be standing in the harsh spotlights of Broadway. Maybe a star. Maybe a bit player. Maybe nothing more than a face amongst the scenery.

But he would be on stage.

Failure never entered his mind.

His family frowned. Robert Porterfield had always walked the straight and narrow, and now he was taking a wrong turn that had more heartbreaks than pot holes. His father was adamantly opposed to the boy's wild intentions, but he was not the kind of man to spit on a dream, no matter how ridiculous it might be.

By 1925, Porterfield was studying at the American Academy of Dramatic Arts in New York. He learned how to walk, what to do with his hands, how to project his voice, and what the world looked like from center stage.

He liked what he saw.

The young man was a beginner, to be sure, but he landed a couple of jobs, saw the curtain rise and fall, and heard the applause, which was not nearly as loud as the sounds of a Great Depression echoing empty across the land.

Banks were closing.

Businesses were locking their doors.

The streets of New York were lined with men searching for a job, a bowl of soup, maybe just a crumb from the bread lines that had infested the city.

New York was broke.

So was the rest of the country.

It didn't matter whether theater tickets cost a dollar or a dime, no one was buying.

For Robert Porterfield, it was as though the edge of the stage was the end of the earth. Step off, and no one would ever see him again. New York shut down is stages. The tumult and the shouting had turned to a faint whimper and the hollow growl of an empty belly.

Robert Porterfield rode into Abingdon, Virginia, and realized that hard times had beat him home. Farmers who had grown cash crops now had crops but no cash. Money had saddled up and gone elsewhere, or, maybe, it had just evaporated like the mist rising atop the Blue Ridge.

Proud men had lost their pride. Pockets were as empty as the bank. Poverty was etched into wrinkles on every face, even those faces too young to have wrinkles. Porterfield wearily glanced in the mirror and realized he had a couple of deepening furrows he had not seen the summer before.

The idea came to him out of the blue, and for a brief moment, he wondered about the sanity of it all. A desperate man, down on his luck, could have all sorts of delusions, he knew, and not all of them made sense.

But this one did.

Up in New York, Porterfield had a few friends with a lot of talent, but none of them were eating regularly. In Abingdon, life was devoid of entertainment, but most of the folks had gardens filled with vegetables, beef cattle grazing their pastures, chickens scratching their yards, pigs in their pens, and tables graced with food.

He could not pack up Virginia and carry it to New York, but he could certainly bring enough actors down to Abingdon to occupy a stage, provided he could find one.

His plan was a simple as it was ingenuous.

Not everyone would be able to buy a ticket with a handful of coins, but just about everyone could swap a peck of beans, a mess of greens, or a basket of eggs for the privilege of seeing a real live Broadway production, even if did happen to be as far off Broadway as anyone had ever been before.

Porterfield thought that the Town Hall of Abingdon might serve well as a theater. After all, its walls had heard the somber words of drama before. The hall had originally been built a hundred years earlier as the Sinking Springs Presbyterian Church, which staged its own theatrical production in 1876 to raise funds necessary for repairing the building.

The stage was still intact, provided actors didn't mind performing discreetly above the cells of an old jail with prisoners, from time to time, shouting out their own drunken, angry, defiant, and sometimes profane lines of dialogue that would have never crossed the mind of any proper and self-respecting playwright.

Robert Porterfield was a man with an idea, a second-hand stage, and a dollar in his pocket. All he needed were actors, a play, and a curtain.

From New York, the actors and actresses came. There was nothing to keep them on Broadway. Broadway, for the most part, was dark. The speaking parts had gone to those who were knocking on locked and shuttered doors, asking, "Brother, can you spare a dime?"

The troupe was hungry, hesitant, and hopeful. Some had pooled the last money in their pockets and bought jalopies for the long trek south. Others came by train. A few hitchhiked their way down a circuitous corridor of decaying pavement that led them to an odd little town beneath the shelter of the Blue Ridge.

They were the outsiders.

They didn't belong.

They looked around them.

It wasn't New York.

And it wasn't home.

It was somewhere in between, not unlike purgatory.

Whispers drifted down the streets of Abingdon, and the whole town was talking about Robert Porterfield.

"The boy's lost his mind."

"He wasn't quite right to start with."

"He ain't never been himself."

"Why do you say that?"

"He's always playing like he's somebody else."

Robert Porterfield heard the grumbling and the complaints. They did not bother him. Only failure troubled him. He would not fail.

In time, Porterfield was advertising: "Ham for Hamlet." He immediately strung up a banner across the outside of Town Hall that said: "With the vegetables you cannot sell, you can buy a good laugh."

Abingdon smiled.

Abingdon had not laughed in a long time.

On the night of June 10, 1933, the curtain rose on a three-act drama called *After Tomorrow*. Admission was thirty cents, but farmers who lived back among the highlands preferred the idea of swapping victuals for tickets.

With money becoming as scarce as hen's teeth, it was a time-honored practice in rural America. Country folks bartered eggs for sugar, corn for tobacco, tobacco for rent, cows for cars, and cars for more cows. In the Blue Ridge, the fine art of bartering had been a way of life for two centuries.

After Tomorrow was played before a full house. Sure the admission had been a nickel more than a movie ticket, but these were real actors, performing so close that those on the front row could reach out and touch them, see the sweat on their faces, smell their breath whether they wanted to or not.

Down below, the prisoners were unruly. Loud. Abrasive. Curses filled the silence. For them, *after tomorrow* would be no different from *the day before.*

The actors were unruffled. Of course, Town Hall also held the fire house, and when the alarm sounded, those on stage merely froze in their positions, waiting until the wail died away before moving steadily ahead with the performance.

As the season ran through the summer, theater patrons found all sorts of ways to pay for their tickets. Live hogs. Dead snakes. Tasted like chicken. At least they did when an actor had an empty table for supper. Toothpaste. Underwear. A dozen eggs. Tobacco. And vegetables. Wash tubs full of vegetables. A jar of homemade liquor, for medicinal purposes, of course, and actors were always sick of the rain, sick of the sun, sick of rehearsals, sick of the prisoners, sick of the howling dogs that replaced the prisoners in the cells below the stage. The dogs were suspected of having rabies.

Robert Porterfield looked up late one afternoon, only thirty minutes before the curtain was scheduled to be raised, and he saw a farmer and his wife walking toward the box office leading a cow and carrying a battered tin bucket.

"How much for a ticket?" the farmer asked.

Porterfield thought it over and answered, "I guess a gallon will be enough."

The farmer tied the cow to a lamp post, knelt down, grabbed a teat, and milked a two-gallon bucket half full. He showed it to Porterfield. The lady in the box office smiled and handed him a ticket.

"How about your wife?" Porterfield asked. "Doesn't she want to see the play?"

The farmer shrugged. "Probably does," he said. "But she can milk her own ticket."

As the first year ended, Porterfield counted the coins and realized that the troupe had eaten well but had earned a mere four dollars and thirty-five cents in cold, hard cash. He promptly sent it to the Motion Picture Relief Fund. The troupe didn't need the money. Members of the company already knew they had notched themselves a successful year. Together, they had gained a total of three hundred pounds.

Playwrights fully expected to receive royalties for their plays that were performed on the theatrical stage in Abingdon, Virginia. They generally received money. No. They always received money. Porterfield didn't send them any.

This was, after all, a barter theater.

Instead of royalty payments, he sent whole Virginia hams to Noel Coward, Thornton Wilder, Tennessee Williams, and George Bernard Shaw.

No one complained, no one, that is, except the crusty and iconoclastic George Bernard Shaw. "How could you do this?" he asked Porterfield.

"It's a perfectly good ham."

"No doubt," the eccentric Irish genius said. "But I am a vegetarian."

Robert Porterfield understood. During the times that tried men's souls, he knew, he needed to make exceptions, and this was one of them.

He apologized profusely.

He swore that such a grievous error would never happen again.

Shaw accepted the apology. He sat back and awaited his royalty check.

Robert Porterfield sent George Bernard Shaw two crates of spinach.

Attorney for Mister Drum

GEORGE GRAHAM VEST and adversity were no strangers to each other. They had met before and would meet again, but never in a trial as unusual as the one facing him in a Kentucky courthouse. Vest had fought a few wars in his time, but now he was sitting in the dim light of a dark room and wondering how in God's great name he would be able to save such a defendant.

It was a case unlike any he had ever witnessed before, the kind he might never see again. A client named Drum was unable to speak for himself, so he had placed his fragile and precarious reputation in the able hands of George Vest.

The attorney closed his eyes and rubbed his temples with the tips of his fingers. A dull ache kept boring into the back of his head. He was aware he had neither statutes nor precedence on his side, and the heavy odds against him were growing stronger with each passing hour.

He would not formulate his case until he walked into the courtroom.

By then, it might be too late.

George Graham Vest was a lifelong politician who had served as a senator in the Confederate Congress and as U.S. Senator when the storm clouds of war finally faded from the landscape. He was a dashing and distinguished figure in Kentucky, and, as an attorney, he handled only the cases of grave interest to the state.

His client was a farm dog, Old Drum, that had been shot by Leonides Hornsby, for killing sheep.

Couldn't prove it.

Had his suspicions.

Had a rifle. Took it down.

Took a shot.

Did not regret it.

Did not deny it.

Old Drum's owner, Charles Burden, without hesitation, retained George Graham Vest as counsel in his suit for damages. Old Drum had been good dog. A faithful dog. A constant companion. A great loss.

A sense of anger worked its way through Leonides Hornsby. He bowed his back, straightened his shoulders and prepared for war.

If Burden wanted to fight,

Hornsby was ready to roll up his sleeves, spit on his fists, and meet Old Drum's owner any place at any time.

In a back alley.

On main street.

Or in a courtroom.

They could settle their dispute with fists, pistols, long knives, or log chains. It did not make him any difference. A bitter Leonides Hornsby promptly hired the renowned and dignified Francis M. Cockrell, a sitting U.S. Senator, to defend him.

All of Kentucky sat back to watch the two statesmen duel with a slam-bang, no-holds-barred whirlwind of words and emotions before a scowling, black-robed referee who happened to look a lot like a judge.

Senator Cockrell was not concerned, which meant that Leonides Hornsby was not worried either. He was competent. He was efficient. He knew the facts. And he carefully placed them before the court in a convincing manner.

He had all of the facts on his side, he said. His client owned a farm.

He raised sheep.

A dog trespassed on Hornsby's land.

Sheep died.

Profits were lost.

The dog needed killing.

His client obliged.

His client only did what other self-respecting farmers would do when facing the sudden demise of their livelihood by a marauding dog. The shooting, he argued in rich baritone voice, was entirely justifiable.

He nodded to the judge, walked stiffly to his chair, and sat down.

All eyes turned to George Graham Vest.

He made no effort to deny any of the facts that his opponent had presented the court.

He called no witnesses.

He cited no legal precedents.

He presented no legal argument.

He did not rant.

Or rave.

George Graham Vest simply stood before the jury and – with a low, calm voice – offered a quiet, gentle eulogy to a dog. He said:

"Gentlemen of the Jury, the best friend a man has in this world may turn against him and become his enemy. His son or daughter that he has reared with loving care may prove ungrateful. Those who are nearest and dearest to us, those whom we trust with our happiness and our good name may become traitors to their faith.

"The money that a man has, he may lose. It flies away from him, perhaps in a moment of ill-considered action. The people who are prone to fall on their knees to do us honor when success is with us, may be the first to throw the stone of malice when failure settles its cloud upon our heads.

"The one absolutely unselfish friend that man can have in this selfish world, the one that never deserts him, the one that never proves ungrateful or treacherous, is his dog. A man's dog stands by him in prosperity and in poverty, in health and in sickness. He will sleep on the cold ground where the wintry winds blow and the snow drives fiercely, if only he may be near his master's side.

"He will kiss the hand that has no food to offer. He will lick the wounds and sores that come when encountered by the roughness of the world. He guards the sleep of his pauper master as if he were a prince.

"When all other friends desert, he remains. When riches take wings and reputation falls to pieces, he is as constant in his love as the sun in its journey through the heavens.

"If fortune drives the master forth as an outcast in the world, friendless and homeless, the faithful dog asks no higher privilege than that of accompanying him to guard him against danger, to fight against his enemies.

"And when the last scène of all comes, and death takes his master in its embrace and his body is laid away, there by the graveside will the noble dog be found, his head between his paws, his eyes sad, but open in alert watchfulness, faithful and true even in death."

Silence gripped the courtroom as Senator George Graham Vest quietly sat down. The silence lingered. Vest glanced around him. Eyes were moist. No one was moving. It was as though everyone had fallen into a trance.

Unexpectedly, a wild storm of applause erupted in the courtroom. Not even the good judge could gavel it away.

He tried. Once.

Then again.

He hammered the gavel with supreme authority.

No one heard.

If they heard, no one paid any attention.

Those in the courtroom cheered.

A few wept.

The jury reached a decision quickly, and it was unanimous. George Graham Vest, like no other, had defended the dignity, the honor, the loyalty of a dog.

Charles Burden had lost a dog.

Leonides Hornsby must pay.

Legally, he might be justified for shooting Mister Drum, but he had to pay.

He had taken the life of a good and faithful dog.

The jury would have been more lenient if he had taken the life of Charles Burden.

The Most Beautiful Woman in Town

MILDRED KITCHENS WAS in the vanity business, and Rachel was the most vain woman in town. Always had been.

The face of a magazine cover.

The legs of a runway model.

Tall.

Thin.

No matter what she ate, Rachel was always thin. Long auburn hair draped across her shoulders. She wore a smile that could knock a man dead at thirty paces and usually did.

Rachel never saw a mirror she didn't like.

She may have grown a little older.

The reflection in the mirror hadn't.

And if she held her head just right, and a gentle splash of sunlight touched her face and wound its way through the curls of her auburn hair, Rachel was, as she had always been, the loveliest woman in Crystal Springs, Mississippi.

She knew it.

So did everyone else.

"Look at Rachel," they would say.

"A beautiful lady."

"She grows more beautiful every day."

"Always had such class."

"And she still looks so young."

"The passing years don't stick to Rachel.

"I wish I knew her secret."

Only Mildred Kitchens knew her secret. She should. Mildred Kitchens was in the vanity business. She operated a small beauty salon on a back street across the alley and behind the Savings & Trust in the small town.

But she just didn't do hair.

Not Mildred.

She did faces as well.

Mildred possessed the deft hand of an artist and was, it was whispered far and wide, something of a magician when it came to mixing just the right combination of powders and lotions – some she concocted herself – lipstick and rouge, eye shadow and sparkle gloss.

An old woman would walk into her salon.

A young woman would walk out.

At least, they felt that way, and the mirror on the back of the shop told them so, and beauty was no longer merely skin deep. When Mildred finished with them, beauty attached itself to the bone.

She didn't merely hide wrinkles. She erased them.

That's why Rachel had been coming to see Mildred for so many years.

"Keep the wrinkles away,' she would say.

The women both laughed.

And Mildred kept the wrinkles away.

They had grown up together in Crystal Springs, Mississippi, had swapped dolls back and forth as young girls, and shared mustard and onion sandwiches beneath the shade of those ancient Southern oaks.

But they hadn't gone to school together.

Rachel was white.

Mildred wasn't.

Rachel graduated from the University of Mississippi with a degree in marriage.

Mildred went into the vanity business.

Some people in town collected stamps and coins and designer dolls.

Rachel collected husbands.

She had buried two, left one outright, and another suddenly showed up at the train station one morning with a suitcase and a bullet hole in the sleeve of his suit coat.

He bought a one-way ticket West.

"Where to?" the agent had asked.

"Don't care," the man said.

"We only go as far as Tucson," the agent said.

"That'll do," the man said.

Rachel only laughed it off. "It wasn't really a fight," she said. "It was just a simple disagreement."

"What about?"

"I wanted him dead. He didn't want to die."

She laughed again.

Rachel had said on more than one occasion that she remained in Crystal Springs just so the gossips would have something new to talk about over knitting, quilting, baking, and coffee each morning, trading opinions about which men were worth keeping around and which ones had run out of gas.

Men ran out of gas a lot in Crystal Springs, Mississippi.

Mildred Kitchens could always count on seeing Rachel before every party, grand opening, celebration, or social gathering in town. During holidays, Rachel often came in to the salon twice a week, maybe more.

"Keep me beautiful," she would say.

"I'll keep you just the way you are, Miss Rachel," Mildred would tell her.

And Rachel smiled. The way she was happened to be just fine.

Rachel always preferred to be front and center during the most special of occasions, and this one was the biggest of all, a high society collection of fine frocks and neatly pressed suits. It was important for Rachel to look better than the rest of the ladies in the room

She had always trusted Mildred to make her beautiful.

Today would be no different.

Mildred added one final touch of rouge. It looked so natural. The lipstick was flawless. And her hair had never looked better. A touch of gray perhaps, but hints of auburn still shone through.

Those who saw Rachel all said, as usual, "She's such a beautiful lady."

"She grows more beautiful every day."

"Always had such class"

"And she still looks so young."

"I wish I knew her secret."

Mildred Kitchens stood to the side and out of the way. She kept smiling, which is what a woman does when she's in the vanity business. Before her was a woman who had always reflected her finest work. She was still smiling when she gazed on Rachel's face for the last time, just before they quietly closed the lid to the coffin.

Escape when the Leaves Are Gold

SHE FLED DURING the autumn of her thirty-eighth year.

No one saw her go.

No one knew where she had gone.

Phone calls to her apartment had gone unanswered for days, and the director of the downtown Rosenberg Art Gallery dreaded what he might find when he unlocked her door and walked in.

Nothing was out of place.

Her clothes were still hanging in the closet.

The black gown she had worn to the opening of her new show lay in a pile of silk on the floor at the foot of her bed.

The only thing missing, as far as he could tell, was her purse and, of course, Abigail Kern. Edward Rosenberg did the only thing he knew to do.

He called the police.

He was waiting on the sidewalk just south of Central Park when the balding investigator with weeks-old wrinkles in his rain coat ambled back down the stairs.

"What did you find?" Rosenberg asked.

"No much."

"Any sign of a struggle?

"Not that I could tell."

"What do you think happened?

"I think she's gone."

"Foul play?"

"Possibly."

"Should I offer a reward?"

"It's your money."

"Has a reward ever brought someone back?"

"Not alive."

Rosenberg posted a two hundred-thousand-dollar reward.

No one called.

No one ever collected.

Abigail Kern, virtually overnight, had become the hottest new commodity in the New York Art community, which meant her impressionistic paintings of street scenes, especially those blurred by the rains, were selling for a quarter of a million dollars, and her last work, entitled *The Mist Comes Mourning*, had been purchased at auction from an anonymous online bidder that, rumors said, paid north of a million dollars.

If you were among the art world's rich and fashionable, it was important and almost essential to have an Abigail Kern hanging on your wall.

Now she was missing.

Maybe kidnapped.

Maybe dead.

But definitely no longer painting.

Abigail had shown her latest collection on a grand and special night at the gallery, and by the time the art critics had posted their rave reviews in the early editions of the *New York Times* and *New York Post*, she had vanished.

Edward Rosenberg mourned her. He grieved for her. After all, he had discovered Abigail and was responsible for her ascension as an acclaimed artist, the brightest young star in the business.

"Do you have any news about her?" he asked the detective.

"No."

"What are the chances of finding her?"

"Alive?"

"Yes."

"After forty-eight hours, hardly any chance at all," the detective said.

Rosenberg nodded, walked sadly back to the gallery, and quietly doubled the prices on his Abigail Kern paintings. He kissed each canvas and smiled in spite of the tears.

THE WOMAN HAD driven into the struggling little community of Elkmont, Tennessee, shortly after sunrise on an autumn morning. It was only a dozen or so funerals away from being a genuine ghost town, but the tourists came through on their way to the Great Smoky Mountains National Park, and, she decided, the town looked and felt like home.

She bought an old abandoned building on a downtown corner, patched it up, applied a new coat of paint, hauled in a few display cases, and opened a small curio and gift shop.

She paid cash.

Nobody asked any questions.

That's what she liked about Elkmont. Nobody asked any questions. Even when she signed her name, no one asked any questions.

Everyone smiled and gossiped a little too much, they no doubt talked about her behind her back. The eggs were fried in too much lard at the little café on the edge of town, but she was left alone, and she liked it that way.

In the early morning hours, she would hike back among the hemlock and pines on the far side of the mountain, search the ground for flat rocks, stack them in a bucket and bring them back to the Elkmont Curio and Gift shop. She had painted single autumn leaves on a half-dozen of them before the first car stopped outside.

She didn't have a lot to sell.

Only a half dozen rocks.

"They're beautiful," the lady said.

"Thank, you."

"They look wet."

The artist smiled.

"They looked like they have been lying in a soft rain."

The artist kept smiling.

"How much are the rocks?" the lady wanted to know.

"Do you really like them?" the artist asked.

"I've never seen anything more beautiful in my life," the lady said.

"I'll take a dollar apiece for them," the artist said.

The lady walked out the door with all six rocks, and the gift shop was empty again. The artist didn't mind.

She locked her door and drove back into the mountains. Everywhere she looked, the ground was littered with rocks. They were free, and there were enough of them in the Smokies to keep her busy for the rest of her life.

Abigail Kern was sitting beside a small mountain creek in the autumn of her thirty-ninth year when Edward Rosenberg found her.

His small staff began each day, scanning through every newspaper in the country, large or small, looking for stories about art and artists. A travel editor in Knoxville had mentioned a woman painting autumn leaves on flat rocks down in Tennessee, and even published a photograph of one.

Edward Rosenberg immediately thought he recognized the style and technique. He looked again, closer this time. There was no doubt about it.

He was on his way to Knoxville as soon as he could find a flight leaving LaGuardia.

Abigail smiled when she saw him scramble awkwardly down the rocky side of the mountain, past the hemlock and toward the creek bank.

He was definitely out of place.

She knew how he must have felt.

"You've been hiding," Rosenberg said.

"No," she said, "I've been painting."

He picked up the rock she was working on. "Exquisite," he said.

"I'm glad you like it."

"Why did you leave?" Rosenberg asked.

"I'm an artist," she said.

"And a very successful one," Rosenberg said. "Your work is worth a lot of money."

"Once," she said, "people bought my art because they liked my art." She shrugged. "Now, they just buy my name. They don't care about the art. Here, no one knows me. They buy the rocks because they like the painting of the leaves."

"You want to paint rocks," Rosenberg said. "Come back to New York, and I'll let you paint rocks. I'll have them hauled in by the truckloads."

She smiled, took the rock from his hand, and tossed it into the creek."

"You've just thrown away fifty thousand dollars," Rosenberg said.

"No, I didn't."

"What makes you say that?"

"I didn't put my name on it," she said.

Abigail Kern had walked back up the mountain by the time Rosenberg, on his hands and knees, had retrieved the flat rock from the crevice where it lodged among the boulders.

He looked at the painting of the autumn leaves.

He had been right.

It was exquisite.

No artist he knew possessed her talent.

Rosenberg took a deep breath and tossed the rock back into the water.

He would have kept it.

He would have sold it.

But Abigail had been right, he admitted to himself. Without her name, the painting was as worthless as the fallen autumn leaves lying beneath his feet.

The Troubadour: A Writer of Songs

GUY CLARK MADE his living writing songs.

It was a good living.

They were great songs.

But as I think back over his life, I realize that Guy Clark was not really a songwriter.

He was a poet.

His heart added the melodies.

As he once said: *Most of the really good songs are dead true. The song had be there, just waiting for me to write down the word. Every time I've tried to make stuff up it just kind of falls flat. The majority of my work is something that happened to me, I saw happen to someone else, or a friend of mine told me what had happened. There is a certain amount of theatrical and poetic license. People are supposed to like it, that's why you're doing it. It's supposed to be fun. It's not brain surgery. It's heart surgery. They're just songs.*

I spent most of the 1970s listening to the songs of Guy Clark. He was an enigma like so many of the songwriters during the madcap era of Progressive Country. He hung out with Townes Van Zandt, Jerry Jeff Walker, Gary P. Nunn, and Billy Joe Shaver.

They played taverns and beer joints and chili parlor bars and anywhere someone with an extra ten dollars in his pocket would let them play.

Sometimes they got paid.

A lot of nights they didn't.

They woke up many mornings and had no idea who they were, where they were, or why they had showed up at all. They would pool their money and buy a beer, then pass the bottle around.

They were rich one day and broke the next, but none of them ever let money get in the way of their songwriting.

"What was it like back then?" I asked him.

He grinned.

He shrugged.

"It was like yesterday," he said.

Guy Clark finally made it to Nashville.

He never made it big in Nashville as a singer of songs.

But his songs made him a legend. He won Grammy Awards. He was inducted into the Songwriter's Hall of Fame. The *New York Times* even said "he patented a rugged, imagistic brand of narrative-rich songwriting."

His songs were honest.

They were powerful.

They spoke of eternal truths.

I spent the day with Guy Clark during the 1980s, interviewing him for a magazine article. What do I remember about him?

He had a quick smile.

He had a quicker wit.

"Some people play golf," he told me. "I play with words."

Many of us string words together, but no one bunched them together any better than Guy Clark.

We sat in a basement down where his music resided, where he made his own guitars, where he lived on a steady diet of black coffee, peanut butter crackers, and hand-rolled cigarettes, the room where those words all came together, a mecca for every young songwriter who came to Music City with a dream.

Guy Clark had time for them all. He would lean back and listen to their songs. He might help them add a word here, a phrase there. But they always left with a better song than they had when they came knocking at his door, wayfaring strangers who had nothing but a satchel full of songs.

His influence on the music scene was immense. He was, some swore, the godfather of Nashville's songwriters. He was door was always open any time day or night.

Having trouble with your lyrics?

Looking for the right word?

Tired, frustrated, and down on your luck?

Guy Clark's light was always on.

Many came with a single line they had written.

Maybe it was only an idea.

Maybe it was only bits and pieces of a conversation.

They left with a song.

Guy Clark considered himself a rambling troubadour who had the good fortune of surviving forty years of hard living, hard drinking, long nights, and scarred microphones where the big stars never came to sing.

Bob Dylan called Guy Clark his hero.

He didn't have many.

Guy Clark was enough.

It was written of him: "The patron saint of an entire generation of bohemian pickers, Guy Clark has become an emblem of artistic integrity, quiet dignity, and simple truths."

His voice was worn gravel.

His words were as smooth as creek water rolling over stones at the bottom of a waterfall.

From "Desperados Waiting on a Train:"

I'd play 'The Red River Valley,
and he'd sit in the kitchen and cry,
run his fingers through seventy years of living,
and wonder, 'Lord, has every well I've drilled run dry?

From "That Old-Time Feeling:"

That old-time feeling
goes sneaking down the hall
like an old grey cat in winter,
keepin' close to the wall.

From "Dublin Blues:"

I wish I was in Austin
In the Chili Parlor Bar
Drinkin' Mad Dog Margaritas
And not carin' where you are.
But here I sit in Dublin
Just rollin' cigarettes
Holdin' back and chokin' back
The shakes with every breath

His songs were recorded by such stars as Johnny Cash, Ricky Skaggs, Emmylou Harris, Brad Paisley, Alan Jackson, George Strait, Bobby Bare, Willie Nelson, and Kris Kristofferson.

Vince Gill was in a studio to record with Guy Clark, and the troubadour began singing "Randall Knife," a tribute to his father.

My father had a Randall knife
My mother gave it to him
When he went off to WWII
To save us all from ruin
If you've ever held a Randall knife
Then you know my father well

If a better blade was ever made
It was probably forged in hell

Vince recalled, "I started weeping, bawling all over my guitar. I couldn't sniff because there was a live mike. Guy Clark may be the greatest storyteller. He paints the coolest pictures of all."

Guy Clark grew up in Monahans, Texas. His father was a lawyer. And every night, the family would sit around the table and listen to him read from one book of poetry, then another.

The words struck Guy Clark like bullets.

They penetrated his brain.

They seared his soul.

Sitting alone in his Nashville home, Guy Clark would close his eyes and listen to recordings of the works of Dylan Thomas.

"The rest of us spread words around," he said. "But that old boy could write."

A major recording label paid him a ridiculous amount of money to write five songs a year. Sometimes he waited around until the first of December, then wrote day and night.

The recording studio had to wait, but the songs were always worth it.

However, Guy Clark never spent a day of his life worried about the money he made or threw away.

Sometimes he had a lot.

More often he didn't.

And when his pockets were full of money, he gave it all away.

He said, "What's important in life and in music is dignity. I'll bet that when you're dying, you're not going to think about the money you made. You're going to think about your art."

Guy Clark's art was a portrait of life, painted richly and in color one word at a time.

Serenade of the Worm Fiddlers

IT IS THE late summer of 1981, and Billy Wayne Bailey would rather be down on the muddy banks of the Choctawhatchee River dragging out shellcrackers, but his honor is at stake, and Billy Wayne Bailey's not about to run, not when he's king, and he is, and nobody forgets it.

He wants a beer.

It's the heat, he says, not nerves that's parched his throat, cracked his lips, and left his mouth as dry as August corn shucks. Billy Wayne Bailey doesn't have time for nerves. They just get in his way, and nothing gets in Billy Wayne Bailey's way, not for long anyway, not as long as he is the king, which nobody disputes.

A politician hands him a beer.

"It ain't cold," Billy Wayne says.

"It's free."

"It's flat."

The politician quickly grabs another can, squeezes crushed ice against it with a callused fist, and shoves it toward Billy Wayne Bailey before the cold can drip off the side. The politician grins. It's good to be shoulder to shoulder with the king, and he is.

He's part of the inner circle, and folks are watching him, and they're all envious. He's sure of it. He passes out a handful of campaign cards, never straying far from the shadow of the king, and that's about as good an endorsement as he can get on a hot Labor Day that's sweating down the panhandle of Florida.

Billy Wayne Bailey frowns and turns to his brother Elbert. "Who the hell was that?" he asks.

Elbert shrugs. "Some local politician."

"What's he want?"

"Votes."

"I thought he was after worms."

"Just votes."

"He doesn't look smart enough to find them."

"Votes?"

"Worms."

Billy Wayne Bailey sucks the can of beer dry, crushes it with one hand just to show he hasn't forgotten any of his high school education, throws it into the rusting bed of a '67 Ford pickup truck, wipes his hands on the stained front of a white T-shirt, and walks out onto the field of battle.

No.

He struts.

Where's the beer?

The day's young.

He's looking for a tub filled with ice.

That's the way it is with World Champions, the undefeated kind, the legends who stand alone at the top, the king that everybody is gunning for and wants to bring down.

Some were born with talent.

Billy Wayne Bailey was.

Some have a God-given calling.

Billy Wayne Bailey has.

Some are possessed.

Billy Wayne Bailey is.

"He's the greatest," an old-timer tells me.

"Can't make no money betting on him," swears another.

"Why?"

"Nobody bets against him."

"Can't nobody beat him," points out a third.

"What's he do?"

"He fiddles worms."

Down amidst the thick pine stands of Caryville, Florida, crackers get together once a year – on Labor Day – to hold the International Worm Fiddling Contest, a social gathering, a competitive sport, a political rally, a spiritual revival that's as traditional as an all-day dinner on the ground and graveyard working.

For the past four years, the championship has gone to Billy Wayne Bailey. He would have won more, maybe, but up till then he always went fishing on Labor Day, and nobody told him about the glorious affair going on down along the third base side of Caryville's deserted baseball field.

He sometimes thinks it was a conspiracy to keep him in the dark.

He might be right.

Worm fiddling is a classical scientific art that began, old-timers swear, when the moon was "little bitty and there weren't no stars at all."

What you do is take a two-foot-long wooden stake and hammer it about twelve inches into the ground. Then you rub a board or a brick or an axe blade across the end of the stake. You may even want to pour a little sand on top if you're looking for a grittier pitch, and some people are.

Not Billy Wayne Bailey.

His sound is a pure as an alley cat in heat.

The vibration causes rumbles way down in the ground. It sends shock waves deep into the earth. The soil throbs with strange, even sensuous tremors that drive the worms wild, propels them into a seething frenzy, and ejaculates them crawling and squirming up out of the ground to see what the commotion is all about.

In the beginning, worm fiddling wasn't a sport at all. It was survival. Preston Hewitt knows. His great-uncle taught him all there was to know about the hand-me-down, family secrets of worm fiddling.

His great-uncle called it snoring – others call it grunting – considering those odd, unearthly, unholy, high-pitched groans that his axe blade made while sawing across the wooden stake.

The Great Depression had emptied the tables and most bellies. All that stood between the Hewitts and hunger was a good stringer full of shellcrackers. And the shellcrackers loved those good, old, juicy Florida panhandle earthworms. They couldn't resist a mess of worms even if there was a hook in the middle of them, which there usually was.

So, to keep his belly full of shellcrackers, Preston Hewitt learned to coax those elusive little worms out of the pine thicket topsoil.

He became a fiddler.

"You can't dig up worms with a shovel or grub hoe," he says.

Billy Wayne Bailey nods. "What you do is wind up cutting them in half," he points out.

"And the shellcracker won't bite at all unless both ends of that danged old worm is wiggling," Hewitt explains. "We used to drive an old Model A car over worm holes. Then we'd take a piece of hay baling wire, attach one end to the spark plugs, and stick the other end into the ground. Rev up the engine real good, and those old worms would singe the dirt getting to the top. It flat shocked them out."

Billy Wayne and Elbert drain their last cans of lukewarm beer and amble over toward a long row of eight-by-ten-foot rectangles blocked off with white chalk and string. Each contestant has drawn for a patch of earth that's thick with weeds, slim on promises, and, maybe, rich with worms. They've all paid three dollars a team to find out. Most have wasted their money.

Billy Wayne wants another beer. "Scared?" asks his brother-in-law Joe Bracknell.

"Only of people like you," Billy Wayne says. He turns to the crowd and yells, "You gotta watch folks like Joe. Them's the kind that try to get a head start on you. They'll stuff their mouths full of worms before they get to their square. Slap them on the back, and you might cause them to swallow first place."

Elbert laughs. Billy Wayne wouldn't be the king without him. Elbert is the picker upper. He's the one down low to the ground, belly flat and eyes in the weeds, scampering after the earthworms that scamper out of the ground, chasing them down before they get away, or, God forbid, crawl into somebody else's hallowed, blessed rectangle of Florida dirt.

Elbert Bailey is tense. He spits on his hands and rubs them together. He wipes his eyes and stares at the ground. It's tough when you're the champion picker upper of the world. There's no place to go but down. And he's already on his belly.

Joe Bracknell yells, "Now, remember, Elbert. No foot stomping. No praying. No begging. And don't get over the line unless you want to leave a couple of fingers in my bucket.

The starter's gun fires. Wooden stakes are hammered into the dry soil. And a ten-minute serenade of grunts and groans, belches and moans, echo back amongst the pines. The stakes are tortured and splintered, uttering the squeals of the damned, the wail of the dying, the lament of the doomed.

Billy Wayne Bailey grins. "The secret's in the wrist," he says with a hint of arrogance in his voice. "It's all in the stroke. It's like playing the violin."

The notes are sour.

He doesn't mind.

It's music to the worms.

His patch of earth is suddenly alive with worms. It was empty, bare, and then the whole earth began to wiggle and quake. Elbert has a handful of runts and is diving for more.

Around him a mad scuffle erupts in a little chaos and a lot of confusion amidst the dirt and dust and dried grasses. The weeds didn't wilt until the fiddling began in earnest.

Arms are flailing.

Fingers are ripping weeds out of the ground, grabbing anything that wiggles or moves or dances like a sidewinder.

Grown men curse.

Grown women spit.

The boards are begging for mercy.

The worms aren't finding any.

The challengers are old and young, gray and not yet out of the second grade. All are stooped over, on their hands and knees, wives cleaning up the sacred ground for husbands, daughters kneeling beside fathers, cute little ladies in short shorts trying to trade worms for engagement rings, brothers squaring off against brothers.

"Make it grunt," a woman yells to her man. "They won't come up unless you make it grunt."

"I'm trying."

"Bear down."

"I'm doing the best I can."

"You got to bear down to get the deep ones."

He stops and stares at her. "Maybe we'd do better if you just bitched them up," he snaps.

It's a hard ten minutes. The noise fades abruptly, and the ground is suddenly quiet. So is Billy Wayne Bailey.

He's the king.

His bucket isn't full.

He waits.

The politician ambles past. "I sure hope I got more votes today than worms," he mumbles. "I only fiddled up twenty-nine of them." He's not pleased.

Neither is Preston Hewitt. "I'm gonna throw my worms away," he says. "I'd be ashamed to go fishing with no more worms than I got."

"How many?"

"Not enough to hide a good-sized hook."

The Caryville City Council down under the shade trees begins laying out the worms. Theirs is a grubby task of untangling those oily balls and underbellies of the earthworms, then counting them, making sure no one has doubled his catch by breaking any of the crawlers in half. The crowd is hushed.

Billy Wayne Bailey is slumped beside his pickup truck, his gimme cap pulled low over his eyes, which are as slumped as his shoulders.

He wants a beer.

It's the heat, he says again.

Not the nerves.

Two grown women from Albany, Georgia, have a hundred and forty-one worms.

The day is getting hotter.

Billy Wayne reaches for another beer without finishing the one he's drinking. His can of worms looks even smaller. He reaches for his personal pine board, stares at it, and shakes his head. "This board ain't worth a dime," he says. "I sawed all the grunts out of it before we got here." He pitches it into the dust.

Two nine-year-old girls from Caryville surprise everyone by gathering up a hundred and forty-nine worms.

Billy Wayne Bailey wants a beer.

No. He needs a beer.

It's the heat, he says.

Elbert is frantically searching through his pockets to see if he can find any stray worms he wadded up and forgot to throw into the bucket.

It's not the nerves.

"That's a lot of worms for a nine-year-old," the king mumbles.

"That's a lot of worms for anybody."

Billy Wayne crushes the beer can. It's still full and splatters lukewarm suds over the front of his T-shirt. The stain turns to mud. "Board let me down," he says. "It's washed up."

The mayor, his voice as dry as Labor Day, says, "For Billy Wayne and Elbert Bailey, the defending champions, two hundred and seven worms."

Elbert grins and quits digging through his pockets.

Billy Wayne doesn't bother to look up.

His face is free of emotion.

The king does not applaud himself at all.

Kings just don't do that.

He simply reaches down, picks up his personal pine board, and looks at it for a moment. Then he holds it up to Elbert. "You know," he says, "we sold last year's board for thirty-three dollars. Might get twice as much for this one. I think I'll go ahead and sell the board while it's still in its prime."

Elbert doesn't look up. Elbert is too busy selling souvenir worms to answer. It's good to be a blue blood, he says. It's good to be the picker upper of the king.

The Promise of Father Red

FATHER RED STOOD on the steps of his St. Nicholas of Myra Catholic Church and watched the storm fester and boil beyond the marshes and explode above the gulf.

It would be a monster.

That's what the weathermen said.

The storm was on its way.

It was coming for Father Red.

He was not afraid.

Fire Chief Joe Perez drove nervously down a little road that snaked its way across a bridge of land separating the fishing village of Lake Catherine from the ragged edge of New Orleans.

He had seen reports of the storm.

He had heard the warnings.

Get out, they said.

Get out now.

The storm was less than twelve hours away from attacking the coast and taking out its vengeance on New Orleans.

You've seen bad storms before?

You've seen hurricanes?

You've never see a storm like this one.

They called it Katrina.

Joe Perez drove into the churchyard, climbed out of his rescue truck, and walked toward Father Red.

The air was thick and heavy.

It was full of rain not yet fallen.

And wind.

Especially wind.

Father Red stood with his arms folded in defiance.

His eyes were hard and stubborn.

"It's time to leave," the fire chief said.

"I'm not going," the parish priest said.

"This one's a killer."

Father Red allowed himself a small smile.

He shook his head.

"You know I may not be able to come back," Perez said. "This is crazy. You've got to go with me. There's no telling what this storm will do."

"No, *cher*," the priest said softly, "if it's God's will, I'll get washed away. If's it's God's will, I'll go down with the church."

Joe Perez drove slowly away.

He glanced in his rearview mirror.

He saw Father Red standing beside the Church's front door, arms folded in defiance, staring at the storm and doubted he would ever see the priest again."

Father Red had lived through a lot of hurricanes.

He had never evacuated.

He swore he would never evacuate.

He couldn't leave.

Someone might need him.

He would not abandon anyone.

On the late afternoon of August 28, Father Red stood alone.

He was the only one left.

He had grown to manhood as an Irishman in the Ninth Ward of New Orleans.

He was tough.

He was rebellious.

He had done his share of smoking.

And cursing.

Once in his life he had devoured far too much whiskey.

He understood temptation and the foibles of sin.

He was not unlike his parishioners.

They were fishermen and alligator hunters, men of the earth, men of the marshes.

In the past, the Diocese, on several occasions, had tried to move him to another parish.

Father Red refused to go.

"I'll quit before I leave," he told the powers that be.

He didn't quit.

He didn't leave.

His congregation loved him.

His sermons were five minutes long and mostly shorter.

The priest once said, "If I can't say what I want to say in five minutes, it's not worth saying." He shrugged. "People stop listening after four minutes anyway," he said.

Father Red preached his last sermon on the evening of August 27. The church grounds were already soggy from high tide. Water crept into the backyard of the church.

He spoke of love.

He spoke words of comfort.

Then he said *amen* and *goodbye.*

The church, St. Nicholas of Myra, had been named for the patron saint of sailors and travelers.

No one was at sea.

Travelers had gone elsewhere.

The bridge of land was now at the mercy of the storm, and Katrina blasted its way ashore.

The waters took the church.

The waters ripped away the old 1950s model trailer where Father Red lived.

The waters stole his jukebox.

When the storm cleared and the skies cleared and the road cleared, the priest was nowhere to be found.

No trace of him was ever recovered.

But the parishioners understand a simple fact of life.

Father Red was no longer among them.

But he remained to provide them comfort among the marshes and alligators of Lake Catherine.

They feel his presence.

They cling to his words of love and comfort

He said he would never leave them.

No one believes he has.

When the Dead Speak

THERE IS AN unusual feeling of tranquility in the unusual town of Cassadaga, located on the side of the road between Orlando and Daytona Beach. The houses with high-pitched roofs and the buildings – simple and austere – all seem to have come from another time. There is a distinctive feel of New England among the Spanish moss of Florida.

The business signs, attached or swinging, advertise mediums and psychics and spiritual counseling within the thirty-five-acre camp of Cassadaga, where spiritualists call home.

Cassadaga itself has no police department, no doctor, no hospital, no school, no fire department, and not really enough water to put out a fire if there was one.

When there is any trouble, if there is any trouble, the county sheriff drops by, but he's hardly ever needed unless some outsider comes to harass the meek who meditate in the pines and talk to the dead.

George Colby was led to the land of the seven hills in 1875 when bad health ran him out of New York. He journeyed by train and by boat to the blue springs of Florida and found shelter with a few other stranded travelers inside an old palmetto shed.

Seneca appeared without warning in the dull glow of a kerosene lantern and told George Colby that one day Spiritualism would be recognized as a religion. One day Spiritualists would have their own community within the land of the seven hills.

Colby had been a medium since the age of twelve and wasn't particularly surprised to see Seneca. It almost scared the rest of the travelers to death.

Seneca had been dead for a long time.

Nonetheless, they all followed the old Indian in a mule wagon to Jenk's Place and reverently established the Southern Cassadaga Spiritualist Camp Meeting Association.

It was a lonely, out-of-the-way place that allowed them to hide away, find peace, and have their daily conversations with those who has already made their journey beyond the grave and to the summer land, to the other side of life.

THE TROUBLED, the worried, the grieving, the tormented, the frightened, the lonely, the confused, and the haunted can always find their way to Cassadaga's humble doorstep.

Sometimes they come under assumed names just so no one beyond the boundaries of the quiet little town will ever know they've sought the advice of a psychic or perhaps let a perfect stranger carry on a personal conversation with a loved one adrift somewhere out there in the spirit world, if a spirit world does exist, and it must exist, or they wouldn't all be coming to Cassadaga in the first place. That's the belief, and usually the prayer, and sometimes the last hope they have.

Lillian Weigel in the autumn of 1982 moves slowly through the austere lobby of the hotel she manages. At the moment, she is waiting for the doubters, the unbelievers, the skeptics to arrive.

They always do.

But these are not merely those needing a job or wanting to change jobs, in love or searching to find love, hoping to find help with their children, looking for lost children, or wondering if their husbands are cheating, and what's her name, and will she be convicted if she shoots him.

These have rock-solid, high-academic, professorial credentials from the University of Florida. These are the men determined to prove that Lillian Weigel is a fraud.

She smiles.

So many have tried before.

She glances at the clock on the wall.

They should be arriving any minute now.

She is not worried and has no reason to be concerned.

Those with degrees, diplomas, and tenure have no idea what lies beyond the grave.

Lillian Weigel knows.

She's seen it.

She's been there.

And, frankly, sometimes she gets a little anxious to go back.

It has been twenty-one years since Lillian Weigel died. She was in a dentist's chair, strangling, and suddenly she saw a tunnel, then a great light, and it led her to the peaceful crest of a mountain.

Across the meadow nestled a small cabin, and she saw her grandmother and grandfather slowly step off the front porch and walk toward her. She had not seen either of them for a long time, not since the lids had been closed on their caskets and the last prayer spoken over their graves.

"Go back now," said the grandmother.

"I don't want to go back."

"You must."

"Why?"

"It's not your time."

The jolt of some physician pounding on her heart snatched Lillian Weigel back into the world of the living, decidedly against her will.

She hears the slamming of car doors on the tree-lined street outside the hotel and knows that the doubters, the skeptics, the unbelievers are walking toward the porch. She straightens her graying hair and waits for the door to open.

The professor, the researcher, the investigator walk quickly into the lobby.

One nods.

One smiles.

One is carrying a briefcase.

Separately and collectively, they are all business.

For too long, they have listened to wild and probably outlandish rumors about the psychics and mediums and spiritualists of Cassadaga, that curious array of men and women who tell Wall Street brokers which stock to choose, give Saturday afternoon gamblers the right football games to bet, and confirm to real estate developers which land has potential and which parcel will leave them in ruin.

The scholars don't believe anything they have heard. Not for a minute. No one talks to the dead. Well, maybe they do, but the dead never talk back.

Life may only have a few certainties.

That is one of them.

The pleasantries are over in a word or two. The professor, the researcher, the sad-faced investigator have work to do. They appear awkward and uncomfortable. The world of academics has trained them to deal in reality and hard truths.

They believe that all of Cassadaga is fraudulent.

Still, they wonder if the small, gray-haired, grandmotherly lady standing before them can read their minds. Their nerves are jangled and on edge.

They have come pompously to make a fool of Lillian Weigel.

She smiles again.

It scares them to death.

Lillian Weigel is led into a small alcove, and the door is shut behind her. It locks. The noise sends an ominous echo rattling down an empty hallway outside. She is asked to sit in a straight-backed chair that has been moved into the middle of the room.

The professor looks at the researcher. They step back.

The investigator is in charge. He is the man who has been chosen to test the raw, hidden powers of psychometrics held within the deep recesses of Lillian Weigel's mind.

She is blindfolded.

The curtains are drawn tight.

A drape of black velvet is hung over the window.

The lights are turned out.

The day has turned to night.

The room is black on black.

No light, not even faintly, spills into the room, and Lillian Weigel is left in the darkness of her own thoughts.

The investigator takes a piece of jagged metal from his briefcase and gently places it in the lady's hand. It is not quite like anything she has ever felt before.

Silence.

There is the distant ticking of a clock.

Nothing else.

"I hear screams," she says at last. Her voice is soft and distant. "I hear groans. Some soft. Some louder. All in agony. It's like someone dying, like everybody dying."

She pauses.

"And there's smoke everywhere," she continues. "thick layers of smoke. I feel it sharp and pungent in my nose. It burns my throat. My eyes are beginning to water. I'm having trouble taking a breath. The smoke is so thick and so close and so suffocating."

Silence.

The professor, the researcher, the investigator shuffle their feet. It is the only noise in the room. I know they are looking at each other even though I cannot see them. Only they know what Lillian Weigel is holding in the darkness before them.

But only she smells the smoke.

Only she hears the sound of the dying.

Only she has ventured beyond the grave.

"What is it?" I ask the investigator.

"A piece of grapeshot," he says.

"Where did you get it?"

"Petersburg," he says. "On a Civil War battleground. Thousands died in the fighting. It was one of the deadliest battles of the war."

He pauses.

Silence.

"How did she know?" he asks.

Nobody saw her, but I'm sure that Lillian Weigel was smiling as all traces of doubt and skepticism found a crack beneath the door and left the room. The rustle of degrees and credentials weren't nearly as loud as they had been before.

Handy Man with the Blues

HE WAS NOTHING more than an itinerant musician, a young man with a horn, black and down on his luck, provided William Christopher Handy had ever experienced any luck, and mostly he hadn't. Somewhere he knew in his heart, the songs of the South were just "pinin' to be written," and he had no idea that he had been the chosen one to write them.

Nobody knew who he was, and nobody cared.

W. C. Handy sat beside an old stained piano in a Beale Street dive in the late hours one night and thought about a woman in tears, a woman abandoned, a woman ready to die. And he sang softly the words he had heard a grief-stricken woman say in the shadows of a world all alone: "I hate to see de evenin' sun go down, 'cause my baby, he done left this town …"

Handy had gone to the St. Louis Fair with a little band but left disappointed. He had found a little work in a switch yard and was cheated out of two-weeks-worth of pay. He slept on the cobblestones of St. Louis and in a horse stall at the race track. He didn't have but one dime in his pocket with nowhere to go, nowhere to sleep, and nobody to care if he were even still around the next morning. Like dirt, he could be swept out on the street.

As he said, "I understood those folks who hated to see the evenin' sun go down."

Handy wound up on the levee one night where the Mississippi roustabouts were shouting and singing and drinking their cheap hard whiskey. He heard a drunken woman moaning over and over: "That man's got a heart like a rock cast in the sea."

William Christopher Handy reached for his trumpet. The blues were one note away from being born. He based his sound on folk songs he had heard his people sing in the streets, in the railroad yards, in the factories. He said,

"I find music all around us – in the ripple of a brook and the sigh of wind in the tree."

It was 1909, and he was sitting beside a mahogany cigar counter in Pee Wee's Saloon on Beale Street. He gambled on a new melancholy sound, and he wrote the "Memphis Blues." He first titled it "Mister Crump" and used it in a political campaign to help elect E. H. "Boss" Crump mayor of Memphis.

He was great at rallies, this young black boy with a lot of trumpet and even more soul. But when the elections died away in a chilled Tennessee wind, Handy was back on the streets again.

Mister Crump did not need him anymore.

Neither did anyone else.

Alone, hungry, broke, he sold the copyright of "Memphis Blues" to a flimflam music clerk in a downtown department store for fifty dollars.

The clerk made a fortune on royalties.

Handy found himself without money or a song.

He was even forced to pay a ridiculous price to reproduce his "Memphis Blues" in the first edition of his song book on the blues. William Christopher Handy did not merely write the blues and play the blues on his old trumpet. He lived the blues.

He later confided, "There was a time I became discouraged and wanted to give it up, but I was given encouragement by a barber in Atlanta, Georgia. He told me: 'Don't you quit. Keep on trying. Lincoln didn't quit. Jesus Christ didn't quit.' That has been the one thing most of all that changed my whole life."

W. C. Handy went back to the nightlife throb of Beale Street, walking among the "Beale Street Mamas," as the composer called the sexy, light-colored ladies who flirted with their "sweet daddies," the "easy riders" that ambled jauntily through the neon jungle of laughter, loud music, and a street where nobody slept, at least not as long as the music disturbed the night, and the night had insomnia.

In 1914, he gave the world "The St. Louis Blues," and, this time, he held on to the copyright. The lonesome lyrics became one of the top-selling songs of all time.

During a performance in Vicksburg, Mississippi, one night, a little old lady slipped up to Handy and whispered, 'I wish you all would play something religious instead of these blues. Please play something nice and pious."

Handy looked at his band. He slowly shrugged his shoulders. Their repertoire, he knew, didn't included anything "nice and pious."

But the clarinetist said, "Just follow me."

W. C. Handy said later, "He played a slow sad piece that sounded as solemn and religious as a hymn, and we all joined in. It was my old 'St.

Louie Blues' played as slow as cold molasses. That lady congratulated us for such a fine religious piece that we played for her."

The blues.

A funeral.

A funeral hymn.

It all sounded the same.

Handy's blues were gospel, whether they pierced through the tears of a stale-smoke tavern or found their way to a lonely back row pew in a country church. He wrote such sacred songs as "Steal Away to Jesus" and "'Tis the Old Ship of Zion."

William Christopher Handy had a church-going upbringing. He was born the son and grandson of Methodist ministers. His father proudly looked forward to the day when Handy, too, would stand behind the pulpit and deliver up sermons of hope, comfort, and salvation. His son, however, earned every coin he could by picking berries, nuts, and making lye soap, and he came home with a guitar he had bought at a pawn shop.

Why not?

Handy was ten years old and already reading music.

His father was not pleased.

No.

His father was upset. He believed all professional musicians were sinners, and he demanded that his son go back to town and trade his guitar for something useful.

Why not sell the guitar and buy a dictionary?

Somewhere between home and town, the boy found a trumpet.

Lord, it made pretty music.

It made his kind of music.

His father was not pleased.

No.

His father was upset. He angrily told the boy, "You are trotting down to hell on a fast horse in a porcupine saddle."

It was full frontal condemnation, but Handy had his trumpet. And it possessed the soul of all mankind. It spoke of grief and heartbreak, love gone wrong and men gone bad, those down and dirty, down and out, down on their luck and faces pressed against the lace of tear-stained pillows, wallowing in those days without wine or roses when the only fear of getting up was getting knocked down again.

The trumpet kept crying long after the tears had dried and love had died, and the problems of yesterday were only a prelude to the bad times of tomorrow.

Years later, Handy lost his sight when he fell off of a subway platform in New York. Along the way, death took his wife. But the music and the merry-go-round never stopped. Bars, beer joints, honky-tonks, concert halls, back alleys, small towns, and big ones alike, he played them all.

Even as an old man, unable to see for fifteen years, stricken by the aftermath of a stroke, W. C. Handy still clung firmly to his trumpet. He knew he would not outlive the blues.

He said, with all of the pride and optimism he could muster, "Life is like this old trumpet of mine. If you don't put something into it, you don't get nothing out."

William Christopher Handy, the Alabama musician who knew how to squeeze a new sound through the bell of an old trumpet while an impoverished world around him cried the blues, died in New York in 1958.

A Harlem minister had the final world. "Gabriel now has an understudy," he said. "When the last trumpet shall sound, Handy will blow the last blues."

King of the Gate Crashers

PINKY GINSBERG WATCHED the first gentle rays of February pierce the back alleys of New Orleans with chilled fingers. It was that curious time of morning when Bourbon Street was silent, and the warm glow of midnight neon had faded from sidewalks stained with spilled whiskey and concoctions that Pat O'Brien had sold for years as Hurricanes.

The back alleys of sin had lost their glitz, their glamour. They were as plain and homely as a table-top dancer who had wiped the paint and powder from her face. Only Pinky Ginsberg had bothered to come out and face the sunrise, and he stood leaning casually against a crooked street sign, wide awake and grinning as he had done for most of his seventy years. Some even swore that he had been known to grin out loud.

I certainly didn't recognize him, but neither had the masked and drunken, wine-soaked masses of Mardi Gras who had shoved their way past Pinky Ginsberg the night before. There was no reason why any of us should have recognized him. But then, that's what made Pinky Ginsberg so famous.

He is everyman.

His face blends in with all others, young and old.

He is almost never what he seems to be and never seems to be who he really is.

Pinky had traveled around the world. He had rubbed shoulders with royalty and celebrities. He felt at home among high society and the rich, especially the very rich. None of them ever recognized him either. That was important to Pinky Ginsberg.

He was, in his own humble opinion, the greatest gate crasher in the world, and he had two dozen scrapbooks, bulging with photographs, to prove it. It was a passion that had afflicted him for a long time. Go where you want to, he believed, even if you don't belong, and see if anybody kicks you out, and, if they don't, stay as long as the lights are burning, the women are smiling, and the wine is flowing, none of which lasts forever.

He remembers that day years ago when temptation found out how weak little Pinky Ginsberg really was. Inside that big old baseball stadium across the street, the Dodgers were playing in the World Series, and he wasn't in there with them. That could indeed be a tragedy when you were eight years old and lived in Brooklyn. He heard the muffled roar of the crowd, but his own voice was lost amidst the tumult and the shouting. He could smell the popcorn and parched peanuts. He just couldn't taste them.

Little Pinky Ginsberg felt like crying, but he couldn't, or at least he wouldn't, not in front of all those strangers who passed him by. To them, he was just another barefoot street urchin and probably in their way. Nobody knew him nor recognized him. There was no reason why they should.

Early that morning, Pinky had broken his piggy bank and scattered around the shattered colored glass he found twelve cents, not nearly enough to buy a ticket, but certainly enough to get him started in business. He knew how to get by on a shoestring. The streets had made him wise that way. But, usually, Pinky was too broke to afford the shoestring. For once, he had his ante.

Little Pinky Ginsberg trotted down to the magazine stand and bought six newspapers for two cents apiece. Then he set himself up beside the front gate at the stadium, holding a sign that pleaded: "Please buy a paper from me so I can see the baseball game." He sold the papers for a nickel each. The well-to-do even tipped him a quarter. And he bought himself a ticket with a dime to spare.

As Pinky walked up to the gate, he glanced around and saw a little girl crying. She didn't care how many strangers were passing her by. She had dreamed of seeing the World Series game, had always wanted to watch her hometown Dodgers, but knew she would never find a way to get beyond that beckoning, yet foreboding, gate.

Pinky Ginsberg, perhaps, didn't have any money. But he knew she was poor. Real poor. As she smiled at him through her tears, Pinky Ginsberg gave her his ticket.

He would always be cursed with a soft heart.

He would always be a sucker for any girl who smiled at him through her tears.

She clutched the ticket tightly and disappeared into the crowd that had become a mob. Pinky didn't even know her name and would never see her again.

He rummaged through his pockets and found his last dime.

He still had an ante.

Returning to the magazine stand, he purchased five more newspapers. He ran back to the stadium, well aware that time was running out on him. By now, it was the third inning, and nobody was left on the streets.

Pinky rolled the five newspapers into a tight wad, struck a match, set them ablaze and ran toward the stadium yelling, "Fire, fire," as loudly and as desperately and as often as he could spit it out.

The ticket sellers, the security guards, the police all ran frantically past him to investigate the sudden outburst of flames, and he ran madly past them, hurrying into the ballpark just as the Dodgers moved a runner into scoring position.

That was the beginning.

It had been so easy, he thought.

It would have no ending.

We sit in his small, one-room apartment that has no fan to cool him in the summer, no heater to chase away the cold, damp winds of a New Orleans winter. It was a sad little room until Pinky carried his grin inside. He is wearing an old tweed suit that someone has either given him or thrown away. It is the only winter suit he owns.

Pinky doesn't mind.

"I make a rag picker look rich," he tells me.

As he hands me the album, a loose picture falls out and slides to the faded and braided rug beneath our feet. I glance down at it, and, sure enough, there is the image of Pinky Ginsberg grinning back at me, standing alongside a square-faced little man who is wearing a scowl and the specter of a black, clipped mustache. Pinky, in the photograph of a thousand words, is being escorted, rather rudely, out the door by a band of storm troopers with swastikas on their shirts.

Adolph Hitler didn't look too pleased at all.

"He didn't like my last name," Pinky says.

"So he asked you to leave."

"He threw me out in the streets."

"What were you doing there?" I ask.

"I came in from the cold."

"Who let you in?"

"Getting in is always easy," he says. "You just walk through the front door, grin a lot, shake the first hand you see, and, if you see somebody's wine glass is empty, you just find the wine bottle and fill it up. Staying in, however, takes a little luck. Mine didn't last long."

"What happened?"

"Everybody there was mad." He shrugs. "I was the only one grinning. I should have kept my grin to myself."

A change of clothes would have helped.

A Nazi uniform, perhaps.

In the 1920s, Pinky Ginsberg had been standing in the snows of Copenhagen when he saw a group of dignitaries pushing their way down the street. He had no idea who they were or that they were all on their way to a private meeting with the King of Denmark.

It didn't matter.

The day was cold.

Pinky noticed they all had buttoned up their coats. So he buttoned his coat, too. With his head bowed against the chilled wind, he became one of the group, tramping steadily down an ice-clad walkway that led him toward the King, boldly and confidently shoving his way past the hard, suspicious eyes of the royal honor guard.

No one said a word to him.

No one recognized him.

Inside the reception parlor, the men all began removing their coats, and all were wearing black ties and tails, all except Pinky Ginsberg, who still had yesterday's soup stains on a hand-me-down brown suit that nobody else wanted.

The meeting between Adolph and the King of Denmark went on without Pinky Ginsberg, who was shown the back door, and who slid on his back all the way out to the street, his broken fingernails clawing at the ice that broke his fall.

But he had learned a hard lesson.

He would not forget it.

By the time King George VI of England was ready for his coronation ceremonies, Pinky Ginsberg had polished and refined his own personal out-of-the-dark, quick-striking approach to gate-crashing. He went out and rented a tuxedo. Then, at a pawn shop, he picked up four rows of old war-time, military medals to pin on his coat. "I looked like a battleship commander when I walked in alongside those diplomats," Pinky remembers.

Nobody stopped him.

Nobody recognized him, but everyone saw those medals and knew he must be somebody important, somebody whose heroics and exploits had made a major impact on the annals of British history, and they all bowed and scraped and curtsied when Pinky Ginsberg swaggered like royalty itself through the room.

Nobody threw him out.

He was dressed as well as anyone and better than most. Nobody even bothered to ask his name, ashamed that they didn't already know him, certain they had seen his smiling face on the high society pages of London's most famous newspapers, simply proud that he seemed to know them.

Other than King George VI, Pinky Ginsberg didn't recognize anybody in the place.

He developed quite a formula for crashing swank and ritzy parties, the kind whose doors are open only to the rich and famous, and, more than likely, to Pinky Ginsberg.

"First, I find out if it is formal or informal," he says, "and then I dress accordingly. I always show up outside at least twenty minutes early. I wait until a car pulls up and several people get out to go in. Then I walk in right along with them, talking earnestly with whomever seems to be the most talkative.

"I don't stop or ever look back.

"If I did, I'd give myself away.

"Once inside, I never mingle with the good-looking women. They have plenty of attention already. I just look around until I find a lady who is unattractive and neglected, and I spend all my time with her. When the hostess sees me giving the wallflower so much attention, she no longer cares who I am. She just wants me to hang around long enough to make her guest happy, and a little attention makes anybody happy."

Of course, that was the problem with Adolph Hitler's little party.

There was no homely, neglected woman for Pinky Ginsberg to look after.

Adolph had no women at all.

Pinky had gotten himself into all sorts of trouble that night, trying to make small talk with Rudolph Hess, speaking his broken-down, hap-hazard German with a Brooklyn accent.

Pinky Ginsberg had crashed the Super Bowl, Rose Bowl, Cotton Bowl, forty-four World Series games, the oval office of ten presidents, the wedding of Franco's daughter, and the royal palaces or headquarters of Egypt's Nasser, Russia's Khrushchev, Cuba's Castro, and Red China's Chou En Lai.

He doesn't do that much anymore.

"In the old days," Pinky says, "if you got caught, somebody would just smile and shrug apologetically, pat you on the back, and throw you out the back door. Now, I'm afraid, they'll smile, pat me on the back, take me out the back door, and shoot me."

His gall through the years not only let him walk beside the rich, it made him rich as well. It helps to bend elbows with the right people. They let him in on a lot of good deals, some better than others.

All he ever needs is an ante.

Pinky Ginsberg has always been able to find one.

He made money, or so he said.

He managed to lose it all, which is obvious.

As Pinky points out, "I just never had the sense to fear a bad man or a good woman who turned out bad."

His heart was always too soft. He has always been an easy touch, and a bad woman who was good to him could make a sucker of Pinky Ginsberg by the time her lipstick was smeared, and he never even cared. A few good times were worth an awful lot of hard ones.

Everybody likes a good loser, and they loved Pinky Ginsberg.

On a yacht one night, an acquaintance - a big man in the steel industry - grabbed Pinky by the arm and whispered, "I need five grand quick. Can you help me? I'll pay you back tomorrow. I swear it."

Pinky nodded. He reached into his wallet, pulled out the five thousand dollars and handed it over without a word. The big man in the steel industry took the money with trembling fingers. He hugged Pinky and hurried away. "I won't forget you as long as I live," he said.

That wasn't long. During the late, dark hours, someone put a bullet through the big man in the steel industry and pitched his lifeless body into the ocean. So much for Pinky's five grand. Pinky probably could have dug the last few hundred dollars out of the man's pockets, but, frankly, he just wasn't willing to dive that deep.

Being broke was better than being twenty thousand leagues beneath the sea.

On one occasion, gambling backed him into a corner, so Pinky ambled on down to a pawn shop, he says, and hocked his massive diamond ring, which he always did when he needed cash in a hurry, and that's the only time to need cash. The pawn shop was his bank.

But when he returned to get the ring, he found a shop full of policemen. It had been robbed. The massive diamond ring was gone and gone for good.

He has never forgotten his Baby Doll. That's what he called her, and that's what she was: soft and tender and warm and beautiful.

Pinky just couldn't do enough for her.

So early one morning, in the romantic glow of sunrise, he gave her his house.

That night, she kicked him out.

The house wasn't big enough for the two of them, she said.

She broke his heart, but not for long. He shrugs, grins out loud again and confesses, "God will heal any heart if you just give Him all the pieces."

Pinky Ginsberg leans back in his rumpled bed, closes his scrapbook and closes his eyes. "I've crashed every important gate there is," he says, "except the gates of heaven." He pauses. "And I hear old St. Peter is a tough sonuvagun to con."

Pinky Ginsberg has done a lot of unusual deeds to raise money for charity, especially for kids. He has pushed a peanut down the street with his nose, stuck his head into a lion's mouth, had a cigarette shot out of his mouth, been shot out of a cannon eight times, dropped from an airplane five times, jumped off a hundred-foot bridge into cold water, even sat on top of a flagpole for four months and thirteen days, or until enough money had been tossed into a barrel below him to send two thousand poor children to summer camp.

Pinky hopes those few and isolated moments have not been misplaced in the Lamb's Book of Life. But just in case, he is making plans as I leave him. He needs to find out if heaven is formal or informal, and he hates to do it this time, but Pinky knows he'll have to get there at least twenty minutes early.

It works every time.

"I haven't been to church in a long time," he calls out as I step into the dimly-lit hallway. "Maybe St. Peter won't recognize me."

Or maybe heaven has a homely, neglected wallflower who's just standing around with an empty wine glass and waiting for the man who grins out loud to fill it.

One Vote Short on Election Night

THE LITTLE MISSISSIPPI town thought it might amount to something one day.

It had a bank. On the north side, past the creek, was a gin for the cotton coming out of the delta. A railroad track ran so close to downtown a freight train barreling West would rattle the windows in City Hall.

But the Great Depression sapped the little town of its money and its energy. Boll weevils stripped the cotton fields. And the little town began to dwindle away. Only a couple of dozen hardy souls managed to hang on.

Abe Patterson was the only rich one amongst them. He owned a plantation. He had inherited it from his daddy. Abe drove the first car to bounce its way down the dirt road some folks called Main Street.

He laughed loud. He laughed a lot.

He kept is money at home and didn't spend a lot of it. Abe didn't have to. A man who has everything already has everything.

When the cotton was ready to pick, Abe hired everybody who wasn't working, which meant he hired every man in town with the exception of the Mayor, the doctor, the post mistress, the cook frying eggs in the downtown diner, and Old Ferdie, who wasn't quite right but met the train with a mailbag every day.

Abe didn't own the town. But he could have if he wanted to write the check. Then again, he couldn't write the check.

He never put a nickel in the bank.

The town got along fairly well.

But nobody trusted Abe.

"He's a Republican," said the whispers.

"He's against us."

Always has been.

Always will be.

As far back as anyone could remember, the Democrats formed the power base for their little town. It would have been a solid voting bloc, but every time an election rolled around, someone had the audacity to vote the other way.

Every man and woman who carried a paid-up poll tax receipt came down to the polling place on election day, circled a candidate's name, handed their ballot to the election judge, and went on about their business.

The results were always the same.

Democrats 24.

Republicans 1.

As the years slipped on past, the final tally never varied.

"Must be Abe."

That was the rumor.

"He's never been one of us."

"He's a money man."

"Owns it all."

"Always trying to get more."

"Hell, when the bank's in trouble, the bank even has to borrows money from Abe."

"Can't trust him."

"He's high society."

"He's out to get us."

Abe Patterson was the Republican.

Who else could it be?

Every so often, they all shuffled down to vote again.

"Don't know why."

That's what they thought.

"It's a waste of time."

"It'll be just like last year."

"Twenty-four good, honest, hard-working Democrats."

"One stinking Republican."

But still they all gathered outside City Hall on election night and waited for the mayor to write the results on the slate bulletin board.

Here he came. It didn't take long.

Polls closed at seven.

The mayor was walking out front with a piece of chalk in his hand by seven minutes past seven o'clock.

"How'd it go this year?"

"No surprises."

"What'd the Democrats get?"

"Twenty-four votes."

"And the Republicans."

"They got their one vote."

Damn Abe.

He was the one reprobate they could do without.

During a wet and chilled winter – it was the third of December – Abe Patterson came down with the walking pneumonia. That's what the doctor said.

Abe was old.

He was growing feeble.

He went in his sleep.

The grave digger dug a hole. The preacher did his best to get a good-for-nothing Republican past the Pearly Gates. Everybody said *amen* and went home.

No one remembered Abe until election night.

He wouldn't be voting that year.

Death had taken their only demon away.

Nothing left now in town but Democrats.

Abe's vote couldn't mess up the results this time. Somebody cheered, and somebody passed a bottle of bourbon, and the Democrats felt as good as they had felt in a long time.

Promptly at seven minutes past seven, the election judge walked out with his chalk.

He began to write.

Democrats 23.

Republicans 1

No one spoke. They all eyed each other with suspicion and quietly walked home. Now they couldn't trust anybody.

Who among them was a traitor?

It might have been Old Ferdie.

But they didn't let Old Ferdie vote.

That night, they knelt and said a prayer for Abe Patterson.

Some even wept.

A damn good Democrat had gone to the grave

The Trail Where They Cried

THE OLD WOMAN believed and was betrayed, stumbling along the pine needle and red-clay ridge where she would never walk again. The child had merely learned to hurt, but not yet to hate. And they clung together in the rain that washed away their footsteps from the soil that held the bones and the ashes of their fathers.

The old woman would not speak.

The child would not cry.

Both the words and the tears had left miles ago.

They were gone.

But then, so was home.

The drizzle matted a patch of gray hair, then plastered it around the wrinkles of a face that had forgotten how to smile, a soul that passed away without dying. By morning, the rain would be ice, and she would no longer feel the cold earth beneath bare feet that had grown numb. The old woman wondered if it was death beginning to slowly creep up her body, and she prayed that it was and feared that it wasn't.

The child held a baby duck tight to her heart, small hands protecting it from the chilled winds. The duck had no name. It was merely something to love, and the child desperately needed something to love. The baby duck snuggled close against her.

She smiled. It was the first time she had smiled since she asked, "Where is mama?"

And nobody answered.

The child bent forward and felt the sting of sleet against her cheek. She was cold but paid no attention to it. Only the duck was warm. She kissed it and brushed the ice off its golden down with her lips, trudging on through the mud that seeped in through the cracks in her decaying leather shoes.

The child glanced up at the old woman who stared ahead, her eyes searching for the promise, believing she would never find it.

The others looked back.

But there was no promise behind them. There were only the graves of those who had gone as far as they could go, and no farther.

They prayed. And they blasphemed their misfortune. The wind swallowed up their words and spit ice in their faces. Some fell and died where they lay, and some waited to be buried but could not die. Their feet, but not their hearts, were turned toward the West.

Count de Tocqueville watched as the band of immigrants as they struggled and fought for life down on the banks of the river. He wrote in his diary:

It was then the middle of winter, and the cold was unusually severe; the snow had frozen hard upon the ground, and the river was drifting huge masses of ice. (They) had their families with them, and they brought in their train the wounded and the sick, with children newly born, and old men upon the verge of death. They possessed neither tents nor wagons, but only their arms and some provisions. No cry, no sob, was heard among the assembled crowd; all were silent. Their calamities were of ancient date, and they knew them to be irremediable. (They) had all stepped into the boat which was to carry them across, but their dogs remained upon the bank. As soon as those animals perceived that their masters were finally leaving the shore, they set up a dismal howl, plunging all together into the icy waters, and swam after the boat.

Home had been stolen from them.

Ahead lay the promise.

As one army officer reported, "Death is hourly among us. The road is lined with the sick. Fortunately they are people that will walk to the last, or I do not know how we could get on."

They barely did.

The old woman watched with hardened eyes as cholera and influenza crept like thieves into their camps at night, as the rains spread misery in their footpath. Some went blind. Some went mad. They had only cotton shirts and thin trousers to protect them from the winds that mourned their journey. Their tracks stained the new fallen snow with traces of blood. Smallpox cut down on the number of the tracks.

The old woman would write: *Many fell by the wayside, too faint with hunger or too weak to keep up with the rest. A crude bed was quickly prepared. Only a bowl of water was left within reach, thus they were left to suffer and die alone."*

Only the baby duck did not suffer. It was warm in the little girls' arms. It snuggled. She smiled. She never asked, *where is mama* again.

A leader for the immigrants had made one last eloquent plea for a chance to hold on to a homeland that a callused government was tearing away from their fragile grasp, not unlike the wind ripping the last brittle leaf from a hardwood tree in winter. He wrote to the men who made such decisions:

The cup of hope is dashed from our lips, our prospects are dark with horror. Are we to be hunted through the mountains like wild beasts, and our women, our children, our aged, our sick, to be dragged from their homes like culprits and packed on board loathsome boats for transportation to a sickly clime?

Already we are thronged with armed men; forts, camps and military posts of every grade already occupy our whole country. With us, it is a season of alarm and apprehension. Our only fortress is the justice of our cause. With trembling solicitude and anxiety, we most humbly and respectfully ask, will you hear us? Will you shield us from the horrors of these threatened storms? Will you sustain the hopes we have rested in the public faith, the honor, the justice, of your mighty empire?

The men who made such decisions heard. The men who made such decisions were not moved. They wanted land, property, expansion, conquest, the gold fields of Georgia and the Carolinas.

Someone must be hurt.

Someone must suffer.

Some must be cast out as animals to prowl in hungry packs across an unforgiving terrain that could not comfort them.

It definitely would not be the men who made such decisions.

It would be the old woman, her eyes dim, but not from age.

It would be child who owned only the tattered clothes on her back, the cracked leather shoes on her feet, the baby duck in her hand.

They were driven away in herds were the immigrants. Their homes, their furniture, all their belongings and worldly possessions fell as prey to plunderers who followed their bloody tracks like wolves whose hunger could not be satisfied.

A preacher saw the pack stagger past his church, and his words were their only eulogy. "It is the work of war in a time of peace," he said.

The preacher wrote: *It was pitiful to see the poor folks, many old and sick, many little children, many with heavy packs on their backs, and all utterly exhausted. In the confusion, some had left behind their children, who chanced not to be at home; other children had run away from their parents in terror."*

They wept.

They searched.

They stumbled on in a herd, but alone.

They slept on the ground.

A child would be born, and a child would die.

Campfires burned cold and campfires remained unlit.

The promise lay many miles ahead of them. The promise was a new home, a depository for the herd, where they would be cut loose, set free, the survivors and the old woman, the exiles and the child who gave a baby duck the last flicker of love she had.

A stranger saw the immigrants, misplaced and burdened, and he wrote of them: *Even aged females, apparently ready to drop into the grave, were traveling on the sometimes-frozen ground, and sometimes muddy streets, with no covering for their feet except what nature had given them. We learned from the inhabitants on the road where (they) passed, they buried fourteen or fifteen at every stopping place.*

He grieved especially for a young mother. The stranger noted: *She could only carry her dying child in her arms a few miles farther, and then she must stop and consign her much loved babe to the cold ground and that, too, without pomp or ceremony. I turned from the sight and wept like childhood.*

The immigrant silently cursed the military that pushed him onward. He waited and he watched. And he escaped with his family, finding a refuge in the canyons of the high country. Others followed his flight, eating roots and berries to stay alive on the land they would not leave.

The military was disgraced. It had sworn to rid the pine-needle and red-clay ridges of their rightful owners, and the military swore it would not fail.

A general dispatched his chief negotiator into the high country to reason with the leader who had fled. If you, your brother and three sons come out of hiding and surrender, the negotiator told him, the military will leave the other refugees alone.

The leader, his brother and three sons all marched down out of the mountains, their backs unbent and unbowed, their heads held high with defiance. It was the least they could do, sacrifice a few freedoms for many freedoms.

Besides, the soldiers weren't really unscrupulous, the father told his sons. They were just tired men doing their duty, representing righteous and ambitious men who make such decisions. He did not agree with them, perhaps, but he respected their authority.

The general looked at the prisoners, his face a mask of pomposity without circumstance. Then he promptly lined them up by the side of the road – an immigrant, his brother and three sons – and he had them shot down by a firing squad.

The herd could go on without them.

The men who made such decisions had made another one.

The old woman did not look back at the sound of the shots. Perhaps she did not hear them. Perhaps she knew better. The child only hugged her duckling tighter and kept walking, moving ever closer to the promise.

Maybe she would find her mama there.

She hoped, she prayed, and she squeezed the baby duck with all the love and enthusiasm she had left. The child trudged on for another hour until she touched the edge of darkness, before she realized that the duckling was dead, crushed between her tiny arms and finger.

She would live to be an old woman herself.

But she would never smile nor ever love again.

The days bogged them down, then the months. But at last they all crossed the river beyond the trees and stepped upon the Promised Land.

Thus ended the removal of the Five Civilized Tribes from the Southeast to a land that became Oklahoma. President Andy Jackson had decided that Georgia, Alabama, Mississippi, the Carolinas, Tennessee and Florida were much more important to Anglo settlers than to the Choctaw, Chickasaw, Cherokee, Creek, and Seminole Indians who lived there. So he and Congress got together and passed the Indian Removal Bill in 1830, promptly kicking them all out of the land of their ancestors.

For the next dozen years, the Indians made the long trek West. More than a fourth of them died along the way, along a pathway that became known as "the trail where they cried."

As the old woman knelt on promised land, one leader of the immigration turned to a government agent who had walked beside him for all those miles, and he said: *You have been with us many moons. You have heard the cries of our women and children. Our road has been a long one and on it we have left the bones of our men, women and children. When we left our homes, the great general told us that we could get to our country as we wanted. We wanted to go in peace and friendship. Did we? No. We were driven off like wolves. And our people's feet were bleeding. We are men ... we have women and children, and why should we come like wild horses?*

That had merely been a decision by the men who make them.

The immigrants sat down and waited to be fed. But the agent, he would later report, found only *damaged pork, damaged flour and damaged corn. A part of the corn was weevil-eaten. Some of the corn was so injured that our horses would not eat it. The flour was sour. The pork was so bad that (the doctor) told me that if the emigrants continued to use it, it would kill them all off.*

A few ate it anyway.

And they were buried in the land that was the promise.

The old woman turned away. That night, she slipped down to the corral where the military had fed its horses, and, on the ground, she found a few scattered kernels of corn that horses had left behind.

She filled her pockets, and the old woman fed the child.

But she did not speak.

The child no longer cried.

Their words and their tears had been taken from them and scattered by a wind that knew nothing of the promise

Puzzle of the Runestone

IT WAS A message from the past, carved into stone by an unknown hand, leaving behind an unknown message on a land that was known only by the reptiles and varmints who made sure that no one came unless he was lost and never stayed for long, whether he was lost or not.

Perhaps it was merely a road sign where no road passed by, or maybe a marker left above a tomb obscured by cobwebs of age and neglect, spun by spiders that found refuge among the strange assortment of timber that hung onto the steep slopes of Oklahoma's Poteau Mountain.

The lady with the purple bonnet had ventured upon the grand and mysterious stone when she was a girl, so long ago she couldn't remember when, so far up into the high country she couldn't remember where, so unusual that she couldn't figure out what it was or who beside the gods had put it there.

Somebody surely had.

At first, she simply wondered why a stone so tall and so wide had been jammed into the good earth like a road sign. After all, it was a good seven feet higher than she was, even when she stood on tiptoes, and she couldn't reach across the great gray-freckled rock no matter how far she stretched open her arms. Then she noticed the writing. So old she could barely read it. So odd that it frightened her. Then she realized she couldn't read it at all.

"The early settlers came up here when bear hides were a better cash crop than cotton," she told me. "They found the stone, but my grandfather said they weren't puzzled or perturbed by it at all. They figured it was an Indian rock."

Nobody doubted that it was, nobody except the Indians. In the 1830s, a band of wandering Choctaws had found the curious stone, and they weren't able to make sense of the writing either. They left it alone and rode elsewhere.

What they were supposed to know, the spirits would let them know.

The unknown should remain unknown.

The gray-freckled stone remained lost in its own solitude, sheltered by the bramble bush of a rain-hewn ravine, hidden from the sun, weathered and worn, an ancient trace of an ancient breed that left few other traces and no footprints at all.

It was ignored, and then it was forgotten.

That's when the scholars came to stare with a solemn reverence at a rock so old they could barely read the writing, so odd that it taunted and intrigued them. The letters had been carved meticulously and miraculously into the sacred face of the stone, maybe with bone, maybe with metal.

"According to the scholars, the symbols on the rock slab were GNOMEDAL," the lady in the purple bonnet said.

"What did it mean?"

She smiled and sat down among the wildflowers that crept out from the ravine on Poteau Mountain. "One said it was a man's name," she said. "G. Nomedal."

It was a reasonable assumption.

"Another said it meant, 'Give Supplication God Man Before Day Has Set.'"

His reasoning was hidden behind more fog than his message.

Other wise and learned translations, according to the lady in the purple bonnet, had been: "Give Attention to This," or "Sun Dial Valley, " or "Monument Valley," or "Boundary Valley," or "Earth Spirit's Dale."

"They were all certain of one thing," the lady said.

"What's that?"

"They had no idea what the stone was trying to tell them." She shrugged and glanced back at the rock. "Then again," she said, "maybe it wasn't trying to tell them anything at all."

Someone was.

Once upon a time.

The scholars were sure of it. They knew the etching on the gray-freckled rock was old, and it was odd, but they walked back out of the mountain at sundown both confused and confounded by the secret that lay embedded in thick underbrush on the steep slopes of Poteau Mountain.

It just wasn't right.

GNOMEDAL, no matter how old or how odd, just shouldn't be that difficult to decipher. The scholars whined and wailed, wringing their hands and gnashing their teeth, silently cursing the gray-freckled rock that defied them, standing mute and insolent on land known only by reptiles and varmints, and the reptiles and varmints had nothing to say either.

Alf Monge laughed at them all. Alf Monge was a U.S. Army cryptographer and code breaker, and he said that upon the western face of the great rock slab, carved amidst the lichen on Savannah sandstone, were eight Norse runes, strange letters of a strange alphabet that dated back almost seventeen hundred years.

"What's more," said the lady in the purple bonnet, "Alf Monge said he understood the runes. He had been born in Norway, and his hobby was studying Medieval Norse Ecclesiastical Calendars. As far as he was concerned, the symbols weren't particularly baffling at all. They were simply a date – November 11, 1012 A.D."

The inscription, Alf Monge said, was in the form of a crypto-puzzle, the kind developed by Benedictine Monks and used by intellectuals around the year 1000 A.D. to hide their messages from the prying eyes of the masses, who had no business trying to read other people's stones in the first place. There could be no mistake, Alf Monge said.

Others doubted him. Most eyed the gray-freckled stone with skepticism. Alf Monge, they whispered among themselves, was as crazy as everybody else.

What was a runestone anyway, and what in the Good Lord's name was it doing in the high country of Oklahoma?

Besides, why would any runestone be dated 1012 A.D., which was at least four centuries before Columbus and his motley crew ever reached the outer shores of the New World, which was nowhere near Indian Territory or Poteau Mountain.

Yet, a closer examination of Norse history revealed that Thorfinn Karlselfni led four Viking ships to the eastern shores of the United States to set up a colony in 1008 A. D.

He failed.

On the way home, one ship reached Greenland, one was driven off course and drifted to Ireland, and one sank.

No trace was ever uncovered of the last ship.

"A lot of people believe that the vessel left to explore southern waters," said the lady in the purple bonnet. "It supposedly sailed around Florida and into the Gulf, came up the Mississippi River, then the Arkansas River, and finally the Poteau River. If those calculations are correct, and who's to say they aren't, such a route would have put the Vikings within a mile of where the runestone is standing."

On board had been a Benedictine monk.

On Poteau Mountain he could easily have celebrated November 11 and considered the date important enough to be written in code upon the gray-freckled face of Savannah sandstone.

Alf Monge was roundly criticized and ridiculed by the scholars whose loose translations of GNOMEDAL were just as cryptic, maybe more so. But, at least, they did not have the audacity to talk out loud and in public about Vikings roaming the far country of a land-locked piece of America when, as everyone knew, a Viking's heart and soul belonged to the sea.

On a September day in 1967, two boys climbed Terry Hill in search of arrowheads. Hard rains had washed the rocky slopes, and, on a stone ledge, rising out of the red mud, they saw a row of strange runic inscriptions.

The boys dug out the ledge with a hammer, broke it, stuck it back together and hauled the writings back down the mountain.

These, too, were old.

And odd.

The symbols were immediately sent to Alf Monge. He grinned a wry grin and reported: "The inscription was made by the same man who composed the Heavener runestone. It is as unmistakable as a thumb print."

The date of the new stone was November 11, 1017 A.D., a holy day, St. Martin's Day, the first day of the fast for Advent Sunday, surely a day to be remembered, honored and celebrated by a man of the cloth, a Benedictine Monk, for example.

At least, the composer had not forgotten his holy days.

At least, he had hung around the mountains for five years, if the myth could be believed, and it was becoming easier to believe the myth all the time.

The gray-freckled rock on Poteau Mountain is protected behind Plexiglas in the wooden shelter of Heavener Runestone State Park. The carving is clear, even after all these years.

The mystery remains.

Did the Vikings really come to the Oklahoma high country and lose their way?

Why didn't they leave?

What could have kept them there so far from the sea, so far from home?

No one really knows for sure.

The lady in the purple bonnet is quick to say: "Many skeptics go up the mountain, but none come down."

"So you believe the Vikings were here?" I said.

"I believe in the runestone."

"Why did they stay?"

"They followed the river." She smiled sadly. "During the rainy season, the river can be as wide as a lake," she said, then shrugged, her eyes gazing back to a far time when all the world was a puzzle. "But when the skies dried up, the river dried up, and, perhaps, their ship ran aground, they were trapped. There was no way out of here. It was as if the sea itself had abandoned and then forsaken them."

"What happened to the ship?"

"It was probably dismantled and the materials used for housing."

"What happened to the houses?"

"The land is filled with the ruins, the ashes, the dust, the splinters of homes that, like man's own footprints, have vanished with the years." She laughed lightly. "You have to remember that the Vikings came, if they came, a long time ago. Not much ever lasts for a thousand years."

"Only memories," I said.

"Especially if they are written on the stone," she said.

"It's not much of a diary," I told her. "A single date. A holy day, if Alf was right. No message. No words of wisdom. No explanation. No signature."

"I don't see a message when I look at the stone," the lady in the purple bonnet said as she stood to make her way back down the mountain again. "I simply read the sadness etched into the letters. For someone, lonely, adrift and without hope of ever seeing home again, it may have been the beginning of the end."

On November 11.

1017.

A.D.

GNOBEL.

It took a thousand years before the stone could be read, even longer before the meaning will be believed, if, perhaps, it's ever believed, six hand-carved letters separating truth from myth, and one is just as puzzling, as uncertain, as the other.

The carving is either old, very old, or the last ancient testament of a monk who sailed with the Vikings into the valley beneath Poteau Mountain and could never find his way out again.

The passing years have preserved the mystery but never solved it.

The passing years have no reason to explain it.

The passing years have only one responsibility.

They just keep on passing.

A Soldier's Last Anthem

THE RAINS CAME just about the time daylight slipped back beyond the fog, hanging thick in the trees, and a bullet took the life of the soldier lying beside him.

Young boy.

Hadn't even begun to shave.

He had spent the night before crying in a ditch beneath a rampart on a Vicksburg hillside. Maybe he had known the end was near. Then again, maybe he was just afraid.

Everybody was afraid.

Seth looked at his pale, waxen face for a moment, then turned away and watched the fog crawl up the ravine, a fog as wet as the rain falling on his face.

A life had passed by.

That's all.

A life had passed by and was gone.

Seth didn't even know the boy's name.

The silence of the night was broken only by the occasional sharp crack of gunfire. A Yankee sharpshooter chasing shadows no doubt. He was hiding in the gray mist, probably high in a tree on the far side of the hill, shooting at any sign of movement, no matter how slight, hoping to get lucky, and sometimes putting a boy into such a deep sleep he would never awaken again.

Seth looked back at the boy beside him.

His gray coat was splattered with blood.

His throat was gone.

His eyes were open.

Seth only hoped that the boy was dead before he knew he was dying. It was better that way. He probably never heard the shot. If he did, he probably suspected it was meant for someone else.

Everyone feared he would be dead by morning.

No one believed it.

Seth inched his way farther down the hillside. The darkness had wrapped itself around him, and even the fog had turned black. The earth, the trees, the sky, it was all the same.

It was as dark as the innards of a grave.

His grave.

Seth lay back and placed his head against a log.

There were thousands on the hills around him, dressed in blue, dressed in gray, and yet he felt as if he was alone, abandoned, betrayed.

In the distance, he heard the strains of a tune he knew well.

An old tune.

Sad and always mournful.

Played on a harmonica.

He mouthed the words but made no sound.

Only the harp was playing *Dixie.*

It was an old show tune, or so he had been told. But somebody down South had picked it up, somebody in *the land of cotton where old times there are not forgotten*, and *Dixie* became the song he was destined to live for and die for, and he had no idea why he was fighting and why he had been ordered to kill a bunch of boys no older than he and why he was lying on a godforsaken patch of earth, torn by shells, stained with blood, and hammered by the rains, or why his country had left him or why he had left his country, and he never could figure out which was which.

A gunshot.

Silence.

Then the harmonica began playing again.

Seth prayed that the night would not end.

Morning brought daylight.

Morning brought the dying.

Morning brought the mourning.

It always did.

The fog was so moist he could taste it. The ground beneath him was turning to mud.

A gunshot.

And even the harmonica quit playing.

All was silent again.

Seth closed his eyes and tried to remember better times, but they were far beyond the reach of his memory.

He had found them once.

They would not be coming back.

Seth sat, his head bowed against the rain.

He missed his home.

He missed his mama.

He even missed the cows that needed to be milked and the old mule that pulled his plow and the hoe he used to chop those endless fields of cotton.

He missed the blisters on his hands and the ache in his back.

Times had been hard but not as hard as dying on a piece of ground that belonged to somebody else, being thrown into a grave his mama would never find, lying there beneath a headstone with only a number and never a name.

The harmonic began playing once more, a lonely dirge shaped by a dying breath.

Dixie.

It was pretty enough, he guessed, but the song wasn't his, not really. He had never heard *Dixie* played anywhere but at a barn dance until the shots were fired at Shiloh, and a band struck up *Dixie* to encourage a ragged bunch of boys to fight back.

Seth listened to the tune.

It meant nothing.

He missed his country.

Where had it gone?

He had seen the bombs bursting in air.

He had witnessed the rockets' red glare.

But it wasn't the same.

There was no land of the free, not anymore.

There was no home of the brave.

He mouthed the words once, then sang them, softly and tenderly.

Most of all, he missed his anthem.

His anthem was his country.

He prayed silently that someone would play his anthem and not *Dixie* when they came to throw dirt upon his grave.

The Unexplained

WE LIVE IN a strange world that is filled with mysteries. No one ever gets around to explaining them.

Maybe we don't want them explained.

Ghosts stalk the countryside.

Every graveyard looks darker when the sun goes down.

Strange spirits wander the hallways of old houses.

Who died?

Who came back?

Are they coming for me?

Can't be coming for me.

I'm gone.

Our eyes search the skies.

It's out there.

What?

Don't know.

But it's watching us.

You can always tell.

The hair stands up and crawls across the back of your neck.

A Dead Man Walks

THE MAN WAS discombobulated. That's what the deputy figured. Odd night. Strange circumstances. And his partner needed help. His partner was a straight arrow, took his job seriously, didn't drink much and never while on duty.

Still his voice didn't sound quite right.

Odd, the deputy thought.

Strange, he decided.

Discombobulated.

The deputy sighed and glanced at his watch. Midnight, maybe a few seconds on the morning side. That figured.

That was all he needed. A radio full of static and a discombobulated cry for help in the dark.

The highway stretched out straight before him, white lines and asphalt patches that tore out madly toward Brit Bailey's prairie, and old man Brit was on the loose again. At least that's what it sounded like when his partner made that frantic call. The night was even darker than before.

The deputy had heard a lot about Brit Bailey but had never come face to face with the cranky, Tabasco-tempered old prowler before, and he liked it that way. The deputy decided he wasn't frightened, just troubled.

After all, what do you say to a man who walks the prairie, tramping around above the grave that has held his mortal remains for the past hundred and fifty years.

James Britton Bailey had loved to fight. On street corners. In back alleys. In saloons. Anywhere he might tear into either friends or strangers. It didn't matter to Brit Bailey.

He was crazy, some whispered.

Then they found out how much money he had and simply referred to him as eccentric, going out of their way to be polite when he walked down the village streets of Brazoria, Texas.

Brit Bailey bought a lot of whiskey and drank even more, and a lot of people danced away Saturday night to the music of his gunfire and the rat-a-tat of his bullets ricocheting off the hardwood floor at their feet.

Most feared him.

But to death, he was just another wayward soul whose time finally ran out. On the morning of December 6, 1832, a fever struck him down, and Brit Bailey had taken his last drink and fought his last fight.

When the eccentric's will was read, it was discovered that he had requested to have his body buried erect and facing toward the West.

Some of the gossips in town only believed he wanted to be interred standing up so he could get a running start on judgment day.

Old Brit had not planned to go to the grave alone or empty-handed. According to his last will and testament, depending on which rumor happened to be making the latest rounds, he had demanded that his favorite hunting dog, gun powder horn, matched pistols, a pouch with a hundred and fifty bullet, lantern, and a jug of whiskey all be jammed inside the coffin with him.

That was too much for his poor widow.

She grew angry, then pious, and finally religious.

She had no idea where he was heading in the hereafter, but she was adamant that Brit Bailey make the journey sober.

She threw the jug of whiskey out the window.

They buried James Britton Bailey in a hole eight-feet deep and about as big around as an old-fashioned wash tub. And they left him standing up.

They prayed, or at least bowed their heads, and shrugged, and some snickered, and they went back to their fields and did their best to forget about Brit Bailey.

He did not forget about them.

Two years later, another family purchased the old Bailey place and moved in. Ann Raney Thomas was sitting by herself the night she looked up and watched as a figure, draped in the ragged edges of a shadow, quietly walked into the room. It was a man, she said, and he had witnessed the wonders or the horrors of whatever was beyond the great beyond. Ann Raney Thomas could see it in the hollow of his eyes.

And he was searching for something he would never find again.

What do you want, she asked.

My whiskey, he said.

And still he searches, wandering an empty stretch of Bailey's Prairie, down between Angleton and West Columbia, trailing after the long beam of his lantern that glows big and bright and orange in the night.

Hundreds have seen the light.

And most were Bible-believing, God-fearing, Sunday-morning church folks too afraid to lie about what they had observed or even admit they had experienced the mysterious *haint* of Brit Bailey.

A colonel saw the light through the drizzle of an autumn night's rain, and he said it looked like fire in the sky.

To one woman, the light hung there like the full moon when it first comes up at dusk.

Another swore she watched it climb across a barbed wire fence before crossing the winding dirt road.

Back in the 1930s, Robert and Joe Munson watched as the light moved through the trees. "It was so still," Robert recalled, "that all I could hear was Joe's heart beating."

A car rounded the bend, and the driver, in fright, suddenly spun the old automobile around and raced away into the dead of night.

"He was doin' ninety miles an hour," Joe told his sister.

"A car won't go that fast," she answered.

"Maybe the driver got out and pushed," he said.

Maybe.

The deputy remembered and grinned. All he knew was that he had been standing beside the dispatcher when his partner's nervous voice came over the radio, reporting: "There's a big red light coming over the prairie toward me. I want somebody else out here, and I want them out here in a hurry."

Ahead of him, the deputy spotted the patrol car in a ditch. He looked quickly around, and there was no light, red or otherwise, and no sign of his partner at all. He parked and ran to the patrol car, poking his head through an open window. He coughed.

The air was thick and pungent with the smell of gunpowder, and a revolver lay on the seat. In the floorboard, his partner sprawled motionless as though dead. His partner opened one eye, then the other.

"What's the matter?" the deputy asked.

"This red light kept coming at me, and nobody came to help me. When it came through my window, I shot it three times."

"Did you kill it?"

"I tried."

"What happened?"

His partner gazed for a moment out across Bailey's Prairie, swallowed up by the darkness, then slowly shook his head. "

His eyes were discombobulated.

His voice was discombobulated.

It was already dead," he said.

Cries in the Wind

IT BEGAN with a storm.

Nothing fierce.

Nothing out of the ordinary.

It was little more than a gale blowing across the sea during the chilled evening of March in 1871. A ship's captain battled the winds, fighting the swells of the Atlantic, headed toward the distant shore hugging the coastline of Maine.

It wasn't far now.

He could see the splinter of beam from the lighthouse flashing at him.

Only a half a mile to go.

Only a half a mile from safety.

The ship suddenly trembled, and the captain heard the deadly, cracking of lumber breaking hard and in agony against the rock ledge.

The captain's muscles tightened.

The ship was taking on water.

It was quiet for a moment.

Then came the screams.

Only a half a mile to go.

He would never make it.

Even the screams died away.

The cold, bitter sea water churned around his knees and kept rising. The winds battered his ship. The rains lashed at his face.

One last scream.

Then the ominous sound of night when there is no sound at all.

Early the next morning, as faint shards of light swept the shoreline, the keeper of Hendrick's Head Lighthouse and his wife began picking through the debris that had washed upon the rocks.

A dying ship was a rest.

A captain, his crew, and his passengers had been drawn to the unforgiving ebony floor of the Atlantic.

No hope.

No prayers.

No survivors.

He stopped.

The keeper heard a faint and gentle cry in the wind. He and his wife found a feather mattress bound with a rope. It held a tiny cargo, a wooden box, and wedged inside was a baby girl. She was alone but had not been abandoned.

Some heart-broken mother had done her best to save the baby, to cast her to the sea and pray that the ocean would not claim her.

There had been a prayer.

And a survivor.

The family of the lighthouse kept her as its own.

They looked for any trace of the mother until all traces had been washed away and buried by the sea.

But on some nights when the sky is dark, and a gale stalks the rim of the Atlantic, the silence is broken by a faint cry caught in the throat of a distant wind.

"It's the mother," I am told. "She walks among the rocks, and sometimes you can see her shadow outlined against the ocean. After all of these years, she is still searching for her baby."

"Has anyone ever seen her face?"

"We only hear her grief."

"She keeps coming back?"

"No." There is a slight shrug. "She never left."

It began with a storm.

So long ago.

It has yet to end.

It Came from Outer Space

DR. ALFRED KRAUS walked patiently and calmly toward the summit of a small shale and limestone rise just beyond Brawley Oates' chicken coop, where the man from outer space had crashed and died on Texas soil.

At least, that's what he had heard for so many years, and his scientific curiosity had finally led him to that hard-scrabble patch of stubborn land on the edge of Aurora and to a hilltop once shadowed by the rusty, complaining blades of Judge W. S. Proctor's windmill, wiped out - so the report said - by the explosion of an unknown spacecraft on that fitful spring day in 1897.

Dr. Kraus paused amidst a blanket of Yellow Stone wildflowers and carefully swept his metal detector across the caliche face of the knoll that rose up from the Wise County prairie like an ancient burial mound.

If there had been a crash, Dr. Kraus reasoned, scraps of hot, twisted metal would have surely been scattered upon the sun-blistered countryside. And if the metal lay hidden amongst the rocks and Yellow Stone wildflowers, he was bound and determined to find it.

Dr. Kraus, possessed by the same affliction that taunts the curiosity of most university professors, simply wanted to know the truth about the fire and thunder that lit up the skies above Aurora.

He would prove that a creature from outer space had indeed crashed into Judge Proctor's farmstead, or he would separate fact from fiction, truth from contradiction, and leave the myth to wither and fade away like those Yellow Stone wildflowers that huddled between the shale and limestone scars of a barren earth.

The metal detector hummed with the enthusiasm of a bored bumblebee. The chickens raised cane down behind the wires of Brawley Oates's little coop, scratching and cackling and bragging about the eggs they had just laid. In the distance, just on the far side of the last turn in the road, Aurora, or what was left of it, lay dying.

Or maybe it was already gone.

Aurora had been built back in the 1870s on a promise. Someday the railroad would be headed the town's way, so fifteen businesses and a few more than four hundred good, honest, hard-working farmers and merchants settled down around the trading post. The Dallas Pacific & Southwest Railroad even had charted and graded a right-of-way through the little community.

But alas, twenty people suddenly died from a strange disease that would later be diagnosed as spotted fever, and the railroad, just as suddenly, abandoned its plans to link Aurora with the rest of Texas.

So long, Aurora.

It's been good to know you.

The town refused to die quietly. The hamlet squared its shoulders and grew despite being shunned.

By April of 1897, Aurora was well occupied with two lawyers, five doctors, one undertaker, one brass band for Sunday afternoon concerts, two cotton gins, one hotel, and a newspaper. It was a quiet little town. Not much of importance ever happened at all.

Then the rumors began to spread about those "mysterious airships" that had been seen in the evening skies above Forney, Tioga, Mansfield, and Waxahachie. Some said, with quivering lips, that the silver ships, shaped like cigars, were at least two hundred feet long.

They're out there.

That was the general consensus.

Are they coming for us?

When will they arrive?

Is it Judgment Day?

Is it too late to pray?

Surely angels don't ride around in space ships shaped like silver cigars.

Some couldn't forget the powerful headlights that beamed down from the snub noses of the ships. Others reported that two gasoline engines turned the propellers that kept each craft aloft. A few even swore that the vessels were piloted by creatures who were dressed in blue sailor suits, and one claimed that three beings climbed down from an airship, sang "Nearer My God to Thee," and passed out temperance tracts.

In early April of 1897, John Barclay was awakened on his Rockland, Texas, farm by frantically barking dogs and a high-pitched whine in the sky.

He ran outside and saw a flying object hovering twenty feet off the ground, he said, with "protrusions and blinding lights." The craft landed, a man climbed out, requested common hardware to repair the craft, paid Barclay with a ten-dollar bill, and took off "like a bullet out of a gun."

The craft landed again near Josserand, Texas, and two short, dark men asked Frank Nichols for permission to draw water from his well. Four days later, an attorney in Aquila, Texas, reported seeing an oblong object overhead as he rode home in a horse-driven carriage. A large, bright light was sweeping the ground around him.

Strange rumors kept on spreading like strange rumors always do. Repeated once, passed on twice, and printed in a God-fearing newspaper heralded any piece of gossip as gospel.

Aurora, however, was undaunted. The town's three thousand good, honest, hard-working farmers and merchants did not pay much if any attention at all to such wild tales, regarding them only as the frenzied results of alcoholic tongues or maybe a good dose of religious hysteria.

They went to bed on the night of April 16, and at three minutes past dawn the next morning, a silver cigar appeared above the southern horizon. It didn't stay there long, remaining only until it hovered at last low over the earth beside those rusty, complaining blades of Judge Proctor's windmill.

Dr. Kraus opened the yellowed clipping and again read the account that the honorable S. E. Hayden, an Aurora cotton buyer, had written seventy years earlier for a Dallas newspaper:

About 6 o'clock this morning, the early risers of Aurora were astonished at the sudden appearance of the air ship which has been sailing throughout the country.

It sailed directly over the public square and when it reached the north part of the town collided with the tower of Judge Proctor's windmill and went to pieces with a terrific explosion, scattering debris over several acres of ground, wrecking the windmill and water tank, and destroying the judge's flower garden.

The pilot of the ship is supposed to have been the only one on board, and while his remains are badly disfigured, enough of the original has been picked up to show that he was not an inhabitant of this world.

T. J. Weems, the U.S. Signal Service Officer at this place and an authority on astronomy, gave it as his opinion that he (the pilot) was a native of Mars.

Papers found on this person - evidently the records of his travels - are written in some unknown hieroglyphics and cannot be deciphered. The ship was too badly wrecked to form conclusions as to the construction or motive power. It was built of an unknown metal resembling a mixture of aluminum and silver, and it must have weighed several tons. The town, today, is full of people who are viewing the wreckage and gathering specimens of strange metal from the debris. The pilot's funeral will take place tomorrow.

For the next several years, there was gossip that the metal had been suddenly and unceremoniously confiscated by the military and never returned.

Maybe.

Probably.

It did sound reasonable anyway.

Those who viewed the wreckage and collected those specimens of strange metal from the debris, were left with empty hands. Maybe they should have asked the military to sign a document or something.

Then again, those wearing starched uniforms and possessing starched faces did not look as though they would have been willing to sign anything. They just took the scattered pieces from the wreckage and left.

No hello.

No goodbye.

No good riddance.

Nothing at all.

Dr. Kraus gazed out across the shale and limestone rise as the earth began to bite off the edge of the sun. He had heard the words of the unbelievers.

Judge Proctor, they said, never even owned a windmill.

T. J. Weems, the so-called authority on astronomy, was nothing more than a blacksmith.

Yet the rumor obstinately hung around that the remains of the creature from outer space had been given a final Christian burial in the community cemetery. At the foot of an unknown grave Dr. Kraus had found a hand-hewn stone marker with no name. Instead, it had been carved with the outline of a flying object that looked a lot like a cigar.

All day Dr. Kraus had scoured the knoll with his metal detector, searching for remnants of the mysterious airship.

Some believed in the man from outer space.

Some didn't.

Dr. Alfred Kraus could only base his scientific judgment on the merit of those antique metal relics that he himself had uncovered among the rocks and Yellow Stone wildflowers that blanketed the small shale and limestone rise.

He walked away from Aurora with old stove lids, horse bridle rings, and a 1932 license plate.

The Hopi Prophecy

HE CAME TO the ancient land of his people because of the saucers in the sky. Dan Katchongva had always known this day would come.

He didn't know where.

He didn't know when.

Now he knew.

Dan Katchongva was a Hopi chieftain, and he had heard the stories handed down, sometimes in whispers, for centuries, and he had never doubted them.

Home was not the earth.

Life was temporary.

He would someday live among the stars.

He didn't know where.

He didn't know when.

Now he knew.

He told the newspaper in Prescott, Arizona: "Our people believe other planets are inhabited and that our prayers are heard there. We, the faithful Hopi, have seen the ships and know they are true."

The Hopi has long had a connection with sky.

The Hopi has long been touched by the people who live among the stars.

They watch the skies.

And they wait.

"It is coming," the chief said.

"What is coming?"

"The Day of Purification."

He is stoic.

His face is solemn.

"The prophecies tell us," he says, "that nature will speak with a mighty breath of wind. It will be the final decisive battle between good and evil. The oceans will join hands and meet the sky. It is the day when all wicked people and wrong-doers will be punished or destroyed."

He pauses.

He gazes into a calm blue sky.

The sky is calling him, he says.

It's been calling for a long time.

"The Hopi believes," he continued, "that those who survive Purification Day will travel to other planets."

The saucers will come for them.

He will be ready.

He waits no longer.

The saucers have come again.

The True White Brothers, he said, are coming to take the faithful away.

Have they come for him?

Some listen to Chief Dan Katchongva.

Others scorn him.

Mostly, his words fall on deaf ears.

He walks out of Prescott early one morning.

He heads across sacred lands.

He moves toward sacred mountains.

It is the tall country where the saucers are seen.

His head is held high.

His steps are strong.

The chief does not hesitate.

He walks all day and into the night.

He is one with the darkness.

And Prescott waits for him to return.

Prescott is still waiting.

No one ever saw Dan Katchongva again.

He left no footprints upon the earth.

Abduction in Pascagoula

THEY WERE JUST a couple of good old boys, never meaning no harm, but harm went out of its way to find them.

It was a cool night.

October cool.

They were sitting on the dock of the bay and fishing off the west bank of the Pascagoula River.

Catfish is what they were catching. Catfish were always biting.

It was a calm night.

October calm.

Darkness had crept across the river. Stars seemed a long way away.

And that's when they saw it – a cigar-shaped craft hovering about two feet off the Mississippi mud, surrounded by flashing blue lights.

They heard the noise first. It was a whizzing sound.

The sound startled them.

The blue lights unnerved them.

When the creatures walked out of the craft and dragged them aboard, the good old boys were downright scared to death.

Charles Hickson felt paralyzed.

He was forty-two.

Calvin Parker felt numb.

He was nineteen.

And they were lying inside the craft, looking up into faces that were pale and wrinkled, had slits for mouths and absolutely no discernible eyes at all.

That's what the two men told officials at Keesler Air Force Base in Biloxi. "It was one of them UFOs," they said.

"We have no affiliation with UFOs," the officer said.

"We read about this Project Blue Book you got," the men said.

"Doesn't exist," the officer said.

He rolled his eyes.

Crazy as hell, he thought.

Charles and Calvin drove to the office of Sheriff Fred Diamond and spilled their guts. "These creatures had one leg," the men said. "They had something that looked like lobster claws at the ends of their arms."

The sheriff smiled and walked out of the room.

He had his doubts.

Crazy as hell, he thought.

But the sheriff was nobody's fool. He had switched on a secret microphone in the room, and he would let the men talk among themselves. If they were lying or pulling some kind of prank, he would find out about it. The men would condemn themselves with their own words.

According to the secret tape, here is what the men said.

You can't make this stuff up.

"I tell you," Charlie said, "when we're through, I'll get you something to settle you down so you can get some damn sleep."

"I can't sleep yet like it is," Calvin said. "I'm damn near crazy."

"Well, Calvin, when they brought you out – when they brought me out of that thing – goddam it, I like to never in hell got you straightened out."

"My damn arms, my arms. I remember they just froze up, and I couldn't move," Calvin said. "Just like I stepped on a damn rattlesnake."

"They didn't do me that way," Charles said.

He sighed.

"I passed out," Calvin said. "I expect I never passed out in my whole life." Calvin's voice was frantic now. "I don't want to keep sitting here. I want to see the doctor."

"They better wake up and start believing," Charles said. "They better start believing now."

"You see how that damn door came right up?" Calvin asked.

"I don't know how it opened, son. I don't know."

"It just laid up and – just like that – those sons of bitches – just like that – come out."

"I know," said Charles, "You can't believe it. You can't make people believe it."

"I was paralyzed right then. I couldn't move."

"They won't believe it. They gonna believe it one of these days. Might be too late. I knew all along they was people from other worlds up there. I knew all along. I never thought it would happen to me."

Calvin shook his head. "It's hard to believe," he said. "Oh, God, it's awful. I know there's a God up there."

The sheriff had expected the boys to start lying about their so-called abduction by a bunch of lobster-clawed aliens from some place way up on the top side of Pascagoula.

Maybe a snicker.

Maybe a laugh or two.

But the good old boys, never meaning no harm, were as frightened when they walked out as they had been when they walked into his office.

They were ridiculed.

They were humiliated.

They heard the laughter behind their backs.

They couldn't run.

They had no place to go.

They stayed and suffered.

Calvin, years later, was admitted to the hospital after an emotional breakdown.

Charles stuck by his story until the day he died.

The boys knew what they saw. They knew what had been done to them.

Calvin had been especially traumatized. He said he had been fondled by the one of the creatures, and he thought she was feminine, but he wasn't for sure, and, Lord God Almighty, he wished he knew for certain.

She came back nineteen years later, he said.

Same craft.

Same girl.

Same pale skin.

Same wrinkles.

She spoke English this time.

And she told him that they shared the same God, that the Bible was an authentic text, and that her species wanted to live on earth, but they couldn't. The earth had too many wars going on.

That's what he said she said, and his story never wavered or changed.

I talked to the sheriff years later. He sort of believed the boys, and he sort of didn't. "There's probably life up there," he said. "But it's not intelligent life."

"What makes you say that?" I asked.

"They could have gone to anyplace in the world they wanted to go," he said.

I nodded.

"They came to Pascagoula, Mississippi." The sheriff shrugged. "You figure it out," he said.

Mystery in the Marfa Skies

THE TRUCK DRIVER saw no reason to be frightened. He didn't believe what he had seen with his own eyes anyway. He poured down a cup of coffee and ordered another, then bought a pack of cigarettes even though he had never smoked before.

"Make the coffee a little stronger this time," he told the waitress. "I want to taste the grounds."

"You must have seen the lights," voiced the Red Ball trucker from the far corner of the little all-night diner.

"Yeah."

"Where?"

"I was headed up Highway Sixty-Seven, coming out of Presidio."

The Red Ball trucker nodded. "Maybe, it was a plane."

"It was flying too damn low," snapped the driver, who saw no reason to be scared. He sipped on the coffee and chewed on the grounds.

"Maybe it wasn't flying at all."

The truck driver knew he didn't believe his own eyes, and now he wasn't believing what he was hearing either. He frowned, stuck a cigarette with trembling fingers into his mouth, and struck a match. A gust of hot wind ripped through the front door. The match went out.

"Back in World War number two," said the Red Ball trucker, "the army had an air base out just east of Marfa. A bomber took off on a training mission one day and never returned."

He paused to drain his coffee cup.

The truck driver reached for another match.

"Some people think those lights out there in the Chinati Mountains are the lights of that bomber still trying to find its way back home," the Red Ball trucker concluded, his words as emotionless as the clock behind the counter.

The clock had struck ten-fourteen years ago and stopped.

Time doesn't mean a lot in Marfa, Texas.

The bomber may still be missing. But the lights, I'm told, were disturbing the holy peace of Marfa long before the army flew into those sun-blistered plains in the first place. They dance in the midnight shadows of the mountains, sometimes white, sometimes blue, sometimes orange. They confuse. They taunt. They are restless, wandering from the Chinatis to the Cienegas to the Dead Horse Mountains.

"They look like headlights in the sky," some say.

"Old-time cowboys thought they were a rustler's campfire."

"They flare with the intensity of fire."

"They're dull."

"They look like an electric light behind frosted glass."

"They're just weird," said Haillie Stillwell, a former justice of the peace in Alpine. "The first time I saw them, they scared me to death. They light up and run across the mountains kind of like a grass fire in a hard wind."

No one has ever explained the unearthly Marfa lights.

Rumor tries.

Rumor doesn't have a clue.

Those dashing, daring young pilots who trained at the air base during World War number two did their best to chase the lights down.

Fritz Kahl had recalled, "I could see them from my plane, a low glow, yellow and red, from the air. They moved around, but they didn't move a great distance. They don't chase you, and they're nothing to be scared of. Maybe the lights are a low-grade form of St. Elmo's fire or static electricity. I only know that when you approach one of the lights, it disappears. It's a lot like trying to catch a rainbow."

Fritz Kahl never caught them.

Some pilots would fly over the lights and drop sacks of flour. Later, when daylight covered the land, they found only busted sacks of flour, no trace of the lights at all.

Around Marfa, you still hear the hushed tales of tragedy that many believe, although none can really prove. It all happened so many years ago. Records were classified and simply filed away or thrown away. "Two soldiers went out in a Jeep to try and track the lights down," I am told, "and they vanished right off the face of the earth. All that was ever found of them was a single wrinkled sock."'

According to rumors, passed along like gossip and gospel, two other soldiers grabbed a Jeep and headed out into the Chinati Mountains one night. Their spotter told them by radio, "You're sitting right on top of the lights."

"We don't see a thing."

There was a crackle of static, and the radio went dead.

The soldiers were found in a smoldering Jeep, burned and scorched beyond recognition.

Another old timer swore, "Two government scientists stumbled up on the lights. Later, when the government finally found them, they were sitting out beside their Jeep, and their Jeep was burned to a crisp."

"What did they say about the lights?"

"Nothing." He paused. "Those scientists never said nothing again," he said. "At least they didn't say nothing that made sense to anybody."

"What happened?"

"They were stark raving mad and were cooped up in a sanitarium the last time I heard anything about them."

"What did the government report on them?"

"The government don't admit they ever even existed. They just shut up about it and they stayed shut up. I guess there are some things that it's best to keep shut up about."

Maybe.

During World War number two, many soldiers believed that the strange, eerie lights were being used to direct German supply planes into a bleak, barren, and isolated country. They were convinced that the Nazi war machine had a large, well-hidden camp just beyond the mountains, that the Germans were planning an invasion of U.S. soil and were marching up from Mexico.

It was to be expected.

After all, during World War number two, it was believed, just as strongly, that the Marfa lights were signals being used to guide German cavalry and pack mules into the Great Chihuahua Desert. An attack was bound to be just around the corner.

Marfa is still waiting.

As early as 1914, however, gossip spread that the lights belonged to Pancho Villa, the Mexican bandit and revolutionary war leader, who had decided to unleash his own brand of vengeance on the United States.

The lights were flickering.

The assault never came.

None of them did.

Through the years, many with scientific and academic credentials strapped on their names, have stepped forward with official explanations.

"It's swamp gas."

The desert has no swamps.

"It's the moon's reflection on a vein of mica."

No large lode of mica has ever been found in the mountains.

"You can only see the lights after a rain."

"You can see them best when the country's bone dry."

"They're little volcanoes."

"They're gases escaping from the ground."

"They're electric jackrabbits."

Huh?

"That's right. When jackrabbits run through luminescent bushes or plants, their fur picks up phosphorous like lint. When you see them running, they're glowing in the dark."

Many just shrug and say that the Marfa lights reflect nothing more than man's imagination, that they're only car lights seen from great distances, creeping along U.S. 67 or U.S. 90 in the dark.

Perhaps.

Robert Ellison always bristled when he heard such a theory. Robert Ellison had been an old cowboy who was first startled by the restless lights in 1883. As an old man, he would always spit with disgust and say, "Automobiles in this country were pretty damn scarce in 1883." He rode the land when there were no roads at all.

In fact, during the 1800s, cowboys depended on the lights as a landmark as they drove their herds of cattle to the railroad in Alpine. As soon as they saw the odd glow dancing across the flats, they knew they were only twenty some odd miles from the stockyards. The lights didn't bother them.

The Indians believed that the lights were homes for fallen stars, for those who had died and not yet chosen their final resting place. Mexican settlers looked upon the curious illumination as the lost, wandering spirit of Alsate, the Apache chieftain they had lured out of the Chisos Mountain, then betrayed. Mexican soldiers had killed many of Alsate's people and had taken the rest as slaves. Now he would haunt them until the day he died, and for all the years thereafter. No one could stop the spirit that stalked the plains.

"The lights are the ghosts of the men who died when the silver mines in Shafter caved in on them," an old rancher said.

"It is the spirit of the soldier who fell asleep doing guard duty," believes another who calls the Big Bend country his home. "The Indians attacked and killed him and his squad. And now his spirit can't rest because he failed to do his duty."

In a cafe, I hear: "It's the lantern of an old prospector who trekked this desert for twenty-five years, then finally struck a vein of pure gold. He was in such a hurry to get to town and have the ore assayed that he forgot to mark his trail, and he never found the gold again. He went mad. He roams the foothills with his lantern, searching for the gold he had in his hands before he lost it all."

On a street corner, I am told, "The Spanish had the Indians dig their gold, then made them carry it out of the mountains. When they could go no farther, the Spanish soldiers killed the Indians and buried them with the treasure. Their ghosts rise out of the ground to dance above the gold that cursed them. If you can find the exact spot of the lights, all you have to do is dig, and you'll find the gold yourself."

For one old cowboy, life was definitely worth more than the gold. Mrs. W. T. Giddens tells of the winter night her father was trapped in a blizzard as he struggled toward home – on foot and blinded by the churning snowstorm. He fought the biting winds, but they drove him to his knees, and he fell, slowly freezing to death, his face numbed, his eyes turned pale.

He saw nothing.

Only the darkness.

Then he saw the lights.

He immediately thought he must be dead, but he heard the lights *speak,* though there was no voice at all. He was told that he was stranded three miles south of Chinati Peak, but off the trail and headed in the wrong direction.

The lights beckoned, and the old cowboy followed them to a small cave, a shelter from the wind and a certain icy death. *We're spirits from long ago,* the lights whispered to him, *and we're here to save you.*

The old cowboy slept. By morning, the lights were gone, and so was the blizzard. He looked around for a landmark and found himself three miles south of Chinati Peak, just as the lights had told him. He staggered home, dazed and confused, but he forever felt a warm and close kinship with the Marfa lights.

George Watson had heard the rumors. They were as common as the grains of dirt beneath his boots and just about as plentiful. He was a respected astronomer who studied the stars and planets for The University of Texas tracking station in the isolated heart of the desert country.

About ten years earlier, George Watson had his first encounter with the lights, and, before the night had ended, he knew them far better than he ever wanted to. Watson was driving home from work in the quiet hour before daylight when he saw a bright glow racing across the prairie.

He thought it was the headlights on a car driving up fast behind him.

It made no effort to pass.

The astronomer glanced out the window and saw disks, pale orange in color, spinning like runaway tops just above the landscape.

They startled him.

Then frightened him.

They would haunt him, and he could never forget them no matter how hard he tried, and he had tried for years.

He believed in man's unshaken ability to explain anything and everything around him. George Watson had no explanations, only nightmares, even when he was awake.

The lights, on another dark morning, would track him down again. He was crossing the Santa Fe Railroad track when he got a glimpse of the light in his rearview mirror.

Watson thought a train was coming.

But there was no noise, only a light, and it grew ever larger, ever closer, and then it quietly disappeared as though the night had unexpectedly swallowed it up.

He recalled, "I left part of my skin out there."

A few years later, George Watson was easing down the dirt road that led from the tracking station, alone in the darkness of morning. He had just reached the hills when, he said, "All of a sudden, a giant light, the size of a building, slowly began to rise out of the ground. It made no sound but lit up the countryside as though it were in the middle of the afternoon."

Watson said he would have left more of his skin back there but said he didn't have any more to leave.

"What do you think it was?" I asked George.

"A UFO," he replied.

"Do you believe in those?"

"No."

"Then why do you think it was a UFO?"

"I saw it." He shook his head. The light that flickered in his eyes was one of fright. "And I don't want to see it again."

In an empty diner outside of Marfa, a truck driver understands. His coffee is cold, and the grounds are dry. He has no reason to be scared, he figures. He's old. He's tired.

His eyes have lied to him before.

He drains his coffee cup, spits out a few grounds that aren't caught between his teeth, and crushes the cigarette against the stained black jukebox that ran out of songs about the same time he ran out of quarters.

He would like to smoke – he needs a smoke – but, for the life of him, he can't get the damn thing lit.

The Literary Side of Life

I GREW UP in that part of East Texas that considered itself in the South. I could go to sleep on our farm outside of Pitner's Junction, wake up in Pine Mountain, Georgia, and never know I had left home.

Maybe I hadn't.

I write because I can't keep a secret.

Tell me story, and I have a burning desire to tell somebody else.

I feel like William Faulkner captured it best when he said, "There is nobody reading in the South. Everybody is writing."

And so we are.

As a Siberian elder once said, "If you don't see the trees, you may be lost in the forest. But if you don't know the stories, you may be lost in life."

So that's our lot in life.

We tell stories.

We don't want anybody to be lost.

So I pay homage to those writers, those storytellers, who have influenced the way I string my words together and give you an idea about a life that's lived among a cast of living, breathing characters who don't exist.

Just because they don't exist doesn't mean they're not real.

The Conscience of America

HIS WAS A curious and a simple life. He would have it no other way. He was a common man who found a curious sense of belonging among common men in common places under common circumstances.

Hidden away among them, he discovered the uncommon rhythm of a life that possessed shape and form but little definition and hardly any meaning at all. He heard only the odd cadence of a nation's voices, often as loud as thunder, sometimes as soft as a whisper, and they spoke to him, and he spoke for them, and very seldom did their diffident collection of words ever rhyme or need to.

His was a crooked road with twists and turns and crossroads, and he seldom knew which road to take, so he tried to take them all. He was a vagabond in the wayward midst of an aimless journey.

It could have turned out far different than it did.

Carl Sandburg was a quiet and gentle little man who wandered adrift in a strange world even when he wasn't lost, and he was never lost. He simply wanted to know what lay beyond the next bend in the road, around the next corner, over the next hill, and who might be waiting for him when the day ended and the bright city lights gave way to the soft glow of moonlight. The narrow highway stretched out before him, and it was, as it had always been, a dead end. Like a fly in the ragged web of a spider, he seldom knew what to do next.

It was not the easiest of times. He had been born on a corn shuck mattress, the son of a Swedish blacksmith who could not write his name, not in English anyway. The birth certificate referred to the child as Carl August, and his family was determined for the boy to be far removed from the culture of the Old Country.

He would speak the language of a bold new land. None would ever speak it with more eloquence. But mostly, during those early years, Carl just listened, and the soul of those who fought and survived a hard life became his own soul, his own conscience. He wondered what God had chosen him to do with his life, and he found few options. None of them dealt with a pen and paper.

It could have turned out far different.

The boy, at the mercy of a financial depression that swept the country in the late 1800s, quit school in the eighth grade. He never had a home for very long. His father was always on the move.

A better job, a better day, a better life always lay somewhere ahead of him.

He chased but never caught it.

Carl was abandoned with a scattered assortment of newspapers, magazines, and books to read. He crawled between their covers and closed the pages around him. He had no other place to go.

Carl Sandburg dressed in old clothes even when he became famous, and fame was one of the few words that escaped his vocabulary. Given his choice, he preferred a simple meal of homemade soups and dark bread. He had never been a stranger to poverty, and the bad times hardened him just as they had strengthened his father.

As a boy, he dug his garden and raised vegetables. He delivered newspapers, scrubbed brick from demolished homes, and cleaned brass cuspidors in a barbershop. He distributed handbills for twenty-five cents a day and worked as a milk slinger on a milk wagon route for twelve dollars a month and dinner. Carl washed bottles in a pop bottling plant, worked as a water boy for mules and men as they graded the hills where trolley cars would run, rented rowboats, stacked heavy blocks of ice in an ice house, and sponged down sweating horses at the Williams racetrack.

Carl could have been discouraged.

He wasn't.

Young, disconnected, and growing older, he was trapped in the midst of a great struggle. It was pulling him somewhere. He had no idea where the struggle would take him. Carl asked for little. He expected little. He found much on a road that allowed him to watch the "fog come in on little cat feet," witness "a sunset sea-flung, bannered with fire and gold," and stumble across "a pier running into a lake straight as a rifle barrel." He could not escape the scenes forged in the back reaches of his mind, and they would not leave him alone. He had no idea what to do with them.

It could have turned out far different.

Carl would always know "hours as empty as a beggar's tin cup on a rainy day, empty as a soldier's sleeve with an arm lost," and he had seen "where the music goes when the fiddle is in the box."

These became the sights he could not forget, the subtle sounds he heard, the pain he felt, the loneliness that gripped him on a road with no end. He was haunted by the memories of a face, a love, a thought he had somehow left behind.

None of them, at the moment, were lines of poetry. But they were lines of life. He scribbled a little now and then but generally had no use for writing pads. The unforgiving battle for survival was much more important to him.

Maybe somewhere along the way from one small, out-of-the-way town to another, he would find a job, a trade, a livelihood that could put a dollar or two in a pocket that was mostly as empty as the streets he walked.

A young man's ambition never stretched farther than his next meal, which often seemed thousands of miles away.

Carl traveled with panhandlers, tramps, thieves, and hoboes that took one road, then another, found one day and lost another, worked for a dime, worked for a meal, and possessed a proud dignity because they endured when the odds had given them up for dead.

Carl said he left home with his hands free, "no bag or bundle, wearing a black sateen shirt, coat, vest, and pants, a slouch hat, good shoes and socks, no underwear, in my pockets a small bar of soap, a razor, a comb, a pocket mirror, two handkerchiefs, a piece of string, needles and thread, a Waterbury watch, a knife, a pipe and a sack of tobacco, three dollars and twenty-five cents in cash."

He considered himself a well-dressed hobo until the rains, dust storms, and railroad yards left his clothes as wrinkled and forlorn as his life.

His father scowled as he watched the boy walk away.

His mother cried.

The road traveled in only one direction. It never brought anyone back. It would go forever or end at the edge of the earth. As he wrote: "I don't know where I'm going, but I'm on my way."

The education of Carl August Sandburg had begun. His teachers would become the great unwashed, the common man in common places, mostly with uncommon ideas. He rode the rails, slept in train yards or fifteen-cent flophouses, watched the cities come and go, saw the countryside change from mountains to wheat fields, then fall away in the long shadows of thick forests.

The rails and the rivers led him on, always on, and he did not know where they would take him, or if they would take him anywhere at all.

Carl chopped wood, picked pears and apples, had a fight or two, was thrown off a few trains, saw the inside of a jail cell from time to time, and shared coffee, stale bread, and burnt frankfurters with those huddled masses who warmed the campfires of a hobo jungle. He listened to their voices, their stories, their hopes, their anger, and the hurt that dwelled deep inside their souls.

Long before he realized it, their trials and their tribulations had become part of his own.

Twice he fell asleep while riding the bumpers of a train.

Twice he almost died.

Many lay in unmarked graves along the side of the road, their names lost, their faces forgotten, their ambitions turning to ashes and dust.

Carl could have been one of them.

It could have turned out far different.

He wrote: "I was meeting fellow travelers and fellow Americans. What they were doing to my heart and mind, my personality, I couldn't say then nor later and be certain. I was getting a deeper self-respect than I had had back home in Galesburg (Illinois) . . .

"What had the trip done to me, I couldn't say. It had changed me … Away deep in my heart now I had hope as never before. Struggles lay ahead, I was sure, but whatever they were I would not be afraid of them."

Carl still had no idea what to do with himself. Words and lines of free verse were forming in his brain. He had no idea what to do with those either. Why write them down? Who would ever read them?

He tried one trade, then another, and none really appealed to him. Carl drove a milk truck, sandpapered houses for a painter, and borrowed every book he could find to read. While the burning, splintered remnants of the battleship Maine lay scattered upon the ocean, he enlisted in the army simply because President McKinley had declared war.

Carl wound up in Cuba by the time the fighting had ended. His was not a bloody tour, he said, but a dirty, lousy affair all the same. Long marches. Hard roads. Fifty-pound backpacks. Never-ending rains. Mosquitoes with blood on their faces, his blood. And graybacks in his uniform.

Carl stood tall during the most miserable of times and impressed his commanding officer so greatly that, with only an eighth-grade education, he was nominated as a candidate for West Point.

That's where his life changed for good.

Carl was still smitten with his "endless unrest." He had spent years looking for a trade, a vocation, even a profession, and he remained on a hard, shadowed road that kept leading him from one dead end to another.

Somewhere in the back of his mind, he began to concoct the idea that maybe he had the ability to put a pen and ink to paper and write. His free verse read like prose, his prose like poetry, full of strength and emotion.

The common man did not read poetry.

The common man would read Carl Sandburg.

His most poetic images and phrasing would not seem alien to either a store clerk or a steelworker.

But he wrote alone, preferred the quiet of the night, and remained a vagabond in search of himself. Carl bought bananas for a dime a dozen and a loaf of stale bread for a nickel. He lived and ate simply.

He traveled the backroads on a rented bicycle, pedaling from farm to farm and selling stereoscopes throughout Wisconsin.

Winding roads.

Never ending.

As restless as always.

But the job did give him the freedom to wander alone and think, to sit beneath the trees in the shank of the day and read, to linger at roadsides and write all kinds of formal verse. The poems were not so good he always said, "but I had the lingering, and that was good."

The lingering would never leave him. His curious journeys had shaped him. The common man molded him.

He read so many words along the way, and finally he began to put his own words on paper. He wrote them his way, free and unstructured, powerful and filled with imagery that came from the mind and emotion of a man who saw America at its best, at its worst, and forgot nothing.

It was his own style.

It fit no other.

It could have turned out far different.

At the end of that unpredictable and circuitous road, Carl Sandburg found pen and paper and finally an old typewriter. He worked on newspapers and magazines, sat down and wrote the Rutabaga Stories for children, and, during the quiet solitude of a long night, began writing the free verse of his poetry.

He had possessed the soul of a poet all along. Although a few holier than thou historians said that a poet's pen should never meddle with history, Carl wrote the six-volume biography of Abraham Lincoln, which may well be the finest biography of them all. His were the stories of a man, a President, and an age.

Carl told his publisher that he thought the Lincoln book might be "a sort of history and Old Testament of the United States, a joke almanac, prayer collection, and compendium of essential facts." The final four volumes, *The War Years*, contained more than 1.75 million words, more than the Bible or the complete works of William Shakespeare. His Lincoln biography, which took almost two decades to research and write, earned Carl Sandburg his first of two Pulitzer Prizes.

Carl Sandburg wrote with his old typewriter mounted atop an orange crate.

"Why not a desk?" he was asked.

Carl shrugged.

"Surely you can afford a desk."

'Carl Sandburg smiled. "If General Grant could command his troops from an old crate," he said, "I can certainly write about it from one."

So he did. Carl Sandburg championed the cause of "the Poor, millions of the Poor, patient and toiling; more patient than crags, tides, and stars; innumerable, patient in the darkness of the night." He celebrated the universal toil, blood, and dreams among lovers, workers, loafers, fighters, players, and gamblers."

And as he said at the end of his days, "If God had let me live five years longer, I should have been a writer."

It could have turned out far different.

If, after his sojourn in the Spanish American War, Carl Sandburg's nomination to West Point had been accepted, he might well have settled down to a military career as an officer and a gentleman. His landscape would have been fogged by the gunpowder of two World War battlefields instead of defined by his poems.

Instead, Carl Sandburg became a poet.

He had no other choice.

West Point glanced over his application and rejected him.

On his entrance exam, Carl Sandburg failed grammer.

Wisdom from the Streets

HE WAS ONE of us. Yet he was so different. Then again, we're all different. We all have our own personal hopes, dreams, flaws, failures, and demons that possess us when walk behind the dark, frayed veil of our own insecurities.

We write books. Denver Moore could not write his own name.

We read books. Denver Moore could not read his own name.

We have homes that are fairly warm or cool, depending on the season. Denver Moore lived on the streets and hid in the sewers.

He was homeless.

He was a drifter.

Not many of us have ever written a bestseller.

Denver Moore has.

His was an odd journey that began on a dusty dead-end road at the front gate of a Louisiana Planation where his aunt and uncle worked as sharecroppers. He worked right alongside of them. They raised him. They fed him. He spent his long days in the field with a hoe in his hand. It was, Denver said, nothing more than stoop labor.

He never asked about school. He didn't know anything about school. School was where the white folks went in the 1950s, and Denver Moore wasn't white, so his shadow never fell on either side of a schoolhouse door. It wasn't something he missed.

Why read? He thought. There was nothing to read.

Why write? He thought. He didn't know anyone who could read it.

During those growing up days, Denver Moore hopped a few freight trains, rode a few rails, slept in a few hobo jungles, walked aimlessly on streets because he had nothing better to do, thought that Vienna sausages from a can was about as good as any meal could get, and made the terrible mistake of taking a gun into a liquor store one night, looking for a little loose change or maybe a wad of dollar bills.

The law took offense.

And, he said, a judge awarded him a ten-year contract for hard labor at the Louisiana State School for Fools, better known as Angola Prison.

It was the first time in a long time that Denver Moore hadn't been homeless.

The road with the dead end finally wound its way to Fort Worth, and for the next twenty-two years, he became one of the sore sights that festered on the streets after the sun went down.

He slept in doorways and back alleys. More than once, during harsh nights of winter, the bellman at the Worthington Hotel found him curled up on a grate outside the hotel and gently kicked the aging black man to make sure the cold and ice and hard winds had not frozen him to death.

On the other side of Fort Worth, Ron Hall was a wealthy and successful art dealer. He and his wife Deborah lived in a multi-million-dollar home, mingled with the highest of high society, and were invited to all of the proper balls, especially when some charity sold you a ticket and asked for you to bring your checkbook along.

The Halls did their duty.

They gave their money.

But Deborah's passion was serving meals to the hungry, hopeless, homeless, and jobless at the Union Gospel Mission.

She and Ron piled up food on a lot of plates and listened to Brother Bill, too blind to even read his own Bible, deliver his usual sermon, always asking, "Are you prepared for the land beyond? You may tie your shoestrings this morning, but the undertaker may untie them before day's end."

Men were quick to say *amen* but slow to give what was left of their hearts to God.

Deborah's heart ached for them.

So many had sullen faces and empty eyes.

So many had given up on life.

She refused to give up on them.

One morning, she told her husband, "I had a dream last night. God told me there was this homeless man who was wise, and by his wisdom our cities and lives would be forever changed."

"Who is he?"

"I don't know." She paused and shrugged. "But we have to find him."

It was lunchtime at the Union Gospel Mission when a wild melee broke out before anyone knew anybody was mad. The hall was filled with screams, and blood spilled on the floor.

Men cursed out of fear and anger.

And everyone who was able to fight did.

Suddenly Deborah was on her feet yelling, "That's him. That's the man I had the dream about."

Only one man was standing. His pants were ragged. He was wearing neither a shirt nor shoes. His fists were clenched, and he was yelling, "I'm gonna kill whoever it was that stole my shoes."

His name was Denver Moore.

Hall recognized the face. The big man had occasionally slept outside his art gallery. Hall had even called the police to haul him away.

For days, then weeks, Hall tried to make friends with the man who wanted to kill somebody. Moore would never even make eye contact with him."

Hall was ready to quit.

"You can't give up on him," Deborah said.

Hall asked Denver Moore one afternoon if he would like to have a cup of coffee. "I'd like to be your friend," Hall said.

Moore stared back with sullen eyes. He was suspicious. He didn't trust anybody, especially not some high-dollar do-gooder who might be out trying to help the poor just so he could feel better about himself. "I ain't interested in being your friend if it's a catch and release program," he said.

Hall smiled. He liked the term. Moore might be poor. But there might indeed be a lot of wisdom bubbling down inside the last soft spot of a heart grown hard.

The two men became inseparable. Theirs was a bond of friendship and respect.

Hall forgot that Moore was poor, and Denver overlooked the fact that Hall was rich.

After awhile, Hall began to understand that he and Denver weren't all that different after all. He had been born poor, too, and grew up in the bed of his granddad's pickup truck.

But he had gone to school.

Denver Moore hadn't.

He had a chance.

Denver Moore didn't.

Ron Hall had a second-grade teacher who taught him to write and draw square houses. She triggered a fascination for art, and art would be his way out of poverty. With an education, his road had no dead ends.

Other than that, he and Denver Moore could have well been brothers with different colors of skin.

The book was Denver's idea. He broke out laughing one night and told Hall, "Ain't nobody gonna believe our story. We gotta do a book."

Hall thought it over.

He didn't laugh.

He liked the idea.

They worked on the manuscript together for three years and produced *Same Kind of Different as Me.*

Ron Hall could write.

Denver Moore could talk.

And both had a lot to say.

The book traced the journeys of two men who became the unlikeliest of friends, and it quickly hit the bestseller list. Hall and Moore toured the country, visiting more than two hundred missions and speaking at more than four hundred events, most of them fund raisers. Royalties from book sales were used to support the Fort Worth mission.

Laura Bush in 2008 invited them to a White House luncheon with the President.

Denver Moore stood, looked at everyone sitting around the table, and said quietly, "I want to thank you for inviting me to ya'll's house. You got a real nice house. I bet you all is proud of it. I'd like to thank you by name, but I can't remember none of your names. All white folks like alike to me."

He grinned and sat down. As he climbed into the limousine to leave that afternoon, he turned to Hall and said, "Mr. Ron, I done gone from living in the bushes to eating with the Bushes." He shook his head. "God bless America," he said. "This is a great country."

Denver Moore was one of us. He has a book with his name on it. And we 've lost him. He went at last to the land beyond. He tied his shoes one morning, and an undertaker untied them before day's end.

He won't be homeless anymore.

Ron Hall could only fight back a tear and say of Denver Moore, "He changed a lot of lives. People who read our book are never able to look at homeless people the same way again. He was a rock star."

Denver Moore, I'm glad you came our way.

May you rest in peace.

From the Belly of the Beast

THE UGLY VAGARIES of life dealt Jack Henry's hand from the bottom of the deck. He was born to an Irish-American soldier and a Chinese prostitute, and neither wanted him. For the first nine years of his life, he was thrown from one foster family to the next, and none of them wanted him either.

He was disciplined.

He was punished.

He was ignored.

He was abandoned.

He was never loved.

But deep within the dark corner of a frayed and fragmented soul, there existed a wealth of extraordinary passion and enormous talent.

Jack Henry was unschooled. He was unlearned. His mentors had been the boys of the streets, the men who used him, abused him, and threw him away like yesterday's trash.

His home at the age of nine became a jail cell.

Cold.

And somber.

Jack Henry found himself being shoved in one juvenile detention center, then jerked out and herded into another.

They didn't want him either.

They kept him.

He was rebellious and violent.

They had no other choice.

He stared at those who accused him, tried him, and convicted him with black, piercing eyes.

Cold.

And somber.

And deep within the dark corner of a frayed and fragmented soul, there existed a wealth of extraordinary passion and enormous talent.

Jack Henry hit the big time when he turned twenty-one years of age. He forged a check and won an all-expense-paid trip to the Utah prison.

He thought life had been hard in the past.

Now he was trapped in the belly of the beast.

It was a hell hole, he figured, where he could kill or be killed.

He stabbed an inmate, stood back, and watched him die.

No remorse.

No regret.

He was sentenced to another twenty-three years behind the walls. He escaped, knocked over a bank in Colorado, and collected nineteen more years of room and board.

Most of it was spent in solitary.

Cold.

And somber.

Jack Henry was left alone to sort through the torn pages of his own thoughts. Time simply stopped running and sat down beside him. He had no idea when it was day, no idea when it was night.

It was always night.

The anger smoldered.

Then it burned.

But Jack Henry could not escape the extraordinary passion and enormous talent that dwelled in the dark corner of a frayed and fragmented past.

In 1977, he chanced to read that author Norman Mailer was writing a book about convicted killer Gary Gilmore who had shocked the penal system and everyone around him by choosing to be executed by a firing squad.

Hell, Jack Henry thought, he knew Gilmore.

Hell, he thought, he was behind the same walls as Gilmore.

Hell, he thought, Gilmore didn't know anything about the decayed decadence of prison life.

Sure, he had murdered a couple of guys.

Sure, he was facing execution.

But if the famous Norman Mailer wanted to know the truth about what poison was churning behind the walls when the lights went out and the guards turned their backs, he should listen to Jack Henry.

That's what he wrote Mailer.

The letters kept coming.

Mailer read them all.

They touched him.

They fascinated him.

They condemned him.

He immediately recognized the extraordinary passion and enormous talent locked away within the dark corner of Jack Henry's frayed and fragmented soul.

Norman Mailer collected the letters. He packaged them. And he released them in a book entitled *In the Belly of the Beast.* The book took New York literary circles by storm.

The critics had discovered behind the walls of a Utah Prison a literary genius.

The book almost instantly became a best seller. Critics read: *The only time they appear human is when you have a knife at their throats. The instant you remove it, they fall back into animality. Obscenity.*

They were mesmerized by such passages as: *Everyone in prison has an idea of violence, murder. Beneath all relationships between prisoners is the ever-present fact of murder. It ultimately defines our relationship among ourselves.*

And they marveled at the raw honesty of his words. Jack Henry was captivating. He was called "a stunning writer and tenacious thinker," a man who had "serious and well thought out views." New York literary giants joined Norman Mailer in an all-out, no-holds-barred campaign to get Jack Henry set free from his dungeon.

In their eyes, he was little more than a political prisoner locked away in an American gulag.

A doctor, however, testified that Jack Henry was a "potentially dangerous man with a hair-trigger temper." And a prison official told the parole board, "I don't see a changed man. His attitude, his demeanor indicated psychosis."

It didn't matter.

No one listened.

New York was talking the loudest, and Mailer was saying that Abbott's talents were of such importance that it would be a crime to ignore them. "Culture," he said, "is worth a little risk."

The New York literary giants prevailed, and Jack Henry became the toast of the Big Apple. He appeared on "Good Morning America." He was interviewed by *People Magazine.* He was offered assignments from *The New York Review* and *The Atlanta Journal-Constitution.* The discovery of a bold new literary talent was celebrated at a luncheon hosted by Norman Mailer and Random House.

Jack Henry Abbott had climbed to the top of the world. He was a writer of rare abilities and insight. He was brutally honest in his writing because he had faced and endured a lifetime of brutality. Publishers were clamoring for the rights to his next book.

Six weeks after walking from behind the walls of a Utah Prison as a free man, six weeks after becoming New York's hottest new writing sensation, Jack Henry stabbed a young actor to death.

No reason, not to a sane man anyway.

It's just that the actor made him mad.

He had to die.

The next morning, *The New York Times* referred to *In the Belly of the Beast* as "awesome, brilliant, perversely ingenuous." Jack Henry didn't read the review. He was on the run. He made it as far as Morgan City, Louisiana, before he ran out of room to run.

The walls were waiting for him.

The New York literary giants celebrated alone that night.

They talked of books.

They talked of words.

They talked of ideals.

They talked about themselves.

No one mentioned Jack Henry Abbott.

My Writing Hero

WE ALL HAVE our heroes. And we lose them. Time and age steals them away.

In the writing profession, I had a hero.

And I lost him.

Jory Sherman isn't with us anymore, but he left behind hundreds of books and poems and disciples who listened to every word he told us and became better writers because we had a chance to grasp the shards of wisdom that only Jory knew.

He was one of a kind. He had traveled a far different road from the one you and I have taken.

For a time, you see, Jory Sherman lived in a dark and frightening place we have never visited, and he had no idea why he had been swallowed up by the darkness of a wayward and tormented mind that had lost its way and carried him far from the agricultural landscape of his South Dakota heritage.

At the age of twenty-two, he found himself in the VA hospital at Ft. Miley, outside of San Francisco. Doctors had decided that Jory Sherman was manic-depressive, and they exiled him to a special ward cursed by intensive occupational therapy.

He hated every minute of it.

He saw his life wasting slowly away, and there was nothing he could do about it.

One day at a time.

That's all he had to live.

One day at a time.

How many days did he have?

With his permission, Sherman's psychiatrist began taping his sessions three times a week, and the hospital staff was astounded at the way he carefully described his complex feelings and thought processes.

Jory Sherman has only one alternative," the staff said.

"What's that?"

"He should become a writer."

So they hauled Jory Sherman out of occupational therapy, led him to an office down the hall, gave him a typewriter and stack of paper and said, more or less, "Apply the seat of your pants to the seat of a chair, and write."

He did.

Sherman remembers, "I began writing with no structure, no purpose, and no plan. I was doing little more than spreading words on paper as they came rushing out of my mind so quickly I had trouble catching them ."

The staff read the pages of his raw manuscript.

"He's a genius," some said.

"He's got what it takes," said others.

"To do what?"

"Be a poet."

Some of the attending doctors only shook their heads sadly.

A poet?

Jory Sherman was just as well off when everybody thought it was crazy.

Writing saved his life and may have even saved his soul.

Sherman says, "After I left the hospital, I made a decision that I would just write and do any kind of work that allowed me the freedom to write. I studied and wrote and what emerged was poetry."

He became one of the beat poets of the beat generation in San Francisco, running in the coffee house circles with good friend Charles Bukowski. But the years passed, and time left him a wiser man.

Poetry wasn't selling.

No matter how great the poetry may have been, the poet was still hungry and often living on the streets.

Jory Sherman took the raw power of his imagery, turned it into prose, and he became one of the most prolific authors of all time, writing more than a thousand articles, five hundred published short stories, and four hundred books in fifty years behind the typewriter and then the computer.

Although he had published several novels and was quickly becoming a name to be reckoned with in America's major publishing houses, his first important break came as he sat in the editor's office at Major Books in North Hollywood.

The art director walked in with a book cover for *Guns for Hire*, a Western, and announced that the author was suffering from writer's block and would not be able to finish the novel.

Sherman grinned and said, "I could write the book just by looking at the cover."

Two weeks later, the editor mailed him the cover and asked him to write the book.

"When do you need it?" he asked.

"Two weeks," she said.

Ten days later, he submitted the finished manuscript. Thus was born the Western writing career of Jory Sherman. He turned out novels as easily as some people turned out letters, and his writing – regardless of the genre – was the stuff of poetry.

Warren French, a professor of literature at the University of Florida, said, "Jory Sherman has a strange and powerful knowledge of language and an almost perfect ear."

His Western novel, *Grass Kingdom*, launched the famed Forge imprint and beat formidable odds by being nominated for a Pulitzer Prize in literature the year that Annie Prouix won the award.

Jory Sherman said, "I think the most enjoyment I get from writing is the feeling I get from using language, the English language, which is the richest in the world. I love seeing ideas take shape in my mind and then using language's powerful symbols to convey those ideas. I have an almost mystical feeling about language and words, as if a sentence is a secret code that can unlock the mysteries of the human mind, can reveal ancient myths and stories that have lain buried in the human subconscious since man came into being on this earth. Language brought me to writing and sustains me even after more than fifty years of putting thoughts into words."

The genre was never important to him.

He began as a poet.

He wrote Westerns.

He wrote horror and paranormal and dozens of mainstream novels.

But they all have one thing in common – the strength and depth of the language that dwelled within him.

As Jory Sherman once wrote in an essay of his mountain homeland: "And so these words, these ephemeral images so fleeting and yet so vivid once, stand as a kind of hymn to the Ozarks. That others might see the paintings, hear the songs being sung, listen to the symphonic music of nature, and have a personal talisman to touch and hold and keep and smell and taste long after I am gone from these hills and have put down my notebook and gone to sleep.

"If only the words remain, that is enough. They hold the images for all earthly time. Enough? The words, ultimately are everything, and are all that may be left to us and generations yet to come."

Jory had been ill for a long time. His health had broken, but never his spirit. He had lost his sight, and it was difficult for him to breathe at times, and he had trouble gaining the strength it took to type a word, much less a story.

But the last time I spoke with Jory, he told me he had written a couple of books in his mind and had started a third. I wish I could read them. Each of the books was always better than the last, and the last was superb.

THE THOUGHT STRUCK me as soon as I walked away and left him in the final fading hours of a good life that, like a good novel, was coming to an end.

As soon as we pass the age of thirty, we become suddenly aware of our own mortality.

I passed thirty a long time ago.

I think the Wright Brothers had just flown.

Or maybe it was Wiley Post.

Doesn't matter.

I have lived a long time trying to outrun my mortality.

It hasn't gained on me, but I can sometimes hear the echo of its footsteps down a dark and rain-splattered alley somewhere.

That's how I want go someday.

In a dark alley.

The darker, the better.

I've spent a lot of time in the dark alleys that occupy my novels.

I figure I'll have company among the shadows.

Writers, more than anyone, keep asking: *what do we leave behind when we are gone?*

Here's the short list.

May God forgive us for our secrets.

We'll leave a few published stories and a few published books.

And, tragically, we leave stories untold.

On our desks, the great unwashed will find scraps of paper that hold our ideas and assorted passages we planned to include in a novel someday before the days finally run out.

"What does it mean?" they ask.

No one knows.

Perhaps no one cares.

Perhaps no one even asks the question.

There will be scattered pieces of wrinkled and yellowed paper where we outlined our plots and plot twists, dressed our characters to meet the world on the outside of the novel, and scratched out potential titles.

Some good.

Some bad.

Most are better left unread, wadded up, and thrown away by the cleaning lady.

If God is as merciful as I hope He is, those scraps will burn before my ashes do.

Here is reality.

What looks like a brilliant idea today may wind up looking downright silly in tomorrow's light of day.

We bleed words.

And not all of them are the right ones.

That's why everything is scribbled on scattered scraps of paper.

Scattered scraps of paper are where we want them to reside.

And forever.

If it were a perfect world, we would leave after typing the final period on the final sentence of the final chapter in our final novel.

It would contain the stories of our lives tucked away in three hundred pages, maybe more, provided, of course, our lives have plodded up one road and down another as we weave our way through an epic.

Then again, others might be better off leaving their legacy among the pages of a novella.

Me?

I figure a good short story will just about cover it all.

I am haunted by those final months of Jory Sherman's life.

He was a legend.

But Jory was old.

He was tired.

He was blind.

He was too weak to write.

He couldn't see the computer screen anyway.

He just lay in bed with a smile on his face.

And he told us all, "I'm still writing novels in my head." He paused, took a deep breath and said, "You know, some of them are pretty good."

We'll never read them.

We'll never know what we missed.

They say you can't take it with you.

But they're wrong.

We do.

Our stories all come with us when we go.

The Man in Charge

FRANK Q. DOBBS. The name is a sentence itself.

No, it's a story, a mini-series and several volumes all packed into eleven letters that meant so much to so many for so long.

Frank Q. Dobbs.

He was larger than life, a bear of a man, a maverick, a renegade misplaced from another time, whose voice could intimidate thunder and whose inventive mind had the sharp crackle of lightning in the hot skies of a summer rainstorm.

And, as screenwriter JP Martin pointed out, "His great mind was matched only by his great heart. He was tenacious and loyal to a fault. He could be gracious and funny and ornery in the same breath. He was a kid at heart with a warrior's soul. He had a kind of genius that left you mesmerized and him frustrated. His integrity could not be altered."

Actor/stuntman/director Dave Cass remembered, "He cared about every project he was involved with and would fight with the most powerful executive to make a point. Never for his own gain, but for the gain of the story being told."

Frank Q. Dobbs would never consider himself to be the story.

He preferred to be the teller of tales.

And no one ever told them better.

He was a schemer.

And a dreamer.

He watched the world around him as though it were flashing on a silver screen, with life as its projector. As Cass pointed out, "His passion for making motion pictures was unsurpassed."

He directed story lines.

He directed scenes.

He directed those on camera.

He directed those off camera.

He directed every one he met whether they were in the film business or not.

Frank Q. Dobbs was the man in charge, and no one ever doubted it.

He made films.

He rescued films that had lost their way.

He put stories back on track when they had drifted astray.

He punched up punch lines.

His pictures were honest and could make you laugh or make you cry, and he could always make you care.

We loved him.

We feared him.

We loved to fear him because, down deep, we always knew that Frank Q. Dobbs, in his own iconoclastic way, loved us.

He was a maverick in search of fight.

A gruff voice.

He sounded like a drill sergeant.

A soft heart.

He cried sometimes but never let you know.

The saddest day of Frank's life was the day he realized that the Western had ridden off into the sunset. Westerns were what he revered most. Westerns had human values, tragedies and triumphs, and you could always tell good from evil by the color of the hats they wore.

Frank Q. Dobbs often told me he should have been born in the 1870s.

He would have had the horses.

And the cattle.

But there were no cameras.

So he wouldn't have really been happy.

It was Frank's duty to come along a hundred years later and portray the Old West the way it was, the way it should be, the way it would always be remembered.

As a young boy, he sat in those dark, cool movie houses on Saturday afternoons in Huntsville, allowing motion pictures to kidnap him away to places he had never been or seen before. And he wanted to go there on his own and take others with him.

Frank Q. Dobbs had no interest in acting.

But he was fascinated with the prospect of telling actors what to do, what to say and how to say it.

The road from Huntsville to Hollywood was long, winding and precarious. He took a job on the set of "Gunsmoke." With a degree in journalism and theater stuffed in his pocket, Frank was quite pleased to be given the chore of holding the horses.

He never complained.

He only learned.

And, in time, the name of Frank Q. Dobbs was being attached to the "Gunsmoke" scripts he had written.

For him, the Old West had never been wilder nor closer.

As the years passed, Happy Shahan's Alamo Village and the high country touching Lajitas and surrounding Big Bend National Park became his personal studios.

As much as anyone, Frank Q. Dobbs invented the film industry in Texas. He brought major film productions to San Antonio, Houston, El Paso and the hinterlands of Brackettville and Study Butte. He knew every inch, every mile, every ruin, every small, antiquated village in Texas. And he wrote scripts to the locations. He never had to scout them. He already knew where they were.

He and I wrote *Hot Wire* and filmed it in Houston. We wrote *Gambler 5: Playing for Keeps* and took the cameras to Galveston, San Antonio, and Big Bend National Park. Those soaring mountains rising above the Great Chihuahua Desert looked like the Bolivian Andes to us. No one ever knew the difference.

When necessary, Frank packed up his talents, his thoughts, his opinions, his guiding genius and hauled them all to Canada and South Africa, to California and Thailand.

He filmed history in the making during his sojourn in Vietnam.

He scaled the summits of obscure mountain ranges.

He traveled roads that didn't come out.

He escaped a Tsunami.

He never knew when he was in danger.

Frank Q. Dobbs preferred to create it or at least direct it.

He was proud of his films. He was proud of his work. He was prouder of those he mentored along the way.

Script writers wrote better, directors directed better, producers produced more effectively simply because Frank had come their way.

He had spoken with the voice of God.

And the smart ones listened.

The smart one succeeded.

Frank and I had written a screen play about an early day search for oil in the vast, barren landscape of far West Texas.

A little drama.

A little humor.

Go ahead and cheer.

The little guy won.

He called about midnight and told me, "I've read an article that CBS wants to shoot seven westerns. We need to write a western."

"When do they need the script?"

"Monday."

I thought for a moment and said, "Frank, let's turn the wildcat oil story into a western. It's already written."

"How do we do it?"

"We change the search for oil to the search for water in a thirsty land." I waited, then added, "In the 1870s, water was more precious than oil. Men fought for it. They killed for it. It'll work."

Silence.

His voice boomed, "Send it."

He marched into CBS with a western about the battle for water on a hot and blistered desert wasteland."

"Sounds interesting," the producer said. "But we've already bought the western scripts. What we're looking for now is a period piece."

Frank grinned.

He reached into his briefcase and removed our old script for *Wildcat.* "How about the battle for oil in 1930 West Texas."

CBS bought it.

Frank never went anywhere without his bag of tricks.

The film business, however, was cruel and inhuman punishment to anyone foolish enough to play the game.

I played.

Frank worked at it.

Since both of us felt a kinship with the Old West, we came up with an idea for a motion picture script about the life of Doc Holliday.

All anyone knew about him was the gunfight at the OK Corral.

He walked in with Wyatt Earp and the Earp brothers.

The guns were blazing.

Men died.

Men prayed.

Men ran.

In thirteen seconds, it was over.

Didn't take long to have a gunfight.

Our story had a simple but powerful theme: *A man's life should not be defined in thirteen seconds.*

Frank pitched the theme to the studio.

The producer loved it.

"That's the greatest idea I've ever heard," he said.

Frank called.

"I need a treatment," he said. "The producer loves it."

"You sure?"

"It's a done deal."

'When do you want the treatment?"

"Monday."

With Frank, it was always Monday.

I glanced at the calendar.

It was Saturday.

I wrote for the next forty-eight hours without sleeping, crawled to the only fax machine at daybreak on Monday, and sent the pages to Hollywood.

Why not?

It was worth the pain and agony of inserting old words into a new story.

It was a done deal.

Frank walked into the studio on Monday afternoon and handed my thirty-two pages to the producer.

He began reading.

Frank sat back with a cocky smile on his face.

The producer suddenly looked up. His eyes were glassy. His hands were shaking

"I can't film this," he said.

"Why not?'

He stammered.

He stuttered.

His voice was barely audible.

"It's a western," he said.

And that's what happened when dealing with a thirty-something studio producer who had never heard of the real Doc Holliday, thought Tombstone was in the cemetery and never a town in Arizona, and had no idea if he corral was OK or not.

Frank's sense of humor was legendary.

When he and I worked on the television pilot for *Backroads* in the mountains of North Carolina, we asked a hotel clerk to point out the east for us since all directions looked the same, and one timbered landmark looked just like the last one.

He pointed.

And Frank Q. Dobbs was standing on the mountain top at four o'clock the next morning, wrapped in a woolen blanket to protect himself from a strong, chilled wind sweeping across Appalachia.

He looked more like a Druid than a filmmaker.

Frank had his camera pointed east. At least it was east if the clerk hadn't been mistaken or lying to him.

He was geared up to catch the first glimpse of morning sunlight as it reached down to anoint the Southern highlands.

He stood.

He shivered.

And he waited.

And suddenly, Frank looked down and saw his own shadow stretching awkwardly across the wrong side of the mountain.

He felt a warm glow burn its way into the back of his neck.

The sun had risen behind him.

He sighed, glanced over and said in his own, indomitable, booming voice, "Hell, I knew Appalachia was backward. But I had no idea the sun rose in the west."

Frank Q. Dobbs gloried in that magic glow of twilight time.

When we worked on "Hot Wire" in downtown Houston, Frank had mentally orchestrated his opening shot of the film.

Twilight.

The golden glow of a setting sun would be threading its way among the streets.

George Kennedy would come driving around the corner as the magic of twilight time ricocheted off the hood of his car.

The camera was set.

Frank was ready.

The sun struck Houston at just the right angle.

He had less than twenty seconds of shooting time.

"Go," he said into the walkie-talkie.

He waited.

Nothing.

The light began to fade, and he heard Kennedy's voice on the walkie talkie, explaining, "Frank, the car won't start."

Sundown.

Frank hit the parking meter beside him with one mighty blow of his fist.

He didn't flinch.

The parking meter bent in the middle and folded over.

The policeman working the set simply turned and walked away.

Frank Q. Dobbs could do a lot of things.

But he couldn't stop the sun.

Now, perhaps, it's all changed.

There may be a minute or two of extra sunlight for those filmmakers who have a car that won't start.

Frank Q. Dobbs is in charge.

Twilight time has a new director.

As costume supervisor Fran Allgood pointed out, "I simply can't imagine a world without Frank Q. Dobbs."

He's still around.

He just has a new job.

Poet on the Run

SHE SAT IN the darkness of a glum and dour afternoon. Autumn had come late to the empty landscape of a country that welcomed only a few and resented those who arrived with downcast eyes and somebody else's name.

A dry chill chased the heat from the arroyos, and a contemptuous wind stormed down out of the rock canyons. The creek beds were dry, and only one road led into town, and if a car passed by, you knew the driver was either lost, misplaced, or on the run.

Nobody ever came to Valentine, Texas, for very long.

The lucky ones were only passing through.

The girl glanced into the mirror beside the sagging bed of a two-bit motel room that was overpriced at two bits. The mirror was cracked. Her reflection was shaded, but not enough for her to realize that she could no longer consider herself a girl. The wrinkles on her face looked like scars.

Once she had been beautiful.

Those in school called her bright.

Now she was alone.

She was always alone.

She picked up an old bankbook, one from the First National Bank of Burkburnett, Texas. She thought for a moment, opened a page, and began to write:

No one must know how I tremble
When I hear a siren moan,
Just fearing for you, darling,
And hoping you're safe at home.

She smiled and read it again. She smiled and had no idea why the tear was creasing her face. There was a time, not so many years ago, when she had been an honor roll student in school, a sassy young lady, brimming with confidence, who won top prizes in scholastic contests for spelling, writing, and public speaking. She even made several introductory speeches for politicians. She was that popular.

Everyone knew she could write. Everyone had long been impressed with her creative mind.

She'll go far, they predicted. *She has the world in the palm of her hands.*

Bright.

Beautiful.

And talented.

But life was as hard then as it was now. Her father had died when she was four-years-old. Her mother worked as a seamstress. She tried hard. She really did. But money was so scarce, and hardly any of the loose change ever found its way to their home.

The lovely girl grew up wanting more.

She grew up dreaming of a better life.

But it always seemed to be just beyond her reach.

And she wrote:

I've seen the world from the gutter up.
It leaves you with a bitter taste.
The multitudes staring down at me
As though I was human waste.

God, she loved poetry. She had written it all of her life. But only recently had poetry begun to sound so much like her own life.

She heard a car stop outside.

She looked up to see if the door would open

It didn't.

She should have stayed in school. She knew that now. But she had grown weary of trying to struggle in a world without money, without hope, without a future.

Roy Thornton had been her ticket to the good life.

She married him six days before her sixteenth birthday. They gave each other Tungsten wedding bands. And she pictured herself as living, where she always belonged, within the pages of a romance magazine.

The romance faded before the magazine subscription ran out.

Sure, she was beautiful.

But Roy Thornton had his pick of beautiful girls, and he wanted them all.

She spent her days alone and her nights lying in an empty bed. She worked as a waitress. She cleaned houses. She was poor, maybe, but she could hold her head high in a world where poverty was the only promise anyone had.

By the time she was eighteen, her husband had broken one law too money and was on his way to prison.

Get a divorce, her mother said.

That would be so unfair to him, the girl said. *I can't leave him while he's locked away.*

She would never divorce him.

But she did find a measure of love in the presence of a young man who said he was going place and wanted her to go along with him.

He loved her.

He was faithful.

He never left her alone, not for very long anyway, and the first time was when he found himself thrown into a jail.

Made a mistake, he said. *It happens.*

Hard times.

Bad luck.

She forgave him. She loved him back. It was a simple relationship. She walked down to the jail and visited him as often as she could.

She brought him smiles.

She brought him letters.

She brought him her poems.

And one day, she brought him a gun.

And now they were in Valentine the way almost everyone came to Valentine.

They were neither lost nor misplaced.

They were on the run.

They had robbed a fruit stand.

That's all.

A lousy old fruit stand.

And then, of course, there was a bank or two.

By then, the Lord had turned his back on them.

By then, the boys with badges and guns were shooting at them.

The light in the sparsely furnished motel was growing dim. And she wrote:

Someday they'll go down together.
They'll bury them side by side.
To a few it'll be grief.
To the law a relief.
But it's death for Bonnie and Clyde.

Bonnie Parker put her pen away and closed her eyes. She waited for the glum and dour afternoon to turn to night. She always felt safe in the darkness.

She heard the key in the lock and saw the doorknob turn.

And she smiled.

All was right with the world again.

Clyde Barrow was home.

On the morning of May 23, 1934, six lawmen from Texas and Louisiana, led by Ranger Frank Hamer, ambushed a Ford V8 headed at high speed down a rural road in Bienville Parrish, Louisiana. They had been waiting two days and were armed with pistols, shotguns, and military-styled Browning automatic rifles, powerful enough to pierce armor.

It was estimated that the first shot fired hit Clyde Barrow and killed him.

Someone heard Bonnie scream when she realized he was dead.

A total of 130 rounds tore into the car as it lay in a ditch.

Smoke rolled from the Ford so thick that it appeared to be on fire.

As Bonnie had written, it was death for Bonnie and Clyde, and they would be buried side by side.

Bonnie was wearing Roy Thornton's Tungsten wedding ring when she drew her last breath.

She had lived her last poem.

I Remember Mama

IT'S A TOUGH life. That's what he said as he waited for the train to come rolling into the Wichita station.

He was a surly little man with a head of full brown curly hair.

Clean shirt.

It was blue with green checks and had been both starched and pressed.

His trousers were black and had a lot of rayon mixed with the wool blend.

His blazer was brown.

From a distance it looked like leather.

He looked out of place.

Train riders were wrinkled folks.

"What's tough about it?" I asked.

"My job."

"What do you do?"

"I generally need to keep it a secret."

I arched an eyebrow.

He shrugged.

"It's my mama," he said. "She doesn't want anybody to know."

"Why not?"

He leaned forward in his chair, pulled a chunk of chewing gum from the sole of his shoe, and said, "I'm a writer."

"That's an honorable job," I said.

"Not for mama."

"What do you write?"

"Fiction."

"What's wrong with fiction?"

"Mama's a real religious woman," he said.

"Most mothers are."

"She's a ten commandments woman," he said.

"The ten commandments don't say anything bad about writing," I told him.

"Have you read them lately?"

I shook my head. "It's been a while."

"I broke the wrong commandment," he said

"Which one?"

"I told you I write fiction," he said.

I nodded.

He sighed.

"I tell lies," he said. "I tell lies, and people believe them."

I thought he might cry.

He did, too.

"Where you headed?" I asked.

"To prison," he said.

I must have looked surprised.

"I'm on my way to visit mama."

"I thought she was a religious, God-fearing woman," I said.

"She is," he said. "And when I wrote my first book, she went a little crazy," he said.

"What happened?"

"She read it, went out, and robbed liquor store."

"Why would she do that?"

"I'm her baby boy," he said.

"So?"

"She didn't want me to go to hell alone."

A Role for Veronica

SHE CAME INTO town about sundown.
She was driving an old Oldsmobile.
But then, there are no new Oldsmobiles.
She may have been forty.
She could have been younger.
It's difficult to tell these days.
Her hair was blonde.
I don't know what it was originally.
But she smiled and said, "Blonde sells."
And so it does.
She was thin, but not anorexic, and tall.
She was wearing heels.
That made her a lot taller than she should have been.
She wore jeans and a red western shirt.
One button too many had been unfastened.
She sat down beside me on a bench outside of a small downtown café.
"What's your name?" I asked.
I was just trying to be friendly.
"That's up to you," she said.
She winked.
She had to be friendly.
She was looking for a job.
"I think you are a Dolly," I said.
She frowned.
"Don't like Dolly," she said.
I studied her a moment.
"How about Sally?" I asked.
"How about Sally Jo?"

"Works for me."
She laughed softly.
"Why are you in town?" I asked.
"How should I know," she said. "You're the one who asked me to come."
"When?"
"Whenever you decided to write a new novel."
I did have a story bubbling around in my mind.
It didn't have a plot.
It didn't have any characters.
It didn't have a hook.
But it was bubbling.
"You need a girl in your novel," she said.
"Why?"
"Every good story needs a girl."
"It won't be a romance."
"Every good story has a little romance."
She kissed me on the cheek.
I didn't argue.
"Did you want to play the heroine?" I asked.
"I'd rather be the heartbreaker."
"Why?" I wanted to know.
"I've had practice."
"Heartbreakers don't have names like Sally Jo."
She shrugged.
"Then change it," she said.
I thought for a moment.
"How about Veronica?" I asked.
"Veronica's good," she said. "But I'll have to dye my hair black."
"Why?"
"You ever see a blonde named Veronica?"
"No."
"That's the reason."
She kissed me again.
"Promise me one thing," she said.
"What's that?"
"Make sure I'm good for at least fifty-six chapters," she said. "Don't kill me off too quickly."
She smiled.
She winked.
She blew me a kiss.
I had one thought as she walked away.
Veronica would last the whole book.

Saying Goodbye to a Hero

HE WAS UPSET when he walked through the door.

He threw his hat across the room.

He slumped down in the sofa.

His jaws were clenched.

His hands had tightened into fists.

He waited until I finished writing the paragraph before he spoke.

Shelton knew it wouldn't take long.

I write short paragraphs.

"Do you realize what you're doing?" he asked.

I shrugged

I had no idea what he was talking about.

"This is my story," Shelton said.

I nodded in agreement.

"This is my journey."

I nodded again.

"I'm the hero."

"No doubt about it."

He paused a moment, then asked, "What page number are you working on."

I glanced at the screen.

"Page two-forty-two," I said

"That's why I'm mad," he said.

"I don't understand."

"I haven't been in the story since page two-fourteen."

"I haven't needed you," I said.

I must have said the wrong thing.

Shelton crossed his arms in defiance.

I do believe he was sulking a little.

"You're spending too much time on the girl," he said.

"I'm telling her backstory."

Shelton stood and began pacing the floor.

"What's so good about her backstory that you have to spend twenty-eight pages to tell it."

I grinned.

So that was it.

Shelton was jealous.

"Her backstory is better than yours," I said.

"Why?" he wanted to know.

"She's blonde."

"What does hair color have to do with it," he said.

"The blonde hair got her into trouble," I said.

He glared at me.

"How she got out of trouble," I said, "now that's a really good backstory."

Shelton wasn't convinced.

He pleaded his case.

"I crossed the desert barefoot," he said. "I worked behind enemy lines as a spy. I got inside Berlin and mapped the location to Hitler's bunker while the war was still going on. I shot down two German officers during an escape attempt. I kidnapped Himmler and led him out of town on the back of a donkey. I broke into an Italian prison and led a revolt. I flew a glider single-handedly into France and wrecked it in the streets of Paris. I stole ten million dollars from an overseas account and used it to finance the building of the Atom bomb. What else do you want from me?"

"Check the color of your hair," I said

He glanced in the mirror.

"So what?" he said.

"It's not blond," I said.

"You don't need a blonde for this story," he said.

"Maybe not, but blonde helps."

"She just gets in the way."

"I like the cute little way she gets back out of the way," I said.

Shelton hammered my desk with his fist.

"One of us has to go," he said.

He glared at me.

I stared at him.

I looked toward the leather chair at the far end of the room.

The blonde smiled.

She did look good in black.

I wondered how she would look in red.

I turned back to the story and decided to find out.

"I'm leaving," Shelton said.

"You really don't have to go."

"I'm resigning," Shelton said.

"But I'm in the middle of the story."

He threw back his head and laughed.

"So what are you gonna do now?" he asked. "How can you finish the story without me?"

He slammed the door, and I barely caught a glance of his shadow in the darkness outside my writing room.

The blonde raised an eyebrow.

She crossed her legs.

The red did look good on her.

Shelton was out of sight and walking down the road when I wrote the next sentence.

Poor bastard.

He never heard the shot when I pulled the trigger.

Love in the Diner

SHE WAS SEATED behind the counter when I walked into the grill.

She looked thirty-five.

She was probably ten years older.

Her cinnamon brown hair was a little too long, piling itself on her shoulders.

Her lipstick was a little too red.

She didn't mind.

She smiled.

I didn't mind the red either.

On her, it worked.

She was pretty in the glow of the overhead light.

She was beautiful when the shadows touched her face.

She stayed in the shadows.

She was wise that way.

Her name was Mary Beth, she said.

"Got a last name?"

"It doesn't matter."

She smiled again.

She was right.

It didn't matter.

Mary Beth had been reading a *True Confession* magazine when I walked in and sat down at the counter.

"Coffee," I said.

"Just a minute," she said.

She kept reading.

"Must be good," I said.

She nodded.

"Woman's in love with the wrong man," she said.

"Most women are."

"She's cheating on the good guy."

"It happens."

"She's bored with the good guy." Mary Beth Shrugged. "He works hard. He makes a good paycheck every week. He comes home on time. She fixes dinner. And they watch sitcoms on TeeVee together."

"That's what life's all about," I said.

"She wants more."

"Most women do."

"She wants adventure." Mary Beth laughs. "The wrong man wants to take her out of town on a trip, and she wants to go."

"Think she will?"

"She's wrestling with her conscience."

"The conscience never wins," I said.

"Mine didn't," Mary Beth told me. "I had a good man once upon a time." She folded the magazine up and placed it under the counter. "Married six years. He loved me. Problem was, he was an accountant."

"What's wrong with an accountant?"

"He never thought my figure was as exciting as the numbers he figured in his head."

"He must have really loved his numbers."

"I ran off with the football coach," she said. "He was hot stuff. Big. Tall. Lots of muscles. He was drafted once by the Chicago Bears."

"He make the big time?"

Mary Beth laughed.

"He did with me," she said.

"What happened?" I wanted to know.

"We lost the coach."

"Coaches have a habit of getting fired," I said. "All it takes is one bad team."

"He didn't have a bad team," she said. "Never had a losing record."

Mary Beth poured my coffee.

"He got himself killed," she said.

"Wreck?"

"Gunshot."

"Your husband?"

"He wasn't the jealous kind."

I sipped my coffee in silence. Finally, I had to ask her the question that needed to be asked.

"You shoot him?"

Mary Beth smiled.

"The coach only liked one thing better than me," she said.

"What's that?"

"A cheerleader."

"Did they arrest you?"

"They didn't convict me."

"Were you guilty?"

"Judge said I wasn't."

"What convinced him?"

"I had an alibi," she said. "I was with his daughter the night coach died."

"Where was his daughter?

Mary Beth laughed out loud.

"She was a cheerleader," Mary Beth said.

I finished my coffee.

"I only have one question," I asked.

"What's that?"

"You want to be in my next novel?"

"What do you want me to do?"

"Just be yourself."

"Are there any cheerleaders in it?"

"There are."

"Anybody die?"

"Somebody does."

"Am I guilty?"

"Not in my eyes."

"I want my own love scene," she said. "Don't worry about it none. I can write it myself."

She poured me a second cup of coffee and went back to *True Confessions.*

Who Tells the Story?

I BROUGHT THEM all into the same room at the same time.

It was late.

I was tired.

They were tired.

But I had a problem, and only they could solve it.

I turned first to the girl.

She was probably too old to be called a girl, but she still wanted to play the ingénue.

Dark black hair.

Oval face.

A hint of wrinkles below her eyes.

Her eyes were dark.

They were hard.

Her voice was soft.

And she quietly told her story.

Her name was Alicia, she said, and she came to the city from a small Southern town.

Her mother worked as a waitress.

Her father was dead.

She never knew him when he wasn't.

She had been poor all of her life and had run off to Atlanta where all the pretty girls went when they were looking for a rich husband.

She found one.

She was tired of him.

Didn't know why.

Maybe, she said, it was because he had possessed almost as much money as girlfriends.

She smiled.

The sparkle on her diamond ring was blinding.
"Has he been good to you?" I asked.
"Now and then," she said.
The young man across the room was nervous.
He did not look directly at me or at anyone.
He wore a new suit.
It was a cheap suit.
Said he was looking for a job.
"What kind of work do you do?" I asked.
"Anything that pays."
"You ever kill anyone?"
"Judge said I did."
"Would you ever kill again?" I asked.
"Not for money."
"For what?"
"For love maybe."
He glanced at the girl.
She did not look at him.
But she kept smiling.
I thought she might have winked.
Maybe not.
The older gentleman thought he was wasting his time.
His fedora was pulled low over his eyes.
He was wearing a wrinkled raincoat.
It wasn't raining.
He didn't care.
He kept a .38 special in his coat pocket.
He had told me once.
But that was long ago.
He was a policeman then.
He was in business for himself now.
He liked it better.
"No rules," he said.
"Nobody looking over my shoulder," he said.
"Nobody makes a fuss over my mistakes anymore," he said.
"What happens to them?"
"I bury them."
He grinned.
He scowled when he grinned.
His teeth were the color of bleached mustard.
He hadn't slept with a femme fatale for a long time.
Buried a couple.
Hadn't slept with either of them.

He had been a friend for years.

The girl wasn't.

I wished she was.

The young man was a drifter.

He could drift in an out of a story or your life without you ever knowing he was coming or going.

So there they were.

I had a story.

Didn't know the beginning.

Didn't know the ending.

All three of the characters did.

And I was facing the most difficult task that confronts a writer.

Each of them had a point of view.

Only one point of view mattered.

Who would I choose to tell the story?

A Writer's Curse

I DIDN'T SLEEP much last night.

I was worried about Mary Brooks.

She was bright.

Dark brown hair bobbed at the neck.

A dimple in her chin.

Eyes the color of the sea at twilight, and they danced.

She had loads of energy.

And when she walked through the door, her smile would light up the whole room.

Mary Brooks was everybody's friend.

Nobody's fool.

And nobody's lover.

However, she had been moody the past few days.

She still smiled.

But the light wasn't there.

Somebody had turned off the switch.

The last time I looked, Mary had been crying.

Couldn't blame her.

She saw what nobody else did.

She knew what nobody else does.

Mary Brooks witnessed a murder.

It was dark outside.

Not even the moon had made an appearance.

She had worked late and was walking across the parking lot toward her car.

That's when she heard the argument.

"It was a man and a woman," she told me.

"Recognize them?"

"I knew them both."
"Lover's quarrel?"
"I don't know if love was involved," she said.
She shrugged.
I saw the tear in her eye before she wiped it away.
"But it was definitely a quarrel."
"What about?"
"Money."
"His or hers?"
"The company's money."
"Somebody stealing it?"
"That's what he said."
"He blame her?"
"He didn't have to."
"Why not?"
"I saw the look on her face."
"Guilt wears many masks."
I paused.
I liked the phrase.
I took the time to write it down.
I would use it somebody.
"That's when she shot him," Mary Brooks said.
"How many times?"
"I know I heard two shots. It might have been three."
She know you were in the parking lot?"
"I hid behind an old Buick."
"What'd she do?"
"She ran to her car and drove away."
"And left him."
"She did take the time to run over him before she left."
"Hard-hearted woman."
Mary Brooks smiled.
"Aren't we all?"
I didn't argue.
And I didn't sleep well last night.
I was worried about Mary Brooks.
She didn't know she was going to die.
I did.
"You can prevent it," the Muse whispered in my ear.
"I can't."
"You're writing the damn story."
The Muse laughed.

"You can kill anybody you want, and you can save anybody you want," he said.

"Not this time"

"Why not?"

"Mary Brooks didn't think the murderer saw her."

"But the murderer did."

"She knew Mary was there all the time."

"Are they friends?" the Muse asked.

"Not anymore."

"It's a terrible life you live," the Muse said.

I agreed.

Mary Brooks awoke this morning.

She was bright.

She had loads of energy.

And when she walked through the door, her smile could light up the whole room.

Mary Brooks was the kind of woman who should live forever.

She won't.

Mary Brooks will never see chapter forty-three.

Meeting Ambrose Lincoln

I MET AMBROSE LINCOLN the night I couldn't sleep.

It was late, almost midnight, and I was roaming television channels when I stumbled across a documentary that was absolutely spell-binding.

It dealt with secret military experiments.

It dealt with mind control.

It dealt with horrors I had never imagined before.

They all took place sometime during the 1930s.

I had no idea they had ever happened.

It was a secret project that didn't exist, and it took place in a secret hospital that didn't exist somewhere outside a secret little town that didn't exist.

Men volunteered for the experiments.

They came from prisons.

They came from asylums.

They came from the military.

And doctors tried to reshape their minds.

They used drugs.

They used LSD.

They used electrical shocks.

They wanted to re-map the brain.

They were building weapons, human weapons.

Men who walked into the hospital were not the same men who walked out, and not all of them walked out.

I was seated on the sofa.

I was mesmerized.

I was alone.

"That's what happened to me," the voice said.

The words were calm and measured.

I turned my head, and there he sat.

He appeared, for all the world, like a man whose soul had left him even though the last flickers of a pulse stayed behind.

His hair was brown, but the flecks of gray had left it as ashen as lava spilling out into a sunburnt desert. It had been carelessly combed, probably dried by the wind, moistened by the rain, and he needed a haircut. He looked to be somewhere between his early thirties and mid-forties. It was difficult to tell. The years had not been kind to him. His face was pale, his cheeks sallow. He had broad shoulders and hands scarred even worse than his face. When he spoke, his words were as direct as a fatal pistol shot.

"Who are you?" I asked.

"Ambrose Lincoln."

I stared at him.

He stared straight ahead.

"What happened to you?" I asked.

"They took my mind away," he said. "They removed my memory."

"Who did?"

"Doctors."

"Why?

Ambrose shrugged. "A man without a memory is a man who is not afraid."

That, he said, is what the doctors told him each time the electrodes touched the tattered nerve endings of his brain, each time the worn purple switch sent jolts of electricity racing down the dark tunnels of everything he had known in life and could not find anymore.

The electricity wiped it clean.

No memories.

No regrets.

No emotions.

"Why did they do such a thing to you?" I asked.

"I volunteered."

"Why?"

"There was a war coming," Ambrose said. "They needed men who could operate deep within Germany."

"What if the Germans caught you?"

"It didn't matter."

"Why not?"

"A man who knows nothing can reveal nothing."

"And your mind is blank."

"Wiped clean," he said.

"Were you the only one who volunteered?" I wanted to know.

"There were nine of us in the beginning," he said. "They took us one by one."

He shrugged again.
"I'm the only one left?"
"Why did you come see me?" I asked.
"I have a story to tell," he said.
"What's it about."
"Secrets," he said, "secrets of the dead."
I switched off the television.
"Where should we begin?" I asked.
"At the funeral of my wife," he said.
"How did she die?"
"No one ever told me."
"How long had you been married?"
"I don't know."
"Did you love her?"
For the first time he looked at me.
His eyes softened but did not blink.
"I had never seen her before in my life," he said.
I nodded.
I knew it would be a long night.

Los Alamos: Where It All Began

I TRAVEL THE way I write. Mostly that's a good thing. Sometimes it's not.

I wake up one morning and head out.

I'm never for sure where I'm going.

I'm not sure how I'll get there.

But I keep driving.

Or I keep writing.

I'm interested in where the road comes out.

This time I had a destination.

I was on my way to Santa Fe, New Mexico.

It was a last-minute decision to go, and I had no reservations.

It was a long time ago.

It might as well have been yesterday.

I figured I'd wind my way into town, find a decent motel by the side of the road, and hide away for a few days.

There were lots of good motels.

One was as good as the next.

In Santa Fe, I found, there were no rooms.

"Big convention in town" the desk clerk said. "The town's sold out."

I looked outside.

A dark golden glow lay upon Santa Fe.

In a couple of hours, it would be dark.

Maybe sooner.

"Where's the closest town?" I asked.

"You need a room?"

"I do."

"Try Los Alamos."

"Where's Los Alamos."

"Take Highway 285 north and follow the signs."

"How far?"

"Thirty-five miles, but it seems farther."

Los Alamos didn't waste any time. It hooked me immediately.

It felt different.

The mountains were stuffed with secrets.

The town looked like a town named Los Alamos ought to look.

And then I drove past the National Laboratory, tucked back on a hill and wedged into the trees.

"That's where it all happened," I was told.

"What happened?"

"That's where they built the bomb."

"Which bomb?"

"The bomb that ended World War II."

I was looking at a collection of dark, foreboding buildings where an assortment of scholars, physicists, and scientists figured out a way to split the atom and create the deadliest weapon known to mankind.

It may destroy the world, some said.

It may set the universe on fire, some said.

They built it anyway.

The story of Los Alamos and the Atomic Bomb never left me.

I've got to write about that someday, I thought.

I did in the second volume of the Ambrose Lincoln series, *Conspiracy of Lies.*

I wrote of those scholars, physicists, and scientists, as well as the general who oversaw the secret project:

They all began gathering in the heavily forested high country of Los Alamos. It was quiet. It was secluded. It was virtually hidden by the Jemez and Sangre de Cristo Mountains. The general liked the location a lot. It was at least two hundred miles away from the West Coast and the threat of Japanese warplanes that might be intent on bombing the bomb if any of the emperor's warriors chanced to learn about his deadly little secret.

By now, the general no longer had any doubts about the A-bomb. It could be built. He was sure of it. And it would be built. His constant fear was espionage.

The Germans wanted to know about the project. So did the Russians.

They were willing to pay good money for information or kill for it.

The compound had been built as a secret city in and around an old abandoned boy's school at Los Alamos. The brightest of the bunch had all moved into former teacher's homes on "Bathtub Row." The place was weathered and rundown, hidden in the backside of the mountains. It was, the general hoped, beyond the reach of any spy. Still he was taking no chances.

No one must know where the brilliant minds had gathered. No one must know who worked in the labs and what their tasks might be. Men who did not exist had been locked away in a place that did not exist.

The general assigned fake names and bodyguards to protect the senior scientists. Their driver's licenses had numbers instead of names.

No phone lines ran beyond the Tech area of the new facility.

And everyone in Los Alamos, from scientists to the lowest private in Uncle Sam's Army, had the same mailing address: Box 1663, Santa Fe, New Mexico.

Nobody, the general decreed, should ever use the word "bomb" either privately or in public. It was too controversial. It was too dangerous. Up among the trees of Los Alamos, the most frightening weapon of them all was simply referred to as "the gadget."

It was a dangerous time. Los Alamos was a dangerous place.

We were building the atomic bomb.

The Russians wanted it.

The Germans were trying to steal it.

The streets of Santa Fe and Los Alamos had two kinds of men: soldiers and spies. Sometimes it was difficult to know which one to trust. Then again, maybe there was no one to trust.

And that's what makes a good story.

Who's the Baddest Guy in the Room?

WE ALL HAVE our own way to write a novel.

Some worry about the plot.

Others can't get started until they have a title.

Some write prologues.

Others write epilogues.

I only care about the characters.

For *Night Side of Dark*, I had the protagonist already in place.

Ambrose Lincoln was the easy one.

He's the lead character in the series.

He can't be replaced.

I interviewed the prospective heroines.

I didn't pick the girl I wanted.

I didn't choose the most beautiful girl.

I didn't select the sexy girl.

I hired the girl who frightened me, and it surprised me how beautiful a dangerous woman could be.

I called her Celia. It's a bad name. It doesn't fit her.

I'll change it later. I'll change it when she tells me what her name really is.

She did.

It was Devra.

Now comes the villain.

I had three candidates.

One was too young and boyish.

But he was eager.

Roger Richmond tried to look tough.

He was smoking a cigarette he had rolled himself.

He folded his arms across the chest to make sure I saw the tattoo on his bicep.

Born to Lose is what it said.

His face was pale and almost white.

If I were writing about a vampire, I would talk to him further.

His mustache was paper thin.

He had tried to hide the pimple on his nose with a heavy dab of cosmetics.

"Why do you want to be the villain?" I asked him.

He tried to sneer.

It looked more like a smile.

"Everybody wants to be the bad guy," he said.

"Are you bad?"

"I kicked a kitten once," he said.

"Thank you for coming," I said.

He was soft.

I don't think he ever kicked a kitten.

The second candidate was the perfect choice.

A chiseled face.

Ugly in a handsome sort of way.

Tango Lynch had muscles bulging at the seams of his tee shirt.

He had a scar that the blade of some knife had torn down the side of his face.

The scar was almost hidden by a two-day growth of whiskers.

His eyes were dark. They burned with anger.

"Are you as tough as you look?" I asked.

"Try me."

"What's your name?" I asked.

"Call me Mister Lynch."

"Why the Mister?"

"I don't want to have to hurt you," he said.

His sneer might have been real, but it didn't look real.

I picked up a Walther PPK lying on the desk and handed it to him.

"What do you want me to do with this?" he asked.

I nodded toward the old man sitting on the couch.

"Shoot him," I said.

Tango's eyes widened.

His mouth gaped open.

"I got no reason to shoot the old man," he said.

"You don't need a reason," I said.

His eyes fluttered.

His hand trembled.

I took the pistol away from him.

Caples Gusarov stood up from the couch and walked slowly across the room.

He was far too old for the role.

He was road-worn and weary.

He was breathing heavily.

He was grizzled.

He was chewing on a cigarette that had not been lit.

He didn't spit the loose tobacco leaves. He swallowed them.

Caples Gusarov looked as though he had walked a mile beyond his last mile.

He didn't say a word.

He jerked the Walther PPK from my hand.

He turned, still chewing on the cigarette, and fired.

The bullet struck Tango Lynch just below the chin.

He was dead before the blood began to flow.

Gusarov looked at me hard. "I'd rather shoot the bastard that kicked the kitten," he said.

He handed the pistol back to me.

"You're hired," I said.

He grinned. "Was there ever any doubt?" he asked.

"Not for me," I said.

I turned back to the novel and only had one regret.

I wished I had asked him to spell Gusarov before he left.

Beautiful and Deadly

I KNEW WHAT I wanted. At least, I thought I did.

I didn't. I never do.

In *Night Side of Dark*, I had a tormented hero without a past or much of a memory wandering around the edges of World War II, not quite sure why he was there or what his mission might be.

He needed a love interest.

After all, every good sub-plot is a love story.

That's what I've been told by writers both good and bad.

So why shouldn't I believe them?

I promptly set up a casting call just to see who would show up and audition for the role. I didn't know what she might do in the story. I simply needed a love interest.

The redhead came first.

I knew she would.

I'm partial to redheads.

She was tall with auburn hair that fell down in ringlets upon her shoulders.

Long legs.

Thin.

Shapely.

A winsome smile.

A beauty mark beneath her left eye.

Her gown was long, made of satin, and she was wearing six-inch heels, shoes with daggers on the heels.

I asked her to sit down.

She smiled.

"How do you feel about snow?' I asked.

"It's cold," she said.

"You'll spend most of the book walking around in it," I said.

"A ski slope?"

Her smile brightened.

"Slush," I said, "the kind of dirty black slush that piles up among the garbage cans alongside the back streets on the wrong side of town."

She frowned.

I saw immediately that it wouldn't work.

I was ready to dismiss her.

But she had already walked through the door and slammed it.

The brunette came in dressed in lingerie.

Black.

Lacy.

She thought she was going to impress me.

She was right.

The brunette sat down and stretched her legs on velvet lounger.

I started to speak.

Instead, I cleared my throat.

I would worry about the words later.

She said she was a catalog model. If she were selling catalogs, I would have bought one.

"Have you ever acted?" I asked.

"Not in a play."

"How about a book?"

She smiled.

She batted her eyelashes.

"I read one once," she said.

"The book's set in Dalldorf," I said.

"Is that near Cleveland?" she asked.

"Germany," I said.

"I've been to Cleveland," she said.

I hated to dismiss her. I really did.

But I would have dismissed her again just to see her walk across the floor.

I had been a fool, I thought. Next time, I would write about Cleveland.

The blonde was about what I expected.

The color of her hair may have come from a bottle.

Or dishwater.

It was short, bobbed around her ears, and might look better in the sun.

She was small, petite.

She looked like she would break if you touched her.

Her face was pale.

Her face was soft.

Her eyes were like chipped flint.

I smiled.

She didn't.

The blonde was wearing a faded dress that might have once been pink but more probably purple.

Her shoes were scuffed.

Her fingernails were broken.

"Are you an actress?" I asked.

"No."

"What do you do?" I wanted to know.

"I kill people."

"With a gun?"

"I sometimes use dynamite."

"Do you have any regrets?" I asked.

"About what?"

"Killing people."

She paused. Her eyes grew even harder.

"Not when the bastards deserve it," she said.

"Are you carrying a gun now?"

She had a 9mm pistol in her hand before I saw her remove her from a garter belt.

"You have the job," I told her.

I smiled.

She didn't.

My hero, Ambrose Lincoln, wasn't scared of anyone.

But he would sleep with one eye open when she was around.

The bastard would never trust me again.

The Little Man Who Wouldn't Leave

THE LITTLE MAN had no business being in the novel.

He was a bit player.

Come in.

Shoot the scene.

Collect minimum pay.

Go home.

Might not even get a screen credit.

Chester Giddings was frail.

He was frightened.

He had been a private detective before the war.

Mostly he handled divorces.

Now he was with the Federal Atomic Commission.

He was looking for spies. He hoped to God he never found one.

The scene arrived, and I needed Chester.

Mostly I needed his room.

The assassin broke in.

Ambrose Lincoln was waiting for him.

The assassin died.

Chester had nothing to do with it.

Chester wanted to wash his hands clean of the whole affair.

As I wrote:

The sergeant with the Santa Fe police stood up and walked to the little man's side. He spoke first. "And who might you be?" he asked.

"Giddings," the little man said. "Chester Giddings."

"You know the dead man?"

Chester shook his head. "I've never seen him before," he said.

"Yet, you think he was trying to kill you."

"Yes, sir, I do."

"Got a reason?" the sergeant asked.

"I'm with the government," Chester said.

The sergeant glanced around at Ambrose Lincoln and rolled his eyes.

Lincoln grinned.

"You got any government identification with you?" the sergeant asked.

"Yes, sir." The little man placed his fedora down on the side of the bed, removed his wallet, and peeled out a business card.

The sergeant held it up to the light, looked at Lincoln, and asked. "How come you don't have one of these?"

"Guess I'm not important enough," Lincoln said.

"But you're important enough to carry a gun."

Lincoln shrugged. "I've never had much luck in a card fight," he said.

The sergeant rolled his eyes again and turned his attention back to the little man with a dark fedora.

"It says here that you're with the Federal Atomic Commission," he said.

"I'm an investigator," Chester said.

"You carry a badge?"

"Just a business card."

"You carry a gun?"

The little man shook his head. "Just a business card,"

It was time for Chester to go.

He wouldn't leave.

I kicked him out

He came back in.

He was still frail.

He was still frightened.

But every time Ambrose Lincoln was in trouble, Chester Giddings came through the doorway.

He became the hero's shadow.

He was never brave.

But he was stronger than he had been.

By the end of the novel, a lot of Ambrose Lincoln had rubbed off on the little man.

His hands shook.

But he was cocky.

Shoot, Chester thought he was invincible.

When Ambrose was rounding up the bad guys, he couldn't do it alone.

He didn't have to.

Here came Chester wandering into the scene.

As I wrote:

He was walking a little straighter than usual. He wore a crooked and cocky smile on his face.

The little man kicked the SVT-40 self-loading rifle away from the dead man's hands and picked it up.

He had never held a rifle before, not in anger anyway.

"Is the safety off?" he asked Lincoln.

"It is."

"What happens if I pull the trigger?"

"You'll blow a hole in the Russian and spend the rest of the night picking up the pieces."

"I don't think I want to do that," Chester said.

"It gets messy."

"Oh, I don't mind the mess," Chester said. "I called the general, and he's on the way down the mountain. If the Russian doesn't sit down and start counting his toes, I'll leave it to the general to pick up the pieces."

Chester grinned.

Federov sat down.

They had tried to kill Ambrose Lincoln. They had tried more than once.

No one messed with the little man who wouldn't leave.

Conversation with Ambrose

AMBROSE LINCOLN WANDERS down from wherever he hangs out about two o'clock every day.

He knows I'll be writing about him soon.

He doesn't't' want to be late.

He knows I get really upset when he's late.

Ambrose Lincoln is not like any of the characters I've written about in the past.

He is different indeed.

They were friendly and outgoing.

Ambrose keeps his feelings locked away inside.

They joke around.

Ambrose seldom smiles. But then, he has little reason to smile.

They make snide, sarcastic comments and want to fool around.

Ambrose is all business.

They came along for the ride.

Ambrose drives.

His philosophy is a simple one.

Let's get the chapter started.

Let's hit the ground running.

Make something happen.

Deadly.

And chilling.

Then move on.

On paper, Ambrose Lincoln moves in and out of scenes that unfolded during World War II. He's not a soldier. He's not in the scene to fight. He has a mission handed him by the U. S. government.

He doesn't know who's in charge.

He doesn't know where the assignments come from.

His mind has been erased during behavioral experiments. His mind is a barren landscape burned dry by the electrodes of shock therapy.

He's not afraid.

Ambrose has no fear of dying.

He believes he may have already died, and the war and purgatory have a lot in common.

"You've just written chapter sixty," Ambrose tells me.

I nod.

He knows I try to keep my novels somewhere between sixty and seventy thousand words, and each chapter runs about a thousand words.

"I read it," he says.

I nod.

"In fact, I've read them all," he says.

"You should," I tell him. "They're about you."

Ambrose shakes his head.

He thinks about grinning, then decides against it.

"You don't have an ending in mind," he says.

"I haven't figured one out yet," I tell him.

"But you're looking."

"I am."

"You changed the story in the past chapter or two," he says.

"I came to a fork in the road, and I couldn't resist not taking it."

"Know where it's going?" Ambrose asks.

"No."

"You're gonna be surprised," he says.

"I usually am," I say.

Ambrose stares out the window.

The sun has dropped behind an oak tree.

The hillside had turned golden.

It's the magic hour of winter.

"Where did you get the girl this time?" he asks.

"Devra?"

He nods.

"She didn't come from central casting," I say.

"Didn't think so," Ambrose says. "She's a helluva woman."

"She's really pretty."

"I knew she would be pretty." He shrugs. "All your girls are pretty," he says.

"She's tough."

"Hell," he says, "she's tougher than I am."

"Devra has a hard shell," I say.

"I can't crack it," he points out.

"Her heart's tender," I say. "She's like a little girl. Lost. Afraid. Abandoned."

"Could have fooled me."

"I tried," I said.

"How many has she killed?" Ambrose asks.

"Bunches."

"More than me?"

"Lots more."

"That's what I thought." He pauses, and his face becomes grim. His eyes darken. "You're not gonna kill her off, are you?" he asks.

"I don't know."

"You better not?"

"Why?"

"I know where you live."

I grin.

He doesn't.

Ambrose stands up and heads on back to wherever he hangs out when I'm not writing.

"Don't worry about the ending," he says.

"Why not?"

"Just follow me, and stay close," he says. "I'll get you there."

"You got it figured out?"

"If I haven't, then you're out of luck," Ambrose says.

I don't argue. I'd write another chapter, but I can't.

Only Ambrose Lincoln knows the story, and he's already gone

Paranormal Thrillers

I DON'T WRITE paranormal. I write historical thrillers.

Pure.

And simple.

So why did I write about a ghost?

Where did she come from?

She certainly wasn't planned.

As the Nazi storm troopers and brown shirts ransacked Baden Baden during the Night of Broken Glass, an old gentleman captured the following scene with his camera:

I wrote:

The young woman was holding her young daughter's hand when the brown shirt approached her. He leered at her and ripped the buttons off her blouse.

She slapped him.

He shot her point black between the eyes.

The child screamed. She was on her knees crying for her mama to get up, begging for her mama to get back up.

She was still crying when the bullet tore into the back of her tiny skull.

It was a tragedy.

It was insanity.

It was war.

Later in the novel, Ambrose Lincoln is on a plane headed toward Baden Baden.

And as I wrote:

Lincoln's eyes fell on the small, oval face of a young woman, maybe thirty, maybe not, with long raven hair and a beauty mark or a spot of mud under her left eye. She was barely five feet tall and wore a woolen dress the color of the earth. Her skin was pale, translucent, and had not yet been touched by the sun. She was barefoot and carrying a bleached cotton sack.

The small, oval face was pointed his way, and her eyes were dark, filled with bitterness and regret. They would speak long before she ever said a word. She stood and swayed awkwardly with the movement of the train as she walked toward him.

Lincoln tried to look away.

He couldn't.

The dark, bitter eyes were hypnotic.

Any sign of life had dimmed behind them a long time ago.

"They are lying," she said suddenly. Her voice was soft and distant.

"Who is lying?"

"The ones who were there."

Lincoln nodded.

"And the ones who weren't," she said.

She sat down at the table and folded her hands on top of the white linen cloth. They were small, fragile, and scarred. Her nails were torn. Her fingers had been bleeding. Lincoln looked closer. It was a spot of mud beneath her eye.

"Where are you talking about?" Lincoln asked.

"My country," she said. "Their country. It belongs to us all. It belongs to no one."

"What are they lying about?"

"The night of broken glass," she said.

Lincoln waited.

In the distance, he could hear the mournful whistle of the train, and he saw a few scattered lights from a small town outside the window. The lights flew past, nothing more than a patchwork of flickering glares in the shadows, and then it was dark again.

"They will tell you that the windows were broken, that the streets were lined with splinters of glass, that drunken thugs attacked us. But the thugs are gone is what they will tell you, and life goes on as it always has."

"Who will tell me this?"

"Your newspapers," she said. "Your politicians. Your President."

"Why?"

"The war has begun? They run from the war."

"Which war?"

"My war." The trace of a sad smile touched her lips. "Soon it will be your war."

Lincoln shrugged. "My war has never ended," he said.

She reached out with her fingers and gently touched his hand. Her voice had become a fading whisper. "They broke our glass," she said. "The broke our hearts. They burned our homes. They burned our little shops."

She paused.

Lincoln waited.

"They killed us all," she said. "They killed the old. They killed the sick. They killed a mother. They killed a child. They left them in the gutter to bleed."

"How do you know?" Lincoln said.

The woman stood and walked toward the door. "I was the mother," she said.

Ambrose Lincoln frowned. His eyes caught a glimpse of the bleached cotton sack she had left on the table.

He stood to catch her before she could leave the dining car.

She was gone.

It was as though she had never been in the dining car at all.

I didn't know her spirit would confront Lincoln on the train.

Neither did he.

She would come to him again on a flight toward Austria.

Her horror was the horror of war.

Her story became Lincoln's conscience.

He could not fail.

He would not fail.

He kept his word to a ghost.

Do I write paranormal?

I don't know.

She seemed real to me.

My Stories Run Hot and Cold

I DON'T OPEN my novels with a long, flowing epistle about the weather.

That's a sin, I've been told.

That's deadly, I've been told.

And I believe it.

However, I must confess, I did open *Secrets of the Dead* with the line: *Even the late October sky wore black to her funeral.*

But it had more to do with the funeral than the coming rain.

I don't dodge the weather. I do write a lot about it. Some have told me that the weather becomes as important as any character in my novels.

I don't know if that's good.

Or bad.

But I think they're right.

And I generally find that the weather in my stories reflects the weather just outside my window.

I live in Texas.

We have long summers.

We have hot winters, dust bowl dry.

I know all about the miseries of heat.

I learned to sweat before I could talk.

When I wrote *Place of Skulls*, we were in the midst of the worst drought in the history of a state that knows all about droughts.

We had fifty-six consecutive days with temperatures topping the hundred-degree mark.

No rain.

No relief.

It was not surprising that I wrote such paragraphs as:

The air was sticky, the heat stifling, the cooling system working overtime and failing miserably, and it seemed as though even the roses in the garden below him had lost their fragrance.

Even late in the day, the temperature was hovering around the hundred-degree mark, and Blaylock, nearing fifty and looking older, gazed out across a barren patch of the forsaken land that had pried him from his air-conditioned Washington office. He brushed the gnats away from his thin, angular face and adjusted his sunglasses as a droplet of sweat streaked the dust that had collected on the lens.

His gray slacks were badly wrinkled, and his navy-blue tie had been loosened at the collar. His thinning brown hair was clipped short, and his pallid skin, turning a pale shade of pink, was beginning to itch and burn.

I wrote what I felt.

I was hot. My skin was itching and burning.

Once again, we were in the midst of summer when I wrote *Conspiracy of Lies.*

The novel is set in New Mexico.

I had gone to New Mexico.

Blisters and sunburn were the only souvenirs I brought home.

So I wrote:

Lincoln rolled his window down, and a blast of heat and sand rolled off the basin and slammed him in the face. He waited for the winds to cool it off. It would be a long wait. Sweat had begun to gather around the collar of his khaki shirt. He had thrown his jacket into the backseat.

The heat bore down and into his shoulder blades like a poker pulled straight from the flames in a blacksmith's furnace.

The chill had wilted, and beyond the edge of town, he could see the heat rising up off the desert floor. The heat was dry and prickly, working its way into his flesh like a thorn. It had already begun to fester.

But the seasons do change.

So does the weather.

This is, after all, Texas.

When I wrote the manuscript for *Night Side of Dark*, we were experiencing the longest, coldest winter that anyone could remember.

Day after day it snowed.

When it wasn't snowing, it was sleeting.

We were encased with ice.

Without thinking, I set the novel in the winters of Poland, Czechoslovakia, and Germany.

I wrote:

It was a cold and empty morning. Only those chosen to meet their destiny were unaware of what lay ahead of them one mile, twenty-seven meters, and a half bridge length away. Below them, the river would be boiling with a white, icy froth. The river awaited them all. Men would freeze to death long before they had a chance to drown. The snow would blind them. The explosion would rip them away from the train, and this was the way it would end. Fire. Then darkness. Then ice. The river would claim them all.

The snow on the street had turned dirty, a cold and wet concoction of mud, exhaust fumes, and grease. Automobiles were stalled in drifts that piled up beside the curbs. A few trucks had not run in weeks, maybe months. Their windshields were frozen sheets of ice. Their tires had been encased in slush. By morning, they, too, would be locked in a case of ice.

Old women wrapped in heavy coats had turned their backs to a hard north wind. Men paced aimlessly on the wooden platform that ran the length of the railway station. Some were looking for love. Some were headed back to the front lines occupied by the German army, frayed and unraveling around the cold and bloodied fields of Berlin. Some wanted to escape the chill of death. Some were just waiting for a train.

I am a victim of the weather.

I am a slave to the weather.

I look out my window before beginning a noel and ask myself two questions?

Are the birds sweating?

Do the birds have ice on their wings?

As soon as I check the birds, I begin to write.

My stories, as they say, run hot and cold.

Blending Fact with Fiction

BACK WHEN I worked for a custom publishing company in Dallas, we did a lot of business with companies in Houston.

Interstate 45 and I became close friends.

I would leave the house before daylight.

Often, I returned in the dead of night and usually just before daylight.

When I needed a break sometime around midnight on my drive back home, I would stop at the Mile 190 Truck Stop. It sat just off the interstate, always had the floodlights on, and was the kind of place you might expect to find in a dystopian novel.

It was old.

It was rundown.

It was open.

Inside were the night people.

Don't know who they were.

Don't know where they came from or why they came.

It wasn't for friendly conversation.

I never saw anyone smile.

I never heard anyone speak.

The night people simply drank coffee, shoved their eggs from one side of the plate to the other, and waited until morning.

Don't know when they left.

I was gone by then.

But I never forgot their faces, and I never forgot the scene.

When I wrote *Conspiracy of Lies,* my hero, Ambrose Lincoln, walks into an all-night café about midnight, and I stole the scene right out of the Mile 190 Truck Stop.

AMBROSE LINCOLN SEARCHED the machinations of his mind, determined it was twenty-two minutes past midnight, and walked to the all-night diner where the lonely came to eat cheap steaks and ham sandwiches, fried eggs and day-old menudo, particularly if they had been drinking anything stronger than mescal tequila, and to keep from being lonely, even if no one spoke to them, and hardly anyone ever did.

He stood outside and stared through the big plate glass window, quietly surveying the scene of a clean, well-lighted place that smelled of burnt grease, stale cigarette smoke, and pickled jalapeno peppers. His gaze shifted from face to face.

Chances were, the lady looking for love. A little too old, a little too heavy, a little too much lipstick, and a little too eager to smile at any man in the place who needed an extra layer of warmth on a warm night. Money was not important. She probably had her own.

The soldier was sleeping with his head on the table. Sometime after dark, his night on the town had ended in ruin. Alone. Sober. Homesick. Nothing to do. And no one to do it with, except, of course, the lady looking for love, and she could well be his mother in another time and another place, and maybe she was.

A peddler had pushed his plate aside, but he still had his last piece of toast clamped between his teeth. He had opened his case and was straightening his wares, trying to forget a bad day and hoping tomorrow would be better, and tomorrow hadn't been better since leaving Des Moines, if he had ever been to Des Moines, and driving into New Mexico. It was tough selling cufflinks in a town filled with soldiers and farmers and drifters like Ambrose Lincoln who had no cuffs, much less any links. He was the only hope Miss Lonely Hearts had, but the peddler didn't look to be that lonely.

Twyla sat in the back corner across the table from a farmer. At least, he looked like a farmer. Short. Stubby. Straw hat. Red face. Dirt-stained khakis as wrinkled as his face. Chewing a cigar with one side of his mouth and a plate of biscuits and sorghum with the other.

He hadn't lit the cigar.

It lasted longer that way.

The farmer was drinking coffee from a saucer. Hot and black. He kept blowing on the coffee to cool it off.

Twyla was watching the clock on the wall.

The night was late.

Her shift was young.

It was already a slow night.

Lincoln stepped through the doorway and walked straight to her table.

I knew all about it. I had sat at her table before.

Twyla was an old friend, and I never knew her name.

Writing the Wrong Book

WE WERE ON a desolate landscape, a moonscape with mountains and a beauty that worked into your skin like a thorn. It stayed for a long time but never hurt.

We had left the road miles ago and were on foot, headed toward the hard-rock ledge that would overlook the South Rim, where, the old man said, you could see clear into day after tomorrow.

I didn't doubt him for a minute.

Peter Koch paused on the old Apache war trail, reached down, and picked up a hand full of seashells.

"Bet you didn't expect to find these out here," he said.

I nodded.

He was right.

"Back when the world was covered with water, these mountains were the reefs," he said. 'That's why there's no two of them alike. Water shaped them. The winds have sculpted them. The seashells have never left them."

He grinned.

No one knew the backcountry of Big Bend National Park like Peter Koch did. He had lived on the edge of the Great Chihuahua Desert for most of his life. He had walked every square mile of the Texas Outback.

The Big Bend gave Peter Koch its secrets.

He tried to give them to me.

"This country would make a great location for a book," he said.

"It's awfully isolated," I said.

"That's what gives the old Bend its mystique," he said. "Lots of mysteries buried in the dirt around here. Lots of men came in and never left. Nobody knows what happened to him. They're here one day and gone the next."

"Maybe they just drove off."

"Maybe they couldn't leave at all."

"Somebody kill them?"

"Could be."

"Why?" I wanted to know.

The grin widened.

"That's what makes for a good book," he said.

I couldn't argue the point.

But I wasn't interested.

"My novel's set in the city," I said.

"Cities are all alike," he said. "The Bend is different.'

"Lots of interesting characters running loose in the city."

"But they're all alike, too." Peter shrugged. "Out here, only the brave come. The weak don't make it. And the cowards never start. Tough men live back in this country," he said.

"I'm writing about a spy," I said.

"Spies like beautiful women," he said.

"They do."

"We got beautiful women out here," he said.

"Where?"

"They come out at night," he said.

I said I would wait. I figured it would be a long wait.

"See that valley running down toward the Rio Grande," Peter Koch said.

I told him I did.

"There's a lost silver mine buried in there."

"Got a map?"

"Don't need one."

"Why not."

"If you stand atop this peak on Easter morning, the first shaft of sunlight strikes the entrance to the mine."

"Have you seen it?" I asked.

"I've tried."

"What happened?"

"Too cloudy," he said. "But the story of the lost mine would make a great book. You ought to write it."

"I don't write Westerns," I said.

"Wouldn't be a Western," he said.

"Sounds like a Western."

"It's a love story."

"Where do you get a love story out of a lost mine?" I wanted to know.

"Every good book is fraught with romance."

"And a man with a gun."

"You've got them both in the Big Bend," he said. "Takes a gun to stay a alive and a beautiful woman to make the living worthwhile."

He stopped, and his gaze swept from mountain to mountain and fell down toward the river that separated two nations.

"We've got ninety mountains out here more than a mile high," he said.

"My story works better in the city," I said.

"We're standing within a stone's throw of Mexico," he said.

"My story deals with German spies," I said.

"We got a lot of drug smugglers," he said.

"My spies are stealing secrets to the Atom bomb," I said.

"You can't find country more rugged and beautiful than this," he said. "That's the kind of backdrop a good book needs."

"My book needs a city," I said.

"Then that's your problem," he said.

"What is?" I liked.

"You're writing the wrong book," he said.

Maybe he's right, I thought as the sun dipped down below the rock formation known as the Window, and the sky faded into a ghostly shade of blue.

Novels by Caleb Pirtle III

Secrets of the Dead
Conspiracy of Lies
Night Side of Dark
Place of Skulls
Back Side of a Blue Moon
Last Deadly Lie
Lovely Night to Die

Nonfiction Books by Caleb Pirtle III

The Man Who Talks to Strangers: A Memoir of Sorts
Gamble in the Devil's Chalk

Preview

Bad Side of a Wicked Moon

A GENTLE WIND ruffled her long white silk and satin nightgown as Eudora Durant watched the hearse rise up out of the fog. It was that mystical hour when threads of daylight were trying to weave their way in and out of the darkness, and mist above the river lay upon the water like ashes in a fire that had burned too long. The sun had not yet awakened, and the frogs still owned the shoreline. Eudora found herself humming "Swing Low, Sweet Chariot" by the time the hearse rounded the bend and headed toward the distant lights of Ashland. Was the hearse coming to take someone away or bringing someone home? It was, she thought, a mighty fine velocipede for the grim reaper to be driving. Not long ago, he would have been hauling the remains away in a second-hand wheelbarrow. Oil made ladies and gentlemen out of the most worthless scalawags on earth. Eudora should know. She had been one of them.

Oil had indeed changed the complexion of the landscape. It may have stained the land black, but oil had washed more transgressions than a Sunday afternoon baptizing down at the New River of Life Baptist Church. It was easy to tell the difference between the haves and have nots of Ashland. The rich had oil flowing beneath their farms. The poor were still sucking on persimmon seeds and chopping weeds out of destitute cotton fields. The cotton stalks looked a lot like the weeds. Those farmers had drilled, too. But mostly they found dirt at the bottom of a dry hole.

God had cursed them, they said. *God had poured his oil under somebody else's farm.*

No, Doc Bannister had told them. *You boys just bought the wrong patch of dirt.*

The early morning silence was broken only by the banging of metal against metal as pipe from the pump jack in the backyard kept pounding the deep earth, lifting crude to the top of the ground and dumping it into a storage tank. The constant grinding and clanging no longer made it difficult for Eudora to sleep at night. She had criticized the ominous and calamitous noise that disturbed her night and day until she cashed her first check from the Midwestern Oil and Natural Gas company. Now the clanging and grinding, the hammering and pounding that had banged against the back of her skull and seared her senses sounded more like the overture of an Irish lullaby.

Eudora walked back inside the farmhouse, searching through the darkness, her fingers rummaging around inside Doc's trouser pockets for the keys to his Ford Model A Roadster.

She stumbled against the bedpost.

Damn.

She quietly made her way through the darkness and into the kitchen. She leaned against the table for a moment, waiting for cobwebs, leftovers from a deep sleep, to melt away in the early chill. She ruffled her hair with her fingertips and walked on bare feet toward the door. Her elbow upended the coffee pot. It tumbled off the counter and bounced on the floor.

Damn again.

The dead are probably awake by now.

It must be judgment day.

"What's wrong?"

The voiced dripped with sleep.

It belonged to Doc.

"I'm going to town," Eudora said.

"At this hour?"

"Somebody's dead." Eudora traded her silk and satin night gown for a long, bird's egg blue dress, slipped on her black T-strap Oxford shoes, and started for the door.

"How do you know?"

"Saw the hearse go by."

"Did he stop outside?"

"No."

"Then don't worry about it." Doc yawned. "It's not coming for us. The big spinner spun for some sinner's soul, and then spun down another street."

"There's a heavy and a grieving heart out there this morning." Eudora's voice had a soft edge. "Nobody should be left alone at a time like this."

"Who died?"

"That's the reason I'm going to town."

"Why?"

"To find out," she said.

Doc sat on the edge of the bed, rubbing his eyes. His dark, thick hair looked as if rats had been nesting in the crown of his head for the most of the night. An undershirt sagged across his shoulders. It was stained as though he had used it to wipe the grease off drilling pipe. He had.

"We'll go to the funeral," he said. "Funerals are held at a decent hour."

"Aren't you curious?" Eudora paused in the doorway and glanced back at him as the first ragged rays of daylight reflected off her green eyes and danced atop her auburn hair.

"I was up past midnight." Doc groaned as he stretched the muscles in his back." I haven't been asleep long."

"It may be someone we know."

Doc's head slumped back down on the pillow. "If the hearse comes looking for me," he said. "Don't tell it where I am."

EUDORA DROVE INTO downtown Ashland, and its streets were as dark as the inside of a casket with the lid nailed shut. She pulled the Roadster in front of Jim Hamilton's Dinner Bell café and cut off the engine. It was too early for the chickens to be laying eggs, much less for Hamilton's short order cook to be frying them. No lights were shining in any of the windows, not even on the top floor of Maizie Thompson's boarding house for gentleman callers and lovely ladies of questionable repute. Men left their reputations hanging beside the front door, along with their coats and hats. The ladies hadn't bothered to bring their reputations to town.

The hardship days of the Great Depression, when jobs were as scarce as hen's teeth, had turned drifters into cowards and wayward women into whores. She did pity the girls. She seldom spoke to the gentlemen callers, not even when they sat on the same Sunday morning pew, lustily sang "Rock of Ages," and loaned their hearts to God to hold in escrow. They never gave their hearts away to either God or the girls.

Eudora walked down the street to the black Model T hearse, parked next to the live oak tree outside the courthouse. Its driver climbed out when he saw her marching his way. He was unusually tall and thin. Without the broad-brimmed hat and black funeral coat, Eudora thought, she could have slid him through a keyhole. His face was gaunt with high chiseled cheekbones, and he wore a gray mustache that drooped below both sides of his chin. His dark, piercing eyes gleamed like marbles in the last, fleeting moments of moonlight. They left little doubt. The driver was no stranger to dancing with either death or the devil.

He removed his broad-brimmed beaver hat and bowed slightly. "Mortimer J. Thurgood at your service, ma am."

Eudora tipped her head to one side and smiled. "You have arrived awfully early for such a solemn and unfortunate occasion," she said.

"I follow the road," Thurgood said. "The clock doesn't always catch up. I'm here when I'm here and usually never when I'm expected."

"Like death itself."

Thurgood straightened his hat. "We do travel a lot together," he said.

"Do you ever come alone?"

"Not unless I'm invited."

A ray of stray sunlight touched the far end of the street. The fog was lifting across the river and falling into the trees.

Eudora folded her arms across her chest. "Have you come to collect someone?" she asked, "or leave someone."

"I have a passenger."

"A name?"

Thurgood shook his head. "I was given a casket and the name of a town." He shrugged and took a deep breath. "The passenger began his or her travels in St. Louis, came to Arkansas on a train, and rode a mule driven wagon to the upper reaches of East Texas. I picked the casket up just south of Texarkana and was paid eight dollars and fifty-four cents to bring it to the little town of Ashland." Thurgood lowered his voice. "You know, your little village is not on the map, at least not where I come from."

"Then how did you find us?"

Thurgood threw his head back and laughed. "They told me to travel down the Sabine River until I found a town with the richest men and the prettiest women, and that would be my final destination."

Eudora raised an eyebrow. "Is that what they really told you, Mister Thurgood?"

"Well, not exactly," he said. "They said to travel down the Sabine River until I found a town that smelled like Sulphur and rotten eggs and had wooden oil derricks rising upon the farmlands, and I would be in Ashland."

"Doesn't smell like Sulphur and rotten eggs to me," Eudora said.

"No?"

"Smells like money."

"Then maybe I should stay a while." Thurgood glanced up and down the street and back alleyways of the town. "It's not a very big place," he said.

"It's growing."

"You got much dying?"

Eudora leaned against the back of the hearse. "Mister Thurgood, you look like a good and decent man. I'll be honest with you."

"Please do."

"We're digging a lot of holes around here, and none of them are graves."

"I guess you'll have to dig one more."

Eudora arched an eyebrow.

"For my passenger," he said.

"Of course." She paused, frowned, then asked, "Do you know if he lived around here?"

"No one said."

"Has the deceased already been given his funeral service?"

"Preacher in Texarkana said he prayed over the casket." Thurgood shoved both boney hands into his pockets. He was jingling some loose change.

Probably fifty-four cents worth of pennies, Eudora figured.

Mortimer J. Thurgood opened the back doors of the hearse and struggled as he pulled out the casket, letting it slide gently to the ground. It was a pine box with all the pine knots in place. It was rough-hewn, wrapped in leather straps, and had not been painted or stained. It was the kind of coffin that held the remains of the lost, the vagabonds, the penniless, and the poor souls who would be condemned to lie in a pauper's field until the trumpet sounded and God's deliverance fell upon them all.

"I'm sure you will see that my passenger gets to the right place." Thurgood tipped his hat again and straightened his long coat. His face was as solemn as a preacher's final prayer.

"You can't just leave a casket lying in the street" Eudora couldn't believe her eyes.

"I was paid to deliver the box to Ashland." Thurgood ceremoniously rubbed his palms against his trouser legs to wipe the dust off his hands. "I was not paid to dig a hole. I was not paid to bury the deceased. I was not paid to say a good word or a foul word against either him or her. My eight dollars and fifty-four-cent fee ran out at the front door of the courthouse. The carcass now belongs to you and God."

Eudora was grasping for words. "We don't even know who he is," she said.

"It may be a lady."

"Then we don't even know who s*he* is."

"Think you might recognize her?" Thurgood asked.

Eudora shrugged. "I've lived here a long time," she said.

Thurgood returned to the back of the hearse, knelt, and unbuckled the leather straps. "The box isn't even nailed shut," he said. "It's the damndest thing I've ever seen."

He removed the lid.

Eudora bent down for a closer look.

She saw a boy, a young man really. He had hair the color of wheat straw lying in the field after a rain. His face was ruddy and packed with freckles. He wore denim overalls, a little on the large size, and a Gretsch guitar had been wedged into the casket beside him.

Eudora touched his face.

His skin felt warm as if he had been lying for too long beneath an August sun.

She jerked her hand away.

The boy smiled.

He opened one eye.

He winked with the other.

"Name's Johnny B. Goodnight," he said. "I perform at weddings, funerals, bar fights, and will stoop to accept tips for playing my guitar on street corners in rowdy towns big and small. I have been known to partake of good whiskey and am still in search of my first wild and wanton woman, who I've been assured can be found on most any street in Texas. I'm here and now and mostly tomorrow, and I am indeed pleased to make your acquaintance, ma 'am."

He sat up.

He took her hand.

Eudora's face had turned as pale as the specter of death.

"I've been known to dance a good bit, too," he said.

By the time Johnny B. Goodnight had climbed out of the pine box, Mortimer J. Thurgood had the black hearse in gear and was racing madly out of town. The Model T was running hot and doing its best to outrun a pesky dust devil trailing after the back tires as they tore down the ruts of Main street.

Johnny B. was on his feet now.

"It's not resurrection morning," Eudora said. "But welcome to Ashland anyway.

"I usually sing for my supper," the boy said, "but I have a right good song for breakfast, too."

Across the street, a light was on in the Dinner Bell.

And Eudora smelled eggs frying.

Made in the USA
Columbia, SC
24 May 2020

98227867R00183